LCSW Study Guide

2022-2023

Updated Prep + 680 Test Questions and Detailed Answer Explanations for the ASWB Clinical Social Work Exam (Includes 4 Full-Length Practice Exams)

Table of Contents

Important Information About the Exam

The Association of Social Work Boards (ASWB) is a nonprofit organization that is in charge of regulating social work boards in all 50 states of the United States, along with the US Virgin Islands, Guam and the 10 provinces of Canada. The ASWB conducts various examinations, including the clinical exam, which is one of their most popular social work tests.

What Is the Function of the ASWB?

Every state or province has its own social work board. It is the responsibility of the state or provincial social board to:

- Determine an individual's overall eligibility for social work
- Issue a certified social worker with a license to practice
- Handle all of the matters relating to license renewal

The job of the ASWB is to regulate all social work boards by developing the licensing exams that future social workers have to take. In short, the organization's task is to develop the licensing examination, issue test scores, register candidates who want to take the examination and issue score transfers.

Format of the Clinical Examination

Each ASWB clinical license examination has a total of 170 multiple-choice questions. Of these, 20 questions, mixed in with the other 150, are considered "pretest questions" and are used to assess certain questions' inclusion in future tests.

You will have four hours to complete the exam. The examination is conducted on a Pearson VUE computer, which is designed to provide smooth computer-based testing (CBT). It is an interactive interface that allows you to go through the questions, bookmark them and more.

All ASWB questions are designed to be free of all forms of bias, including race, gender and sexual orientation. Highly qualified professionals create the examination, and the questions themselves are subjected to a rigorous review process. The exams all follow the standards developed by the American

Psychological Association (APA), the American Educational Research Association (AERA) and the National Council on Measurement in Education (NCME).

Taking the ASWB Clinical Examination

Step One

First, you need to apply for a social work license from the regulatory board in your home state or province. You must receive official approval to take the examination. You also need to fulfill the eligibility requirements necessary to get this approval. These requirements vary from region to region. You will need to submit an application and pay a small application fee to the local regulatory board. You can also make arrangements for nonstandard testing in case of disabilities.

Step Two

Once you have registered with your provincial or state regulator and received approval, you need to register with the ASWB. You'll be asked to answer a series of questions regarding topics like your education. The ASWB will use your answers to verify your eligibility for the examination. The organization will also use the information that you provide as demographic data. All of the information will be kept confidential.

Ensure that the name you use to register for the exam matches the ID documents that you produce at the exam center. Exam fees must be paid via a credit card like a Mastercard, Visa or Discover. All registration fees are nonrefundable. The associate examination fee is US$230.

Once the payment goes through, you will receive an Authorization to Test (ATT) email directly from the ASWB. Keep this email for future reference, since it will allow you to set up a testing appointment. The ATT is valid for only one attempt at the exam and expires after one year.

Step Three

Next, you will need to schedule a testing appointment for your exam. To do this, you need to use the Pearson VUE platform, which has a portal dedicated to the ASWB exam. The clinical examination has no set time or date; you can schedule a testing appointment according to your needs after you have received an ATT email. It is recommended that you book the test center and date as far in advance as it is possible.

Once you have scheduled a testing appointment with the date, time and test center of your choice, you will receive a confirmation email from ASWB within the next 24 hours. If you do not receive the email, contact Pearson VUE immediately so that they can resend the email to you. You may also reschedule or cancel your appointment if there are extenuating circumstances.

The Day of ASWB Clinical Examination

You should arrive at the test center early. If you arrive late, you will be assumed to be a no-show, will not be permitted to take the examination and will have your registration fee forfeited.

Extenuating circumstances, such as accidents, natural disasters, etc., will entitle you to reschedule your examination at a later date. Contact the ASWB office to learn more.

Forms of ID

When you arrive for the examination, you need to carry two forms of primary and secondary ID documents, including one form of ID from each of the following lists.

Primary ID: An unexpired government-issued ID that includes your first name, last name, a photograph and your signature.

- Passport
- Military ID
- Driver's license
- Permanent resident ID
- Green card
- Any other form of government-issued identification

Secondary ID: An unexpired identification that contains your first name, last name and signature.

- Social Security card

- Work ID
- Student ID
- Credit card

Check-In

- A VUE staff member will take your photograph after your ID documents and admission card have been verified.
- The palm of your hand will be scanned and stored in the database for security reasons.
- All personal items will be taken and stored in a locker. You will not be able to access the locker during the examination. Please note that personal electronics, books, notes, etc., must all be surrendered before the exam and placed in the locker.
- Lastly, you will be asked to provide an electronic signature for the Candidate Rules Agreement (CRA).

Items Not Allowed in the Testing Room

The testing room has various computer stations, each of which has a monitor, a mouse, a keyboard and a pair of headphones. The VUE staff will seat you in a designated spot.

- You will not be able to eat or drink in the testing room. You may visit the break room to eat something, but only if allowances have been previously made under the nonstandard testing arrangement.
- You will be provided with an erasable booklet and marker. Return these to the test center staff after the exam. Failure to do so may result in the invalidation of your score.
- You cannot bring any study materials, reference materials, etc., into the testing room. If you violate this rule, you will be expelled from the test center. Your test scores will be invalidated, and you may find yourself facing civil, administrative or criminal charges.

Unit I: Human Development, Diversity and Behavior in the Environment

Chapter One: Human Development in the Life Cycle

In the field of social work, theories are arrived at by applying scientific deductions and methods to general explanations and available and collected evidence. Human behavior is a very important facet of social work. By understanding human interactions and responses to certain prompts, a theory can begin to explain human behavior.

In the ASWB clinical examination, it is more important to understand the concept of human development theories than to memorize the names of the theories. To prepare for the exam, you need to have a broad understanding of the different theories. You will also need a focused understanding of the theories so that you can understand when something is applicable.

Personality Theories

Personality theories try to uncover the origins of human personality. These are also known as psychodynamic theories, and there are dozens of them. However, all of them emphasize the importance of unconscious motives and childhood experiences.

Psychosexual Stages of Development – Sigmund Freud

Sigmund Freud theorized that a major percentage of a person's personality solidifies at a very young age. He believed most children get their unique personalities by the age of five. He also proposed the five psychosexual stages of development: oral, anal, phallic, latency and genital. He proposed that children gain some kind of pleasure or gratification from the parts of their bodies named in that particular stage. Each psychosexual stage comes with various conflicts, and children's personalities are shaped by how they come to terms with these conflicts.

Freud also introduced the concept of **fixation**, which happens when a child is either gratified or frustrated too much. Fixation is a stage during which the child is unable to smoothly progress from one stage of development to another. This fixation has lasting effects and shapes the child's personality as an adult (for example, anal retentivity).

Stage	Age of the Child	Activities	Consequence of Fixation
Oral	0 to 12 months	Sucking, biting, chewing, etc.	Overeating and excessive smoking
Anal	2 years	Bowel movements	Anal-retentive and anal-expulsive behavior
Phallic	3 to 5 years	Genitals	Guilt or anxiety with respect to sexual intercourse
Latency	5 to 13 or 14 years (puberty)	Latent or dormant sexuality	N/A
Genital	Puberty onward	Genitals; awakening of sexual urges	N/A

Freud was a proponent of the **Oedipus complex** and its female counterpart, the **Electra complex**. The Oedipus complex occurs during the phallic stage of development, when the male child views his father as a rival for his mother's love. Freud said that a male child who sees a naked female for the first time would think that the female's penis has been cut off. The child would fear that his own father would subject him to this for desiring his mother—a fear that Freud refers to as **castration anxiety**. Freud theorized that the male child would begin to identify with the father and accept his father's personality.

Psychoanalytic Theory

Sigmund Freud's other major contribution to the field is the theory that an individual is the sum total of past experiences, and treatment can be done by dealing with all of the repressed thoughts in the subconscious. Personalities come into being due to innate conflicts between repressed sexual and aggressive urges.

Freud posited that behavior and personality take root in the conflicts that occur between conflicting forces operating at the three distinct levels of awareness. These levels are referred to as the **preconscious**, the **conscious** and the **unconscious**.

- The preconscious consists of all those thoughts that are not immediately in a client's mind. However, these thoughts can be retrieved quite easily because they are readily available.
- The conscious consists of all the material that a client is consciously thinking about at any given point in time.
- Lastly, the unconscious consists of those materials that have a lot of influence on the daily life of the client but that the client is ultimately unaware of.

Freud dissected the human personality into three distinct components:

- **Id:** This is composed entirely of unconscious psychological energy, all of which contains the base urges of the flesh. For example, all of the animal impulses of sex, survival, aggression, etc., are the main components of the id. The underlying drive of the id is the **pleasure principle** that says humans want to experience pleasure and avoid pain.
- **Ego:** The ego is responsible for managing all the conflicts that arise between the id and the callings of the real world and society. The ego is very complex; some parts of it are unconscious, while others are conscious. The ego's underlying drive is the **reality principle**, or the knowledge that base desires and impulses have to be delayed to meet the needs of the real world. When an individual's behavior is in line with the ego, it is called **syntonic** behavior. The opposite kind of behavior is called **dystonic** behavior. When the ego is unable to reconcile with the demands of the id, there is a lot of conflict. The distress from all of this conflict leads to a spillover that results in **anxiety**. **Ego strength** is the ability of a person's ego to comprehensively deal with the demands of the id and superego.
- **Superego:** The superego is the moral component of a person's make-up. All of the moral standards imparted by parents, teachers, guiding figures and society are contained in the superego. This component is responsible for forcing the ego to behave in line with reality and the expected standards

of morality. The superego is the reason why someone feels bad for disregarding the norms of society.

Self Psychology

The **self** is the central nervous system of the human personality, according to the theory of self psychology. A developing child's various needs are met as a result of compassionate responses from early caregivers, which leads to the child developing a very strong sense of "self-hood." When caregivers are not very compassionate in their responses to young children, there can be a lack of self-cohesion in a child's personality.

The goal of self psychology is to help the individual develop a better and stronger sense of self-cohesion. The client's frustrated "self-object" needs can be met with the help of **therapeutic regression**. The main self-object needs are:

- Idealization – Children identify with someone they think is more capable, idealize that person, then draw strength from their relationship with that person.
- Twinship – Children seek to create an alter ego so that they can belong with others.
- Mirroring – Children's aspirations for a perfect self are validated.

Individual Psychology

One of Freud's contemporaries, **Alfred Adler**, broke away from him and posited his own theory of individual psychology. Adler believed a person's main motivations were not animalistic urges of sex or violence. Instead, the driving force behind human personality is people's efforts to attain perfection. He said that children feel inadequate when compared to adults. This feeling of inferiority allows them to develop, learn skills and **compensate** for their previous shortcomings.

Some people, however, tend to **overcompensate** because they suffer from a very large inferiority complex. Instead of trying to master and overcome the challenges that they faced in their childhood, they cover up their insecurities with displays of wealth, power, status, etc. People who suffer from these feelings of being "less" are unhealthy. Proper therapy can help a person overcome these unhealthy patterns and start to contribute to the well-being of others.

Ego Psychology

The intelligent and sentient processes of the ego are the focus of ego psychology. Ego psychology is based on a client assessment, such as the one offered here. Because good behavior is completely under the control of the ego, the process of treatment focuses on how the client's ego functions. Here is what ego psychology chooses to address:

- The client's behavior in relation to the situation that a person finds him or herself in
- The client's perception or impression of reality, which is called reality testing
- The strengths of the ego, which are also referred to as coping abilities
- The client's capacity to relate to peers

The goal of ego psychology is to maintain and control the ego so that stress and anxiety are minimized. The mind responds to both internal and external forces.

The Psychosocial Stages of Development

Psychologist **Erik Erikson** postulated that children's personalities develop in a predetermined fashion but are not affected by sexuality. Instead, the sense of self of a child is determined by social interactions. Erikson was also a proponent of the theory that personality develops constantly and identity crises are the epicenter of each stage of development. Erikson came up with a theory describing the eight stages of psychosocial development. Here is a concise representation of these stages and their key characteristics:

1. **Trust vs. Mistrust:** This is a stage between birth and 12 months when children learn to trust others depending on the quality of the care they're given. Improperly concluded, this stage can cause anxiety, heightened mistrust, insecurity, etc.

2. **Autonomy vs. Shame:** This is a stage between the ages of one to three years when children start to assert their independence. If children are not encouraged to be free in this stage, they can develop a sense of shame, doubt, lack self-esteem, etc.

3. **Initiative vs. Guilt:** From the ages of three to six years, children assert themselves and become more independent in their play and projects. If this is not encouraged, they will begin to feel a sense of guilt and will always be followers.

4. **Industry vs. Inferiority:** From the ages of six until puberty, children start their own pet projects. They initiate projects, collaborate with their peers and develop a sense of pride. If restricted, this can lead to feelings of inferiority and a lack of confidence.

5. **Identity vs. Role Confusion:** This stage occurs during adolescence and involves the transition from childhood to adulthood. During this stage, people start to form their own identities. Restriction can lead to role confusion and insecurity.

6. **Intimacy vs. Isolation:** As young adults, people start to explore relationships and become intimate with other people who are not their family. This is a defining stage. Restriction during this stage can lead to isolation.

7. **Generativity vs. Stagnation:** As middle-aged adults, people start jobs, start families and settle down to realize that they are part of a much larger picture. If this stage is restricted, then an individual can start to feel stagnant or unproductive.

8. **Ego Identity vs. Despair:** This is toward the end of life, when individuals become senior citizens and start to slow down. During this time, it is important to stay curious and explore life. Not doing so can lead to a sense of despair.

Object Relations Theory

Developed by **Margaret Mahler**, the premise of object relations theory is that the development of personality is due to relationships with other people. There are various stages of development under this theory, and each centers around an individual's relationships with other people. During the early stages, attachments with parents are most important. An *object* can refer to people, parts of people, physical items, etc. Below is a table explaining the various stages and characteristics of object relations theory.

Age	Stage	Defining Characteristics
0 to 1 month	**Normal Autism**	Detached, unaware and self-absorbed
1 to 5 months	**Normal Symbiotic**	Aware of parents, but no sense of self
5 to 9 months	**Individualization**	Increased interest in the outside world
9 to 15 months	**Practicing**	Explore freely and discover a self
15 to 24 months	**Rapprochement**	Become close to the mother
24 to 38 months	**Object Constancy**	Begin to see themselves as separate and unique individuals

The Process of Social Development

Human beings are social animals, which is why social development is a very important facet of development as a whole. By being properly social, a person's mental health, job competency and interpersonal competency, etc., are enhanced. At the very grassroots level, social development teaches a child how to interact with others. Emotional development is a very important stage during which children learn how to manage their emotions productively.

Social development is also linked directly to various social institutions. In an inclusive and progressive society, it is very important to treat people with fairness and kindness. When peaceful and safe environments are created, social cohesion and togetherness also increase. Institutional change can be carried out only if there are inclusive reforms and policies available.

Impact of Disabilities on Development

Depending on the type of disability and the way it manifests, the impact on development and growth can vary widely. Some disabilities are short term and disappear within a few weeks or months. Others are chronic and lifelong; they become an intrinsic part of an individual. The development of coping skills and proper support is critical.

Disability is a phenomenon that exists in all societies, and that is why it can be classified as **normal**. Despite a largely fractured history, societies all over the world have started to become more inclusive toward people with disabilities. **Disability rights** is a very important topic right now, and these rights are increasingly being enforced by individuals and institutions.

In existing disability literature, terms like ***inclusion, participation and nondiscrimination*** have been introduced. The goal of inclusion and participation is to do away with the social stigma that disabled people face. Whether the disability is physical, mental or cognitive, disabled individuals have extensive rights.

Stages of Adult Development

Humans do not stop developing when they become adults. Even as adults, there are various physical, mental and interpersonal changes that take place. Usually, these changes are gradual, although some of them can be rapid.

Stage #1 – Young Adults

Age: 21 to 39 years

Physical Change: Physical and sexual maturity is reached. Nutritional needs are purely for the sake of maintenance, not growth.
Mental Change: New skills, knowledge, etc., are acquired and used to solve problems.
Interpersonal Change: Seek intimacy, start a family, set career goals and choose a lifestyle.

Stage #2 – Middle Adults

Age: 40 to 64 years

Physical Change: Begin to age. Women enter menopause, and many adults come to terms with chronic health problems.
Mental Change: Life experiences are used to solve problems.
Interpersonal Change: The main issue is to stay productive while also planning retirement and caring for children and parents.

Age: 65 to 79 years

Physical Change: There is gradual aging, which is naturally accompanied by a decline in physical abilities and senses.
Mental Change: Learning continues actively; however, memory is affected.
Interpersonal Change: Take on new roles of grandparents or widows or widowers; learn to strike a balance between dependence and independence.

Age: Above 80 years

Physical Change: Physical abilities continue to decline, and other chronic health conditions can continue to worsen over time.
Mental Change: Memory skills continue to decline, and there can also be some confusion that stems from illnesses (Alzheimer's, dementia, etc.).
Interpersonal Change: Live as independently as possible while accepting the end of life and personal losses.

Interplay of Bio-, Psycho- and Social Factors

The development of the individual is the end result of the interplay between biological, psychological and social factors. Children develop physically and intellectually, and they also gain more emotional maturity. Society and environment also play a major role. All of these physical, cognitive and social changes lead to the formation of a person's unique psychosocial identity.

Spiritual, Cognitive and Emotional Development

Spiritual Development

Spiritual development is difficult to explain, and there have been many models that seek to define it. However, most of these models have one thing in common. They state that spiritual development is a continuum, and some people stay on the same course all their lives. Other people, however, radically change their path. Here are the different types of spiritual development usually observed:

- People who are unwilling to accept that there is a will greater than their own. Usually, such individuals are egotistical and show a reckless disregard for society's rules. This kind of behavior is displayed by young children.
- People who have blind faith in authority figures and see the world in simple black and white. These people are self-righteous and religious. They engage in a simple blind faith with no context or substance. People do not usually shift from this point easily.
- People who display scientific questioning and skepticism. This kind of behavior is most seen in people who work in the fields of science, academia and education. They question spiritual forces and move away from religious dogma.
- The most beautiful stage is nirvana, in which a person enjoys the beauty of nature and existence. This is an individual who does not judge others. Instead, he or she follows a path marked by the loss of all egocentric attachments.

Cognitive Development

Information processing, conceptual capacity, perception, linguistic abilities and other elements of brain development are addressed in cognitive development. It is the emergence of the capacity to reason and comprehend. One of the biggest debates in this section is regarding nature vs. nurture. Over the years, many experts have been divided on whether cognitive abilities depend on a person's innate skill (nature) or the quality of caregivers and education (nurture).

Right now, experts realize that is a false dichotomy. Biological and behavioral experiments have shown that gene activity and experiences both play a huge role in the shaping of a person's cognitive development. In other words, a person's innate skill is a very important factor. At the same time, the quality of caregivers also plays a large role in people's development. The main proponent of a solid theory of cognitive growth is psychologist **Jean Piaget**.

Age	Stage	Characteristics of the Stage
0 to 2 years	Sensorimotor	a. Object retention b. Primitive logic development c. Intentional actions d. Copycat playing e. Meaning signaling f. Symbol meaning
2 to 7 years	Preoperational	a. Concrete and abstract thinking b. Sense of time c. Words and symbols d. Magical thinking e. Difficulty empathizing and seeing another point of view f. Thinking is not generalized **Imaginary friends** usually appear during this stage of development. This is a normal phenomenon and not a sign of an innate disorder.
7 to 11 years	Concrete Operations	a. Think abstractly b. Can play games with proper rules c. Understand how cause and effect works d. Understand how events follow logically e. Reversible thinking
11 onward	Formal Operations	a. Plan for the future b. Abstract at a high level c. Think and dabble in hypotheticals d. Assume the roles and responsibilities of adults e. Start to question conventions

Emotional Development

The milestones of emotional development are much harder to isolate and quantify when compared to spiritual, physical and cognitive development. This is an area where a lot of skills are on display: self-awareness, self-regulation, etc. Social skills and emotional development go hand in hand, with the ability to pay attention, empathize, cooperate with others, etc., being defining qualities. In fact, play is a valuable way for children to experience social and emotional growth

Normal Sexual Development

Babies, children, young adults and elders are sexual beings. Many people have a misconception that sexual activity is reserved only for young adults and middle adults. Actually, sexual activity is not limited to sexual intercourse. As a result, sexual activity is a lifelong phenomenon for the average human.

In infants and toddlers, sexuality can be present even before they are born. By the time they are two years old, children know their own gender and are aware of the differences in male and female genitalia.

During the ages of three to seven, children begin to explore their sexuality. They may begin by doing something innocuous that they have seen other adults doing—holding hands, kissing and more. By the ages of five or six, children start to develop a sense of privacy and modesty about dressing and bathing.

Preadolescence, between ages nine and 13, is when bodies start to go through changes. For example, there can be faint developments of body hair and other secondary sexual characteristics. This is a sensitive time because children are usually very self-conscious about their overall appearance. Some older children begin to date and display romantic interest in classmates or friends. Around this time, young people start to wonder about their identity and sexual orientation.

In adolescent youth, sexuality is more well defined. The average teenager has great interest in sex, sexual relationships, romantic relationships and more. Teenagers start to develop serious romantic and sexual attachments, of which sex is a natural part. By the age of 20, most people have already fallen in love, fallen out of love, had sex, etc. This goes for teenagers of all kinds of sexualities—hetero, homo, bi, pan, asexual, etc.

The story is different in the case of adults. Adult sexuality is varied and complex. However, sex remains an integral part of adult life. Women experience menopause during their fifties, which can affect their sexuality. In the same vein, adult men also start to experience changes in their sexuality. However, the change in men is not as predictable as it is in women. Sexuality is not largely absent among senior citizens. Even if the desire or ability to engage in sex lessens, the need for intimacy and touch is ever present with them.

Gerontology

Some definitions:

- **Aging**, or the process of getting older, is the accumulation of physiological changes that occur with an advance in age. In most cases, these changes increase the risk of death or chronic disease.
- **Life expectancy:** This statistic predicts the average life span in a particular demographic. The demographic can be mapped by geographical region, profession, race, sexual orientation, etc.

Over the years, the average life expectancy in the modern world has increased dramatically due to better standards of living and hygiene. The development of vaccines, antibiotics and other preventive medicine has played a major role in the growth and development of the human race.

Many people think that getting on in years is undesirable, and they live in a state of denial. They invest in a lot of antiaging treatments under the false belief that society does not value them if they become older. To many people, aging means the same as stagnation and deterioration.

As people age, they are subjected to a wide variety of physical changes in their stamina, overall strength, senses, etc. However, the extent of these changes depends on a lot of factors. First, genetics plays a very important role. Second, lifestyle and medical history also affect aging.

Social workers need to understand that older adults still hold a place of value in their family, their community and society at large. However, many elderly individuals have to contend with a lot of challenges as they age. They have to deal with their aging body and the challenges of physical weakness. They also have to face the challenge of gaining access to proper health care and physiotherapy. Some elderly individuals also have to come to terms with decreased economic security, vulnerability to abuse and a perceived loss of importance to other people. A social worker's job is to advocate for these individuals.

The Theory of Attachment and Bonding

Developed by **Edward John Mostyn Bowlby**, attachment theory states that when the primary caregiver is responsive to an infant's needs, the infant develops an innate sense of security and safety. Bowlby posited that children come into the world ready to form attachments with other people because, evolutionarily, this helps them survive. At first, they form a primary attachment with their mother, which is called **monotropy**. Using this attachment as a frame of reference, infants, babies and growing toddlers start to explore the world. Disruption to this attachment can cause serious issues.

Another major theory states that attachment itself can be classified as a set of **learned behaviors**. For example, the child will initially form an attachment to whoever gives it food, thus proving the evolutionary drive of the child to seek out food. The child associates the mother with the comfort of receiving food and hence seeks out the mother whenever it's in distress. The child can also slowly make use of conditioning techniques to get what it wants from people.

No matter what we look at—Bowlby's theory or learned behaviors—it is clear that parents are the first point of contact for any child. Their important role cannot be minimized in any way. In fact, disrupted parental attachment systems can lead to severe psychiatric disorders later on in life. However, these theories have not been exempt from criticism. There are cultural influences and many differences around the world in the way children interact with their primary caregivers. These theories have not taken into account the differences that exist among various cultures.

Child Development

From birth to the end of puberty, a child will go through many physical, mental, social and emotional changes. This is a continuous process and is very important for a person's overall health, adjustment and well-being. This is basically what child development is, and it can vary widely for different people and different cultures. The developmental changes in children can also be influenced by genetic and environmental factors. Below is a concise summary of the various stages of child development, along with the key health-care issues that occur.

Infants and Toddlers

Age: 0 to 3 years

Physical Growth: Rapid, especially the size of the brain

Mental Growth: Learn by sensing, playing and crying and communicating through babbling and elementary sentences

Socio-Emotional Growth: Trust others, depend on them and develop a proto-sense of self

Key Issues:

- Proper communication
- Health and safety

Young Children

Age: 4 to 6 years

Physical Growth: Slow, better motor skills and toilet training

Mental Growth: Vivid imagination, fear of things, memory begins to improve considerably, enjoy stories

Socio-Emotional Growth: Independence, increased assertiveness and sensitivity to others' feelings

Key Issues:

- Proper communication
- Health and safety

Older Children

Age: 7 to 12 years

Physical Growth: Slow, until they reach puberty

Mental Growth: Active, eager to learn, understand how cause and effect works, can read and do mathematics

Socio-Emotional Growth: Advanced sense of self, school activities and more independence

Key Issues:

- Proper communication
- Health and safety

Basic Human Needs

Humans have certain needs that are required to be fulfilled, as described by **Abraham Maslow** in his hierarchy of needs. This theory states that people have an innate drive to engage in activities specifically so that their needs are fulfilled. **Maslow Pyramid**'s five layers are as follows (from the bottom up):

- Physiological: Food, water, oxygen, proper temperatures, etc., are humans' physiological needs. People need these to survive; if they are deprived of one or all of these, they will surely die.
- Social: Humans are social animals, and they need to form social bonds with other human beings. A person needs family, friendship, romantic relationships, etc.
- Safety: A human needs to feel safe from all kinds of threats, including physical harm or immediate danger. As a result, a person requires a routine and some predictability.
- Esteem: People need a stable and firm level of self-respect. At the same time, they also need a minimum level of respect from other people.
- Self-Actualization: The top of the pyramid is self-actualization, which is an ongoing and continuing process. Self-actualization involves the development of one's own potential and working toward being one's best

version. Only 1% of people consistently operate at the self-actualization level.

The bottom four layers of the pyramid are known as deficiency needs, or D-needs. This is because Maslow believed that these needs rise due to a deficiency or lack. On the other hand, the top layer of the pyramid is called the being or growth need—B-need. In the realm of social work, the Maslow Pyramid is a very important topic and can be used to prioritize problems.

Adolescent/Teenage Development

The period of 13 to 18 years is a very critical time in the development of children. This is when they start to understand complex concepts, such as philosophy, mathematics, rights, privileges, etc. They mature emotionally, physically and intellectually during this time.

- **Physical Growth:** Adolescents grow in spurts and mature in other physical ways.
- **Mental Growth:** Adolescents become abstract thinkers and try to look at problems in a deeper way. They also choose their own values.
- **Socio-Emotional Growth:** Adolescents develop a sense of identity, build close relationships with their peer group and family and are concerned about their appearance. During this period, many teenagers go through a rebellious phase and challenge authority.

Key Issues:

- Health and safety
- Communication

Age-Specific Care for Adolescents:

- Avoid treating them as children; try to treat them as adults.
- Show respect and do not patronize them. Be considerate of how you treat and talk to them.
- Provide them with the information they need to make positive choices.

- Encourage them to communicate openly with their peers, parents, etc.

How Self-Image Is Affected in the Life Cycle

Self-image is very important, since this is how people define themselves. It is tied to a physical description, social role, professional position, personal traits and beliefs at large. At the same time, people also have self-esteem, which is a measure of how much a person accepts his or her own self-image. Self-esteem involves perspectives and can be positive or negative. These factors are linked intrinsically and are very important for everyone.

- **Childhood:** Small children have remarkably high self-esteem. Their self-esteem slowly declines as they grow and begin to form a balanced portrayal of themselves.
- **Adolescence:** During the teenage years, self-esteem continues to fall, mostly due to a fall in body image. There is also a lot of peer pressure during this time, all of which is coupled with social and academic hurdles.
- **Adulthood:** During adulthood, people's self-esteem improves gradually as they start professional positions and develop mature relationships with partners, family, coworkers, etc. There is also a stark decrease in body image issues.
- **Older Adulthood:** The self-esteem level starts to decline as a person crosses 70 years of age, possibly due to a loss of employment, partners, friends, etc. Health problems can also affect self-image.

It has been found that during the adolescent years, females usually have a lower level of self-esteem than males do. This gap persists throughout early adulthood, then tapers off as both genders begin to approach old age.

Genetic Issues

It is important to know why clients may seek genetic testing, counseling, etc. Social workers need to know about the process of genetic inheritance. They also need to know about the different types of genetic conditions—chromosomal anomalies, multifactorial disorders, single-gene disorders, environmental disorders, etc. An understanding of the patterns of inheritance is also recommended.

The Dynamics of Loss and Grief

Elisabeth Kubler-Ross is responsible for developing the theory of the five stages of grief. She formulated her initial theory after observing people who were suffering from terminal illnesses. Later on, she expanded this theory to include people suffering from all kinds of personal loss—death of a loved one, loss of a job, loss of income, onset of a major illness and other tragedies or disasters. Here are the five stages:

- **Denial:** A person denies the tragedy and thinks, "This is not happening to me."
- **Anger:** Due to an inability to process the bad news, the person gets frustrated and then resorts to anger. He or she lashes out and finds something or someone to blame.
- **Bargaining:** The person tries to negotiate with someone in order to change something about the situation.
- **Depression:** This is a period of sadness and loneliness, which will definitely occur as the person reflects upon the immense loss suffered.
- **Acceptance:** The last stage of grief is acceptance, in which the person accepts the loss and tries to live with it. This is when someone is at peace with what happened. Hope is possible at all stages.

Biopsychological Responses to Diseases and Infirmity

Disability can place many demands on a family. It can consume time, money, resources, energy, etc., and this leads to many other needs being unmet. Assisting the disabled person daily can be physically and emotionally taxing and can lead to fatigue. There are emotional strains involved, leading to resentment, worry, guilt and anger.

The financial burden associated with taking care of someone who is disabled is also a major worry. Getting the proper health services, education, diet, transportation, therapy, etc., can be a major financial task. The person may be eligible for reimbursement from insurance or public health care acts. However, it can be a challenge for families to be aware of the programs that are available.

It is very difficult to navigate the bureaucratic systems that check for eligibility for receiving these benefits, and this can be a frustrating experience. In such a situation, social workers can be a huge help. They can help families by coordinating with all of the different providers that are needed. Also, different communities have different levels of access to needed facilities. It is a difficult task to deal with stigma, judgment and rejection.

Depending on the kind of disability and the environment in which people are in, the disabled person and his or her caregivers can face a variety of different challenges.

Life Cycle of the Family

Stage 1 – Experiences with the Family of Origin

- Build and maintain relationships with parents, siblings and friends
- Finish education
- Develop the foundations for an individual family life

Stage 2 – Leaving the Home

- Developing adult relationships with parents after coming up with a differentiated sense of self and family of origin
- Developing intimate relationships with peers
- Developing an identity of work and building toward financial independence

Stage 3 – Pre-Marriage

- Selecting a partner to marry or settle down with
- Developing a relationship with the partner
- Deciding to establish a family with someone

Stage 4 – Childless Couple

- Living together emotionally and practically
- Introducing a new partner to the family of origin and adjusting priorities

Stage 5 – Family with Young Children

- Family is realigned to make space for young children
- Perfecting and adopting the role of parents
- Family of origin's relationships with the children are realigned to include roles of family and grandparents
- Helping young children develop successful peer relationships

Stage 6 – Family with Teens

- Adjusting the parent-child relationship to provide the child with more autonomy
- Focusing on midlife and careers
- Caring for families of origin

Stage 7 – Launching the Children

- Developing adult-adult relationships with children
- Adjusting to living as a couple
- Adjusting to include children's partners into the family
- Dealing with family deaths

Stage 8 – Later Family Life

- Coping with one's own decline
- Adjusting to handing responsibilities off to children
- Dealing with the loss of loved ones and peers
- Preparing for one's death

Types of Parenting Skills

Authoritarian Parenting

This is a parenting style in which children are ordered to follow the rules set in place by the parent. Flouting such rules can lead to punishment. This kind of parenting can lead to lower levels of happiness, poor social competence and low self-esteem.

Authoritative Parenting

Like authoritarian parenting, this parenting style involves setting rules that the children are expected to follow. However, the children have a say in the rules and are afforded the ability to ask questions. Instead of punishment, the parent doles out nurturing and forgiveness. This usually leads to more happiness and self-esteem.

Uninvolved Parenting

In this style, parents are largely absent from the lives of their children. They fulfill all basic needs but are not there for their children. This is the worst kind of parenting, since the children will lack self-control and be incompetent.

Permissive Parenting

Permissive parents make very few demands of their children. They do not discipline them, and they let them get away with whatever they want. Children like these usually tend to do poorly in academics. They also have a problem listening to authority.

The Impact of Trauma

Sometimes, people are subjected to traumatic and stressful events and experiences, all of which can have lasting effects. These events destroy a person's sense of safety and can lead to a feeling of being overwhelmed and helpless. Emotional and psychological trauma can be as bad as physical trauma, if not worse. An event can lead to emotional and psychological trauma if:

- It happened without any warning.
- There was no preparation.
- There was a feeling of pervasive powerlessness.
- It happened again and again.
- The abuser was intentionally cruel.
- It happened during childhood.

A child who has undergone trauma sees the world through a distorted lens, and a lack of support and therapy can have lasting consequences. Such children continually experience a fundamental sense of fear and insecurity even as adults.

Emotional and Psychological Symptoms of Trauma

- Mood swings and increased anger
- Anxiety, fear and paranoia
- Withdrawal and isolation from others
- Confusion and sadness
- Numbness
- Self-blame, guilt and shame

Physical Symptoms of Trauma

- Insomnia, nightmares and sleep disorders
- A racing heartbeat
- Pain and fatigue
- Agitation and irritability
- Increased muscle tension
- Jumpiness and jitters
- Difficulty concentrating

There is also a type of trauma that results from **intimate partner abuse**. In all instances of this kind of abuse, abusers' need for power and control over their partners leads to them mistreating their partners. Domestic violence occurs in all racial, cultural and socioeconomic areas and can involve other factors, such as physical abuse, sexual abuse, emotional abuse and financial abuse. Here are some of the signs of domestic violence:

- A suspicious injury or injuries that are inconsistent with a normal history of injury. This includes bruises, repeated minor injuries, new scars, etc.
- A physical complaint without any apparent diagnosis, such as pain in the back, abdomen, pelvic region, etc.
- Suspicious behavior, such as crying, being fearful, making no eye contact, defensiveness, irrational anger, anxiety, having a blank expression, etc.
- Partners are controlling and/or coercive. They are overly concerned; they hover, they will not leave their partners unattended with the social worker;

clients are afraid of speaking to someone without their partners; clients are fearful of partners or defer to their partners.

Chapter Two: How Humans Behave Environmentally

Person-in-Environment Theory

Also known as PIE theory, this theory looks at individual behavior in the context of the environment people reside in. This is a very important and nuanced perspective, especially in the field of social work. The ecology of PIE is rooted in systems theory, in which coping is looked at as a transactional process. In a nutshell, environmental factors can have a major positive or negative effect on clients' development.

PIE's classification system was developed as a better alternative to the disease and moral models, which have since become obsolete. A good example of such a model is the *Diagnostic and Statistical Manual of Mental Disorders (DSM)* and the national civil and penal codes. The main benefit of PIE theory is that it centers on the client and not the agency. This is a field-tested theory and is extremely effective in social work.

The Theories of Human Behavior

There are many theoretical points of view regarding social behavior in today's world. As a social worker, you will be expected to know the different factors and ways in which the environment can affect a human's development and behavior.

Systems Theory

All systems of human behavior are made of a number of interrelated complex parts, and each part affects the others. The way in which all of these interdependencies affect each other and the system as a whole is the summary of systems theory.

Rational Choice Theory

Clients are rational human beings, and all of their behavior is target oriented. All interactions are measured and rational and involve the pure exchange of social resources to reach a certain goal. Like in economics, the main goal is to act out of self-interest and maximize rewards.

Conflict Theory

People see themselves in competition with others and act purely out of their own self-interest. Resources are scarce, and it is humans' goal to gain power and dominate others. Any and all social change is driven purely by conflict and strife.

Psychodynamic Theory

Mental activity—both conscious and unconscious—serves as the primary impetus that shapes human behavior. In particular, the experiences of early childhood and the formative years play a very important role. People also use defense mechanisms.

Social Constructionist Theory

Humans interact with each other socially and develop a common, shared view and understanding of their environment. All cultural and historical contexts play a very big role in shaping the world. Processes are grounded in customs.

Social Behavioral Theory

By interacting with the environment, human behavior is learned. By using the techniques of classical and operant conditioning, undesirable behavior can be removed, and all solutions to problems can be formulated. In this type of theory, association and imitation play a very important role.

Developmental Theory

Physical, psychological and social factors come into play as human civilization develops. Each stage builds upon the others, and this leads to the growth of human behavior in the environmental context.

Humanistic Perspective Theory

This theory centers on the individual instead of the entire society. According to this theory, human behavior is driven by a need for growth and the quest for personal meaning. If people behave in a way that is inconsistent with their true self, they can experience anxiety. Everyone is responsible for their own choices.

Psychological Defense Mechanisms

People also tend to use psychological **defense mechanisms** that protect them from anxiety and worry. Defense mechanisms are involuntary and shouldn't be confused with coping strategies, which are carried out voluntarily and consciously. Here are some common psychological defense mechanisms.

- Acting Out – People get into trouble to get attention instead of talking about feeling neglected.
- Compensation – People adopt behaviors to compensate for real or imaginary deficiencies. Someone who is insecure about his masculinity, for example, can compensate by making jokes of a lurid or sexual nature.
- Conversion – People repress urges; this repression is expressed as some kind of bodily function, such as nervous tics, flatulence, hiccups, etc.
- Denial – People deny the event and refuse or are unable to acknowledge the fact that the event actually happened.
- Dissociation – People split their mental states, which allows them to express all their unconscious desires without having to take any responsibility. This is called a fugue state or daydreaming.
- Idealization – People admire another person and overestimate the individual's good qualities, putting him or her on a pedestal.
- Identification – People see a part of themselves in another person and supplant themselves in the role of that person. This is important in total superego development.
- Inhibition – People lose the motivation to engage in an activity that they enjoy. They do this to avoid conflicting with impulses they think are forbidden.
- Projection – People project their own shortcomings—whether real or imaginary—onto someone else as a way to deflect all responsibility. This is a primitive defense.
- Rationalization – People try to rationalize and explain their irrational behavior by coming up with an explanation that is ridiculous. However, they still try to foist this explanation onto others.
- Regression – People return partially, symbolically or entirely to an infantile and childlike pattern of thinking and acting.
- Repression – People keep all their thoughts, fantasies, ideas, impulses, etc., firmly inside themselves. This is a key mechanism that many people use.

- Sublimation – People channel their maladaptive and unacceptable impulses into something constructive and good. For example, a person who is prone to anger issues takes on an aggressive sport, such as football.
- Turning against self – People turn on themselves and inflict undue hostility, violence and extraordinary amounts of criticism on themselves.

Normal vs. Abnormal Behavior

It is difficult to frame an objective definition of what normal behavior is, and in the same vein, what abnormal behavior is. The definition of these kinds of behaviors depends heavily on the society under consideration. Usually, societal conventions and rules are defined as "normal," which is also synonymous with "good." In the same way, behavior that is taboo and does not fall within societal definitions of normal is almost synonymous with "bad." The best way to diagnose behavior as normal and abnormal is to use the *Diagnostic and Statistical Manual of Mental Disorders (DSM)*. This publication is a concise history of how the definition of normal behavior has changed historically. It also distinguishes clearly between most prevalent mental disorders.

Understanding Dysfunctional Family Dynamics

Family dynamics is the term used to describe all the interactions between the various members of a family unit. All families are unique, and each has its own dynamics. Usually, some of these dynamics are good, while others are bad. Even if clients are not in contact with their families, their previous family dynamic will have a bearing on their behavior. For a social worker, it is very important to understand how dysfunctional dynamics work:

- Each and every member of the family is looked at as an individual person.
- The family has a structure and a regular routine that all members follow.
- The family members have realistic expectations of one another.
- All the members set aside time regularly to spend with each other doing group activities, relaxing and just enjoying each other's company.
- Family members help one another in times of need by providing direct assistance.
- Family members ensure that individual family members' needs are met— not just the collective's needs.

- Family members connect with the extended family and community.

The Dynamics of Sexual Abuse

Sexual abuse is one of the most horrifying experiences that any individual can go through. The effect is multiplicative and far-reaching, especially when victims are children, because their experiences will affect their day-to-day life for years to come. Parental support is imperative to help children adjust. Here are some of the main aftereffects of sexual abuse:

- An unwillingness to trust or invest in others while simultaneously seeking out self-destructive paths and acting out to get attention
- A tendency to self-victimize and perceive oneself as vulnerable, which can involve phobias, oversleeping, eating disorders, etc.
- Shame and guilt for being subjected to abuse, which can result in a pattern of self-destructive behavior, including substance abuse, self-harm, suicidal thoughts, acting out, etc.
- Problems with sexuality, an aversion to sex or, in contrast, hypersexual behavior in an effort to compensate

Here are some factors that can affect the way sexual abuse affects the life of the abused and their family dynamics:

- Extent and duration of the sexual abuse
- Existing relationship between the abuser and the survivor
- How other people react to the news of the abuse
- Age of the victim at the time of abuse and at the time of assessment
- The survivor's related life experience

Here are some risks that an individual faces when the news of the abuse is disclosed:

- Disbelief by loved ones—especially parents, siblings, etc. This is especially true if the survivor is a child and the abuser is an adult or a parent's spouse or partner.
- Rejection by other people
- Blame for the abuse. In some cases, the victim can also have to face the consequences for disclosing the abuse in the first place.

Dynamics of Psychological Abuse and Neglect

Psychological abuse is just as bad as sexual abuse—and it is even more invasive and lasting in some ways. Abuse and neglect constitute a pattern of intentional behavior that aims to threaten, isolate, degrade, discredit, humiliate, ignore, withhold, etc. It can also stem from the abuser placing unrealistic and unreasonable expectations on the survivor and making constant demands.

When sustained, psychological abuse and neglect can result in terrifying consequences. Research has shown that abused individuals have trouble with memory, attention, imagination, perception and even intelligence. Those who are being abused are likely to be paranoid, withdrawn, resentful and extremely pessimistic. They feel unloved and unwanted, and they value themselves only through the eyes of other people.

Dynamics of Physical Abuse and Neglect

Intentional injury or trauma that a person repeatedly causes to another over the course of weeks, months, or years is the basic definition of physical abuse. Actions include punching, kicking, biting, burning, scalding, etc. Physical abuse is the most visible form of abuse, as there are outward signs that you can look for. With children, this kind of abuse usually stems from excessive disciplinary actions. More often than not, physical abuse and neglect occur within the family. It is more prevalent in impoverished families that have drug or alcohol issues.

Neglect is a form of physical abuse that can be classified into three types. The first is physical neglect, in which a child or dependent is denied food, clothing, shelter, physical necessities, etc. The second is emotional neglect, in which children are denied love, affection and comfort. The third is medical neglect, in which a child is denied access to proper medical care. Social workers need to realize that many abusers were themselves subjected to abuse at a young age. Proper support is needed to ensure that the cycle of abuse is not repeated.

Characteristics of Abusers

There will be many individuals with the characteristics listed below who have never committed an act of abuse. However, abuse can stem from a variety of factors— and these factors are more likely to be present in a person who is a perpetrator of abuse. A past history of violence is the best predictor for future violence or abuse. Here are some of the main risk factors to consider:

- A long criminal history and a known record of repeated antisocial behavior
- A documented psychiatric disorder: psychosis, personality disorders, APDs, BPD, etc.
- A psychiatric disorder coupled with a diagnosed or suspected substance abuse problem
- A history of owning, collecting and using weapons against other people
- A history of low tolerance, recklessness and entitlement
- A high anger score with low empathy
- Environmental stressors like poverty, socioeconomic status, job termination, etc.

It is the responsibility of the social worker to take all reports or suspicions of abuse and threats of physical or sexual harm very seriously. Social workers should also be able to distinguish between **static risk factors** and **dynamic risk factors**.

The former includes a history of violent behavior, criminal behavior, demographic information, environmental stressors, etc. The latter can be changed with proper intervention, such as a change in living situations, access to psychiatric help and therapy, abstention and therapy for drug or alcohol abuse, no access to weapons, anger management therapy and so on. The risk factors for any client can be summarized as the following:

- **Stressors** – A history of abuse, low income and sustained financial problems, isolated from society with lack of support, low sense of self-esteem and competence
- **Family Issues** – Evidence of marital discord and infidelity, an imbalance and toxic relationship with spouse or domestic partner, domestic violence, a history of substance abuse
- **Poor Skills** – Low IQ, poor at communication and self-control, poor interpersonal skills, authoritarian and rigid outlook, bigoted politically or religiously

The Effects of Trauma on Behavior

Physical, emotional or sexual trauma can manifest in multiple ways. There can be many physiological or behavioral symptoms of trauma and abuse. Here are some of the most expected behavioral manifestations:

- Self-harm by abusing harmful substances like drugs and alcohol
- Overworking to the point of fatigue on a regular basis
- Isolating from peers and not making any meaningful friendships
- Eating disorders, such as anorexia, bulimia, etc. and unhealthy eating habits
- Doing risky and irrational things on a regular basis
- Displaying anal-retentive behavior and being controlling about minor things

Some clients can also develop anxiety as a result, which can then cause panic attacks. These clients would also become unable to cope in such circumstances. In these kinds of situations, social workers can be a huge help.

How Trauma Affects Self-Image

Trauma can be defined as a response to an overwhelmingly negative event. The effects of trauma can be lasting and debilitating. That is why social workers need to treat the dysfunction that is caused by the traumatic event. To do so, it is important to know the ways in which trauma can affect a person's self-image. A person may experience:

- Anxiety and unrest
- A tendency to get enraged or irritable quickly
- Intrusive memories and flashbacks regarding traumatic events
- Feeling depressed, passive and shutdown
- Difficulty concentrating and learning
- A tendency to self-harm or self-destruct
- A feeling of unsafety and wariness of other people
- Guilt, shame or unlikability regarding one's own self

People who have gone through a lot of trauma feel they cannot trust anyone, and they often think that the entire world is conspiring against them. They become despondent and think that they are powerless. They can also have trouble feeling hopeful. Sometimes, trauma causes a client to display intense emotions toward others, and this can result in isolation. As a result, trauma is difficult for a client's loved ones as well.

Chapter Three: The Effects of Diversity

Navigating Differences in Culture, Race and Ethnicity

The United States is one of the most diverse countries in the world, with a very racially and ethnically diverse makeup. The US Census officially recognizes six racial categories: White American (Caucasian), American Indian and Alaska Native, Asian, African American, Native Hawaiian and Pacific Island, along with people of two or more races. The Census Bureau also classifies some Americans as "Hispanic" or "Latino," which is a very large and diverse minority in the United States.

Ethnicity refers to membership of a cultural, national and/or racial group. Members may share many of the same values, such as religion, race, language or simply a place of origin. Two or more people may share the same race but have starkly different ethnicities. It is important to understand that the definition of **race** itself is ever changing and not fixed. In today's world, races are primarily classified on the basis of skin color.

Social workers always have to remember that there is a huge amount of diversity within the groups themselves. In fact, the differences that lie within a particular ethnic group can sometimes be more profound than differences between different ethnic groups. Social workers cannot stereotype or make assumptions about values, behaviors and attitudes based on a client's racial or ethnic makeup. Doing so is inappropriate and a form of ethnic prejudice.

Social workers need to encourage an environment of respect for all kinds of diversity and stand for policies and practices that promote the rights of minorities. Social workers also need to protect people who are in a position of exploitation by actively speaking up against discrimination. To take into account clients' varying cultural experiences, social workers need to be aware of various cultural competence standards. The *National Association of Social Workers Code of Ethics, 1999,* is a very good reference.

- Social workers should gain an understanding of culture and recognize the strengths that are a part of all cultures.

- They should also be able to obtain education and understand how certain races, ethnicities, sexual orientations, etc., have been historically subjected to oppression.
- Social workers should abstain from using any forms of derogatory language in all of their verbal and written communications with or about their clients.

Social workers also need to possess specific knowledge about the ethnic or racial group of people they work with. They should take it upon themselves to learn about historical experiences, socioeconomic backgrounds, cultural customs, etc. All of the institutions and other barriers that stand in the way of upliftment have to be identified, addressed and duly removed.

The Influences of Culture, Race and Ethnicity

White American (Caucasian)

- **Family:** Parents with young children; personal desires are put above family; parents try to be friends with their children; divorce is common.
- **Spirituality:** Religion is mostly a private affair; most White people in the United States are Christian, either Protestant or Bible-based.
- **Values:** Capitalism and libertarianism; many hold the mistaken belief that poverty is a moral failing; physical beauty standards conform to white skin, blond hair; sports have a lot of importance; democracy, freedom and individual human rights are important.
- **Communication:** Standard American English.

Asian

- **Family:** Patriarchal makeup where the father is above the wife and children; obligation to parents and respect for elders; family structure is hierarchical; there are strict roles and rules that are duly enforced.
- **Spirituality:** Cultures are influenced by Buddhist, Confucian and Hindu philosophies.
- **Values:** Actions of individuals reflect on the family and the extended network of relatives; help is accepted only from those within the family and its cultural community; social norms are enforced by obligations to others and extreme shaming.

- **Communication:** Direct confrontation is avoided; reserved emotional expression and affection.

African American

- **Family:** Strong bonds of kinship; extended families and family friends do not always include blood ties; the informal adoption of children by members of the extended family; all family roles are flexible; women are usually seen as the "strength of the family."
- **Spirituality:** Church is a very important part of community life; the community of others in the same religion is very important.
- **Values:** Strong bonds of kinship; strong orientation toward religion; make use of an informal network of support; ingrained distrust of governments and other institutions; a strong sense of pride.
- **Communication:** Animated and passionate; individuals speak up in an effort to get their opinions heard; physical touch and direct communication are valued; respect is always shown; a history of racism and prejudice impacts their interactions.

American Indian and Alaska Native

- **Family:** A complex and unique organization that includes friends and kin who do not share direct blood ties; multigenerational families that result in very strong bonds; the needs of the many outweigh the needs of the few; sharing of common property; collective decision-making.
- **Spirituality:** Varies vastly from different group to group; unique set of beliefs and customs; spiritual leaders also take on the role of the healer; belief in interconnectedness of living things.
- **Values:** Time is viewed as a circle; harmony with nature and the environment is extremely important; interconnectedness of mind, body and spirit is very important.
- **Communication:** Various forms of nonverbal communication; eye contact is not made when talking with someone of higher status; comfortable with silence and indirectness; fond of listening.

Hawaiian and Other Pacific Islander

- **Family:** Western concept of "immediate family" is not common to anyone who is indigenous to Hawaii; blood ties are unimportant and "found family" matters more; ancestors are loved and cherished; multigenerational relationships.
- **Spirituality:** Polytheistic religions that vary from sect to sect; worship of nature and sources of sustenance; spirits are found in nature and the beyond.
- **Values:** Community welfare is very important; culture is very important; a focus on the health of the community as a whole; everyone is responsible for everyone else; sharing is important.
- **Communication:** There are many different languages and customs; those who can speak English enjoy access to health care and public services; Hawaiian is actually an official state language.

Latino or Hispanic

- **Family:** Extended family system that goes above and beyond blood ties; godparents, family friends and informally adopted children are valued members of the family unit; needs of many outweigh the needs of the few; deep level of commitment to family; family unity; males have greater power.
- **Spirituality:** Most people are Roman Catholic; greater emphasis on spiritual values; community is interwoven with church.
- **Values:** There is great effort to improve circumstances; respect for dignity of self and others; respect for elders and authority; pride in one's heritage and history.
- **Communication:** Mostly in Spanish; depending on the language people are speaking, emotional responses can vary—when speaking English, they can be guarded; while speaking Spanish, speech is expressive, friendly, playful and more emotional.

Effects of Cultural, Racial and Ethnic Discrimination

Here are some of the long-term effects of discrimination due to cultural, racial and ethnic discrimination:

- Loss of motivation and drive

- Restricted opportunities for employment and education
- Depression and increased behavioral issues
- Difficulty in communication
- Lack of education and financial achievement
- Limited access to services like health care and education

People who have experienced discrimination based on culture, race and ethnicity can split off from society and isolate themselves. They can also feel embarrassed about the shame that is being imposed on them, their family and their loved ones. One of the worst effects of discrimination is the internalization of the negative biases that affect individuals and their communities. People can end up discriminating against others and copying the actions of their oppressors.

Understanding Sexual Orientation and Gender

Gender identity, or just **gender**, is the knowledge that people have regarding their state of being male, female or nonbinary. Gender identity usually conforms to a person's anatomic sex, but it can also vary, as is the case with transgender and nonbinary individuals.

Sexual orientation, on the other hand, refers to a person's preferences in a sexual or physical partner. Heterosexual people are attracted to the opposite sex; homosexual people are attracted to the same sex; bisexuals are attracted to two genders; pansexual people are attracted to all kinds of individuals, irrespective of gender. There is also asexuality, which is the absence of sexual attraction to others.

People who are transgender can conform to any one of the various sexual identities that have been listed here. It is very important to let individuals develop and define their own sexual orientation and gender.

Effects of Sexual Orientation and Gender

During adolescence, there is some sexual exploration. Toward the end of adolescence, people discover and come to terms with their own identity. Acknowledging oneself can bring about an end to confusion, but it comes with its own set of risks. This is especially true for LGBTQ+ youth, who are more likely to be bullied and face substance abuse and other high-risk situations. Some face bigotry and abuse from within their families as well. Similarly, gender variance has similar effects on young adults.

Impact of Sexual Orientation and Gender on Self-Image

LGBTQ+ youth can suffer from poor self-image as a result of sustained bullying and abuse. They can also experience a lot of harassment, stigma, rejection by family and friends, social isolation, self-harm, etc. They can develop mental and physical afflictions as a result of bullying. Some people can internalize the abuse that has been inflicted on them and develop self-hatred. Here are the main stages of developing a positive self-image:

- **Stage 1:** People feel different and realize that they are not like all the other people they know.
- **Stage 2:** People are confused because they think that what feels "right" to them is "wrong" or causes shame.
- **Stage 3:** People accept who they are, which includes their sexual orientation or gender.
- **Stage 4:** People take steps to integrate their sexual orientation and gender identity into their overall well-being.

Proper support and guidance can mitigate the lasting impact of bullying, discrimination and misinformation. Reassurance has to be provided so that a positive self-identity is formed.

Impact of Diversity in Communication Styles

As mentioned before, race, culture and ethnicity can have a major bearing on an individual's communication style. Communication is much more than a simple exchange of verbal or written words. Hand gestures, facial expressions, eye contact, etc., all play a major role in defining *communication*. It is important that a social worker understand nonverbal cues.

Social workers need to do the following so that they can communicate effectively with people of different cultures and ethnicities:

- Understand and recognize the various kinds of communication styles, both direct and indirect

- Come up with a large set of verbal responses, nonverbal responses and strategies for all kinds of situations
- Use culturally and professionally appropriate language
- Demonstrate sensitivity to nonverbal cues
- Understand the barriers that inhibit engagement and institutionally remove them
- Understand their own style and assess their strengths and drawbacks

Chapter Four: Addictions

Understanding Substance Abuse and Dependence

In the *DSM-V*, Substance Use Disorder incorporates the different categories under Substance Abuse and Substance Dependence Disorders existing under the *DSM-IV* framework. Apart from caffeine, all of the substances are addressed as a separate type of use disorder. For someone to be diagnosed with mild substance use disorder, the person needs to satisfy two or three of the 11 symptoms in total. Problems with law enforcement have been removed from the list because racial considerations make these criteria very hard to apply.

Risk Factors for Substance Abuse

1. Family – Immediate family uses substances on a regular basis; family trauma is present; there is lots of family dysfunction.

2. Behavioral – History of use of other substances; proclivity for impulsive behavior and risk taking; academic problems stemming from behavior; substandard interpersonal relationships; a history of aggressive behavior from childhood.

3. Social – Peers use drugs and alcohol and subject others to peer pressure; existing social and cultural norms allow substance abuse; most drugs and alcohol are easily available and accessible.

4. Psychiatric – Anxiety disorder, low self-esteem, low tolerance for stress, depression, etc., can lead to substance abuse; desperation and loss of control can also lead to abuse.

Theories of Addiction

Over the years, many theories have tried to explain the causes of substance abuse. Here are the theories that have the most scientific and evidential credibility:

Medical Model

In recent times, the medical model of addiction has received the most credibility from both the scientific community and empirical observations made by professionals, such as police officers, social workers, etc. In the medical model, addiction is looked at as a chronic, progressive and relapsing medical disease. There can be genetic causes, brain reward mechanisms, etc. Habitual use of substances can also alter brain chemistry.

Biopsychosocial Model

This theory posits that there are multiple reasons why a person would start to use and continue using illicit and harmful substances. This is a comprehensive model that takes into account all of the biological, psychological and social factors that can result in substance use disorders. Hereditary factors, emotional issues, psychological issues, mental disorders, social influences, environmental problems, etc., are all very important factors in this model.

Family and Environmental Model

This model explains that substance abuse occurs due to exposure to family and friends engaging in substance abuse. The environmental factors are caused by family dynamics, financial condition, personalities, physical and sexual abuse, school, etc.

Social Model

This model attributes substance use to the social factors present in a person's life. Basically, it posits that all kinds of substance abuse are learned, reinforced and passed down within one's personal circle. Substance abuse is picked up from role models and is passed down to those who look up to a person as a role model. Factors like poverty, sexism, racism, etc., all contribute to this.

Self-Medication Model

Another theory is that substance abuse relieves physical or mental discomfort. Substance abuse is a form of self-medication that is reinforced by symptom relief.

Effects of Substance Abuse on Behavior

Signs That Clients Have Substance Abuse Issues

- Substance use has caused them to neglect or forget other responsibilities—academic, professional, family, etc.
- Substance use causes problems at home, work, school or in interpersonal relationships
- Substance use causes dangerous behaviors—driving while intoxicated, unprotected sex, binge eating, unsafe needles, etc.
- Substance use has resulted in financial or legal trouble, such as gambling or shoplifting.
- Clients have abandoned activities they used to enjoy so that they can consume substances.
- Clients are exhibiting sudden psychological issues, such as paranoia, depression, mood swings and changes in attitude.

The Signs of Drug Use

- **Heroin:** Contracted or dilated pupils (pupils that are unresponsive to light); going to sleep at unusual times; sweating profusely; vomiting; coughing and sniffling a lot; loss of appetite; twitchy behavior
- **Cocaine:** Dilated pupils; irritability and anxiety; excessive mood swings and hyperactivity at times; manic episodes with a lot of talking followed by periods of depression and excessive sleeping; going for long periods without any meals
- **Marijuana:** Inappropriate laughter followed by drowsiness; loss of interest and motivation; weight gain or loss; glassy and red eyes; loudness

The Effects of Addiction on Behavior and Relationships

People with an addiction feel a helpless dependency on the substance and find it very difficult to let it go. They also feel ashamed at the prospect of having their addictions being discovered. They will lie so that their addiction can remain concealed and the extent of their addiction can remain unknown. Secrecy and deceit can erode the trust in relationships with spouses, loved ones and family members. Family members can be frightened and traumatized by the addict's unpredictable behavior. The swings between manic and depressive behavior can be frightening for loved ones.

People who are preoccupied with their addiction stop paying attention to their responsibilities and the needs of their dependents. When clients are addicted to drugs or alcohol, there is a lot of pressure on family and loved ones. They have to take on additional responsibilities around the house and in their professional sphere to compensate for the unpredictability and instability that usually accompany any form of debilitating addiction. They feel strained, and the relationships start to fray. At some point, this fraying leads to a complete breakdown. Family members have to walk on eggshells because they think that the wrong choice of words or actions can exacerbate the situation. Children can begin to feel scared and confused. They are likely to develop addictive behaviors as a coping mechanism.

Unit II: Assessment, Diagnosis and Treatment Planning

Chapter Five: Gathering Information

The Primary Principles of Interviewing

An interview is one of the most powerful tools any social worker has. It involves verbal and nonverbal communication with the client, and the social worker can gain a lot of ideas, attitudes, feelings and insights from the interview. The goal of an interview is to gain information and keep the client focused.

The objective of any interview within the realm of social work is to serve the interests of the client. As a result, all of the actions taken by the social worker during the interview have to be planned and methodical. There should not be any generic questions or statements. Instead, inquiries should be specifically created for a particular client's unique situation.

The same interview can be designed to serve more than one purpose. For example, the overall aim of the interview may be therapeutic, diagnostic or informational. It is possible, more often than not, to have an interview for all three. Specific questions that the social worker asks will elicit specific responses, leading to more inquiries for an unbiased and accurate picture.

Here are some helpful techniques a social worker can utilize to assist clients during an interview:

- Reframing and Relabeling: In this technique, you present the problem in a way that is different from what it usually would have been. Doing so allows the client to look at the problem from a different perspective.
- Confrontation: You can highlight the problem in your client's mind by deliberately calling attention to it. This is confrontational and can be a very effective method of communication.
- Interpretation: You pull together differing kinds of behavior to receive a new picture of the situation.

- Clarification: Ask clients to reformulate a problem in their own words and then repeat it back yourself. This ensures that you and the client are on the same page and prevents any misunderstandings.
- Universalization: When you generalize clients' behaviors or experiences, you can reassure clients that their experiences are valid and shared by others. This can help you reach out and comfort your clients.

The Components of Biopsychosocial History

Biological Section

- Medical history
- Developmental history
- Current list of medications
- History of substance abuse (if any)
- Family history of medical conditions

Mental health issues can exacerbate existing physical health issues and vice versa. It is the social worker's responsibility to refer clients to doctors to ensure that untreated medical conditions get addressed. Clients should also have all of their medications and doses coordinated by a provider, keeping side effects in mind.

Social Section

- Unique context and situation
- Sexual identity issues or concerns
- Personal history
- History of the family of origin
- History of abuse
- In-depth look at the available support system
- History of education and work
- Marital and relationship status
- Summary of all risks
- Legal history

Psychological Section

- History of psychiatric illnesses and symptoms

- History of current psychiatric disorder
- Present or past psychiatric stressors
- Current mental status
- Treatment history
- List of past and current medications

Obtaining Information by Using Collaterals

Social workers use collateral sources, such as friends, families, spouses, etc., to gather an accurate picture of a client's situation. They may also use information and reports from physicians and other social work agencies, etc. The severity and history of the issues can be gleaned by conducting direct interviews with family members and loved ones.

Collateral is a very important consideration, especially when the information received directly from the client is not 100% credible. One good example is a child custody process, which is inherently adversarial. It is difficult to come up with a clear picture of the situation because the data is completely biased. You can easily verify the integrity of the information by talking to collateral sources. During this stage, social workers need to be wary because data from neutrals have more validity. Using multiple sources (triangulation) is an effective technique. Lastly, it is very important for social workers to get clients' consent before they reach out to collateral sources.

Some Standardized Psychological Evaluation Tests

Myers-Briggs Personality Type Indicator (MBTI)

The MBTI is a self-report assessment that seeks to assign a distinct personality type to an individual based on a person's answers to the assessment. There are a total of 16 MBTI types, all of which are permutations of:

a. General Attitude – Extraversion (E) or Introversion (I)
b. Perception – Sensation (S) or Intuition (N)
c. Processing Style – Thinking (T) or Feeling (F)
d. Judging (J) or Perceiving (P)

Beck Depression Inventory (BDI)

This is a test consisting of 21 multiple-choice questions. It evaluates the presence and extent of depression.

Rorschach Inkblot Test

The inkblot test is used to assess clients' perceptual reactions, psychological functioning and makeup. It is a widely used projective test.

Stanford-Binet Intelligence Scale

This is an intelligence scale that assesses cognitive abilities in children and adults. It can be used to measure verbal abilities, performance abilities and full-scale scores.

Minnesota Multiphasic Personality Inventory (MMPI)

The MMPI is an objective verbal inventory that can be used to administer a personality test solely for the purposes of therapy or psychoanalysis. This is a comprehensive test that consists of 550 statements, of which 16 are repeated.

Thematic Apperception Test (TAT)

The TAT is one of the most popular projective tests in the world. The TAT consists of a series of pictures, each of which depicts an ambiguous scene. The client is instructed to make up a story or fantasy based on the scene and accompany that with a description of his or her thoughts and feelings. This test can provide the social worker with in-depth knowledge and understanding of the client's perceptions and imagination. It is part of a larger set of clinical tests.

Wechsler Intelligence Scale (WISC)

The WISC is a simple measure of a child's intellectual and cognitive abilities. It comes with four index scales and a full-scale score. In other words, it is a test of IQ. It is currently in its fifth edition.

Chapter Six: Assessment and Diagnosis

Assessment of Clients' Communication Skills

In all aspects of treatment, clients have to be involved with the social worker who is currently responsible for them. Clients' communication skills need to be assessed so that a feasible treatment plan can be created for them. Clients also need to understand the findings and data, which is why expressive and receptive communication matters.

Social workers need to know how to reach out and communicate with clients who have gone through serious trauma. It is important to understand how these experiences affect the client's communication abilities. The social worker also needs to take into account the client's cultural background and experiences. Sometimes, silence is also a type of communication.

Lastly, social workers need to learn how to communicate with someone who is angry and upset. It is important to understand how certain choices of words or tones can trigger or upset a person. The client's ethnic background, past experiences, etc., can all have lasting effects.

Making Use of Observation

The direct observation of interactions between family members and clients, their nonverbal behaviors, etc., can provide a wealth of information. Apart from the interview, social workers need to hone their observation skills. They can glean many insights by observing behavior.

Social workers can also consider a professional position as observers. While doing so, they can take on multiple roles. They can be complete participants who experience everything along with the client. They can also be participants as observers who interact with the participants. Lastly, they can participate as observers, as participants or as complete observers removed from activity.

Client Strength and Weakness Assessment

In the context of social work, an individual's strength is that person's ability to cope with hardships and remain functional under duress and stress. A strength assessment can be done via a variety of methods, and there is no one-size-fits-all approach. Here are some of the abilities that need to be taken into account while assessing clients' strengths and weaknesses:

Defenses and Coping Mechanisms

- Flexibility – can cope with stressors
- Ability to soothe themselves
- Ability to regulate impulses

Temperamental Factors

- Belief in justice
- Sense of self-esteem and worth
- Sense of confidence and optimism
- Trust in other people
- Ability to cope with negative events
- Good sense of humor
- Ability to grieve
- Ability to take responsibility
- Lack of hostility and anger
- Sense of direction and purpose

Cognitive Skills

- Ability to receive and use feedback
- Creativity and curiosity
- Common sense and presence of mind
- Ability to deal with problems
- Standard intellectual and cognitive abilities
- Patience

Interpersonal Skills

- Ability to construct, develop and maintain healthy relationships
- Ability to confide in other people
- Good problem-solving skills
- Large capacity for empathy

- Sense of security

Other Factors

- Proper physical health
- Proper financial security – source of income
- Part of institutions
- Supportive circle of loved ones

The Indicators of Motivation

Social workers should be able to determine the stage of change a particular client is in. Doing so will allow them to come up with the strategies required to come to terms with these issues. Therapeutic alliances can be severed if social workers and therapists push clients to take on more than they are ready for.

In the stages of **precontemplation and contemplation**, there is often a marked lack of motivation. In the former stage, clients are unaware of or maybe even unwilling to make changes to their lives. There is resistance and a lack of motivation. There is a lot of arguing, denial, ignoring and avoidance. Sometimes, clients even intentionally miss appointments. The best way to deal with this stage is to establish a relationship and a rapport with clients. To do so, keep conversations informal and keep clients engaged. Most importantly, recognize all their thoughts, concerns, fears and feelings.

In the latter stage, clients are generally unsure about their changes in behavior. As a result, they can act out unpredictably. They may be willing to look at the benefits of changing their behavior and, more often than not, be willing to work toward doing so. The best way to deal with this is to emphasize to clients that they are free to forge their own way. It is also very important to inform clients how these changes will be helpful to their situation.

Factors for Intervention or Treatment Ability

Social workers should never make assumptions on the part of their clients—especially regarding any changes that might need to be made. Clients may be unmotivated or unnecessarily oppositional. This is called resistance. Here are some factors that can be used as evidence, especially if you feel that clients are showing resistance:

- Being reticent with the amount of information that they are providing to the social worker, marked by minimal conversation and a pointed silence during appointments; at the same time, this can also be done by changing the topic and engaging in banal small talk instead
- Talking about past issues instead of focusing on more pressing concerns in the present
- Censoring and editing their thoughts when the social worker asks them about a particular thing
- Making false promises and not showing up to appointments
- Using flattery in an effort to soften up social workers, which is a form of manipulation
- Refusing to make payments or intentionally delaying owed payments

Components of the Mental Status Exam

The mental status examination is a structured and effective way of diagnosing and describing clients' current state of mind. Appearance, attitude, mood, etc., provide helpful insights into their present state of mind. This exam is a mandatory part of anyone's client assessment, irrespective of clients' presenting problems. Here are all of the primary components of the mental status examination:

- **Appearance:** Clients' grooming and dress provide helpful insights into their mental status. At the same time, facial expressions are also very helpful.
- **Insight:** Clients' ability to predict the consequences of their current behavior provides valuable insight. This allows them to make decisions that are sensible and allows them to understand how they contribute to their problem.
- **Intellectual Function:** Clients' level of intelligence and memory can be a good way to assess their status.
- **Impulsivity:** Clients' impulse control is very important because it allows the social worker to gauge whether someone is a danger to themself or others.

- **Mood:** Clients' mood or behavior is very important, as in manic, sad, anxious, placid and so on.
- **Orientation:** Clients' awareness regarding things like events, time, place and so on can tell you a lot about state of mind.
- **Speech:** Clients' patterns of speech can also provide insights. For example, tone and speech patterns can be very telling.
- **Thought Processes:** Clients' thinking style and ability to distinguish reality from fantasy is very important.

List of Medications

Antipsychotic Drugs

These drugs are used to treat conditions such as schizophrenia and mania. These psychotropic drugs are of two basic types: typical and atypical.

Typical Drugs

- Haldol
- Loxitane
- Mellaril — Thioradizine
- Moban
- Navane
- Prolixin
- Serentil
- Thorazine

Atypical Drugs

- Abilify /Ariprazole
- Clozaril
- Geodon
- Risperdal /Risperdone
- Seroquel /Quetipine
- Zyprexa

Antimanic Agents, i.e., Mood Stabilizers

These drugs are used to treat the manic stages of bipolar disorder.

- Depakene *Valproate*
- Lamictal
- Lithium
- Tegretol
- Carbatrol — *also used to treat epilepsy*
- Topamax

Lithium is a very serious medication, since the difference between toxic levels and therapeutic levels is very small. Lithium can affect kidney and thyroid functions, so the client needs to be subjected to proper tests periodically.

Antidepressants

These drugs treat depression and are generally of three broad types—SSRIs, monoamine oxidase inhibitors (MAIOs) and tricyclic drugs.

SSRIs

- Celexa /*Citalopram*
- Lexapro /*Escitalopram*
- Luvox /*Fluvoxamine*
- Prozac /*Fluoxetine*
- Zoloft /*Sertraline*
- Paxil /*Paroxetine*

Monoamine Oxidase Inhibitors (MAOIs)

- Nardil
- Parnate

Tricyclics

- Anafranil
- Elavil
- Norpramin

- Pamelor
- Surmontil
- Vivactil
- Tofranil
- Asendin

Others

- Desyrel
- Remeron ~ *Mirtazapine*

Visteral/Hydroxizine
(Anxiety)

Atarax
(Hydroxizine)
Anx &
Insomnia

Antianxiety Drugs

This kind of medication treats anxiety and panic disorders.

- Ativan /*Lorazepam*
- Xanax /*Alprazolam*
- Klonopin /*clonazepam*
- Valium /*Diazepam*
- Buspar /*Buspirone*

These drugs are commonly abused and can be very dangerous if combined with alcohol. These should be prescribed under specific conditions.

Stimulant Drugs

These stimulant drugs are given to people who have attention deficit hyperactivity disorder (ADHD) or just hyperactivity disorder.

- Ritalin (also known as methylphenidate)
- Dexedrine
- Dextrostat
- Concerta
- Adderall (a mix of amphetamine and salts)

The Indicators of Sexual Abuse

There are many indicators of sexual abuse. First, physical and anatomical signs need to be sought out, such as injuries in the genital or rectal areas. Second, there also may be behavioral signs, such as anxiety, fears, recurring nightmares, sleep disturbances, etc. Children who have been sexually abused may show an unusual interest in sexual matters that is inappropriate for their age. Sexual promiscuity and victimization are also signs of abuse.

The Indicators of Physical Abuse

Physical abuse can take the form of various indicators, such as:

- A person can have unexplained burns from cigarettes, cigars, etc., especially on places like the hand, foot, back or buttocks.
- A person can have lacerations or bruises on the face, lips, torso, etc. The article used to inflict the injury can make itself apparent in the shape of the bruise (like a belt).
- The person may also be very wary of other people. This is especially true of children who are being abused, since they are wary of their parents and caretakers. They may frequently resort to extreme behavior, aggressiveness or withdrawal.

The Indicators of Psychological Abuse

Here are some of the main indicators of victims who have endured sustained psychological abuse:

- They have very little empathy toward other people and usually relate to other people in a very flat or superficial way.
- They engage in disruptive or aggressive behavior toward other people. Someone who is being emotionally or physically abused is likely to bully other people.
- They may engage in dangerous, self-destructive behaviors, such as showing little regard for their safety, doing dangerous drugs regularly, drinking too much, etc. In extreme cases, the client may also engage in self-harm and self-mutilation.
- They avoid eye contact in general and experience anxiety, loneliness and despair very regularly.

Risk Factors for Dangerous Clients

Here are some risk factors that need to be considered, especially when dealing with clients who may act dangerously to themselves or others:

- Usually, people who engage with drugs, precocious sex, guns and risky behaviors are prone to violence. In fact, they may be prone to serious violence.
- Someone who is involved with delinquent peers and explores gang membership is at a huge risk of committing violent acts. These are two of the most powerful predictors of violence.
- Young people who commit acts of violence before the age of 13 usually tend to commit more serious crimes as they grow older. They display a pattern of escalating violence as they grow, and this pattern usually persists until adulthood.

Risk Factors Relating to Suicide

- The best predictor of suicide is if a person has attempted suicide previously. The medical seriousness of the attempt is also relevant in this case.
- The presence of some kind of psychiatric disorder can also be a major risk factor, especially when suicide is concerned.
- The client has a history of substance abuse.
- The client has a family history of suicide, has been exposed to the suicidal behavior of family members, peers, etc.
- The client has experienced relationship, financial, professional or social loss.
- The client has easy access to firearms and other methods.
- The client lives alone and has little to no social support.

The Indicators of Traumatic Stress

Here are some of the primary indicators of traumatic stress and violence:

- Addictive behavior, especially with respect to drugs, alcohol, gambling, sex, impulsive spending and shopping, etc.
- Sustained dichotomous thinking pattern: all or nothing
- Repeated suicidal thoughts

- Dissociation
- Eating disorders or poor eating habits
- Anxiety and repeated panic attacks
- A history of self-destructive behavior
- Depression
- Paranoia regarding people, places, things, etc.

Chapter Seven: Planning Treatments

Methods Used to Develop Intervention/Treatment Plans

Before planning treatment, the engagement and assessment steps are very important. These steps ensure that the social worker and client are on the same page. It also shows that an alliance has been created, and all the important information has been collected in an effort to move on to the next stage. During planning, the social worker and the client must:

- Develop **SMART** objectives. The objectives need to be **Specific**, **Measurable**, **Achievable**, **Relevant** and **Time-Specific**.
- Generate solutions that can be used to tackle the problem properly. While doing so, specific driving and restraining forces also need to be properly identified and understood.
- Define the problem properly in a clear and data-driven way.
- Come up with strategies, objectives and interventions that are related to the objectives at hand.

The Importance of Measurable Objectives

When coming up with intervention or treatment plans, the social worker needs to ensure that the goals are observable and measurable. If achievement is not measurable, then the client can become despondent and hopeless. The following elements must be very subtly included:

- **Criteria** – What is the healthy behavior that the client needs to exhibit? How often and for how long must this be done? Under what conditions does the client have to demonstrate this goal?
- **Evaluation Method** – How is the client's progress going to be measured? What metrics will be used to chart the client's growth?
- **Evaluation Schedule** – How often and when will the client's progress be measured?

To help encourage clients, the social worker can divide the intervention and treatment plan into goals and benchmarks. This can help motivate clients and help them reach their ultimate goal. Breaking a goal into smaller goals can provide a step-by-step program, which is an effective idea.

The SOAP Format Treatment Plan

Social workers need to take into account subjective and objective data at the same time when framing their assessment of clients. Treatment plans need to be developed using the SOAP framework—**Subjective**, **Objective**, **Assessment** and **Plan**.

Subjective (S)

This is the subjective data that the social worker gleans through conversation with clients. This usually includes information regarding their well-being, what they've been doing, etc.

Objective (O)

The objective data include measurable and quantifiable information, such as blood pressure, temperature, heart rate, pulse, etc. This section can also include quantifiable indicators, such as test scores, legal issues, disorientation, etc.

Assessment (A)

The social worker can make use of the subjective and objective information received, then consolidate these into a short and descriptive assessment.

Plan (P)

This is the final step that the social worker comes up with. It is very important to involve clients in their own treatment. By being asked to self-monitor and provide subjective data, clients can be involved and can track their own progress.

Applying Research to Practice

In the world of social work, evidence-based research is very important and widespread. The information gathered can be used for clinical decision-making and other clinical practices. By gathering and analyzing scientific data, social workers can translate it into a plan of action that can be applied in various situations.

The client's best interests and well-being is paramount, even in this kind of a treatment policy. It is the social worker's responsibility to use only the best practices available. Any services and techniques used have to be tested and proven scientifically effective.

Social workers also need to know how to locate and make use of all the evidence-based interventions that they come across. Research must be used to guide practice and to help social workers provide high-quality services. Their efforts can also lead to the development of more effective treatments.

Reliability and validity are important criteria that must be kept in mind, especially when working with experimental research findings. It is very important to assess these factors properly. The former asks if the same answer or result can be obtained or reproduced, while the latter tests the confidence in the hypothesized cause and effect.

Unit III: Psychotherapy, Case Management and Clinical Interventions

Chapter Eight: Therapeutic Relationship

Understanding How Feedback Works

Clients' best interests are most important for social workers. They need to talk and interact with other professionals in order to provide the best services for their clients. An example would be a medical professional or a therapist. Feedback is very important. It helps the social worker understand what is working and what can be done even better.

- There is no one method that social workers can resort to while looking for feedback. However, there are some guiding principles that social workers should adhere to when working with feedback, irrespective of them obtaining or providing it.
- When social workers seek to involve other professionals or consultants in the client care and feedback process, the client's express consent needs to be taken no matter what. It is also very important to protect the client's confidentiality, especially if it is specifically requested.
- Social workers are obligated to ask for feedback in difficult situations. It may be tempting to ask for feedback when things are going well, but it is equally important to identify proper information from someone who is critical.
- Social workers need to understand that feedback can be conveyed in a number of ways, both verbally and nonverbally. They need to keep an eye out for what their clients are trying to convey to them, either in words or through behavior.
- All feedback needs to be documented for further review. You should explain to the client clearly why you are looking for feedback. You should also explain what will be done with the information.
- Lastly, social workers need to come up with an appropriate channel of communication when looking for feedback. For younger clients, digital forms of contact, such as texting, emails, etc., is best. For older clients, a sit-down conversation is far more effective. Make sure that the client is not improperly influenced.

The Summarization of Communication

Summarization is very important, as it involves bringing together all the important points and takeaways from a discussion to give social workers and clients a sense of where they stand. It brings about a sense of closure and can be extremely reassuring for the client. It also is an effective way for social workers to ensure that they and the clients are on the same page.

Summarization of a conversation need not be done only at completion. It can also be done periodically throughout the course of the discussion. Irrespective of whether the client or the social worker creates the summary, it is one of the most valuable intervention techniques. Something that is apparently disorganized and unrelated can be put together effectively with the help of summarization.

There are various approaches to summarizing. It can be initiated by the social worker at any point of the discussion. It can also be done by asking clients to review all the points they have picked up during the conversation. Alternatively, the social worker and the client may summarize the progress they have made collaboratively.

Methods for Communication

You need to be aware of the methods you can use to facilitate and ease communication with clients. If you want to form a therapeutic alliance with a person who is seeking help, you need to display **empathy**. Empathy is very important, and it shows that you understand the client's thoughts and feelings. You must have an accurate perception of a person's situation and communicate this understanding properly.

You need to be **genuine** and show your earnestness and sincerity. Only then will you be able to build a connection of trust with your client. To do so, you need to listen and communicate without distorting or misconstruing what someone is saying.

You also have to make use of **positive regard**, which shows clients that they are worthy of care and assistance. It is basically a form of reassurance through which you tell clients that they are strong, capable and have lots of potential. This can be done via respect and nonverbal communication.

Proper communication can be facilitated by the simple act of **listening**. It is also very important to suspend **judgments** and listen to what clients are saying without responding with anything critical. It is very important for you to be aware of behavior that is **culturally appropriate**. Finally, you also need to establish clear and healthy boundaries with your clients so that a safe environment can be established.

Verbal and Nonverbal Communication Methods

Social workers need to be adept communicators if they want to make real change happen with their clients. To do so, they need to be skilled at all forms of verbal and nonverbal communication techniques. A social worker's goal is to help clients. In order to do so, they need to build a relationship of trust and mutual respect. Here are the main verbal and nonverbal communication methods that you should know:

- **Silence** is one of the most powerful communication tools. It can demonstrate acceptance of clients' feelings and the points they raise. It also denotes that the social worker is thinking about what has been said.
- **Questioning** is also a very good way of communicating, since it allows the social worker to glean relevant information in a transparent and nonjudgmental way.
- **Active listening** is a technique that social workers need to master. This involves sitting up straight and leaning toward clients so that clients know that they are being listened to. Maintaining eye contact, making relevant comments, nodding, etc., shows people that they are being listened to.
- **Paraphrasing and clarifying** is a very simple technique in which social workers simply reframe what clients have said in their words and repeat it back to them. This can help clients feel understood and helps with clarification.

Types of Feedback Methods

There are various methods by which feedback can be collected. It can be done in a written or verbal format, and it can be done personally or impersonally. It can come in an unsolicited manner, or it can come via request. It can even be done in formal or informal settings. At times, feedback can also be completely anonymous. Here are some common feedback methods:

One-to-One Feedback

The client sits face-to-face with the social worker and gives feedback then and there. This is the most common form of feedback, and it needs to be delivered in a sensitive manner. Professionals need to strictly adhere to the codes of conduct when they are receiving feedback in this manner.

Group-to-Group Feedback

When two or more groups are working together toward a common goal, they can each provide feedback on the other. This kind of feedback can be unidirectional as well, depending on context. Particular individuals may be the recipients of the feedback, or it may be meant for the entire group.

Intragroup Feedback

Feedback can also be provided by the different members of a single group that is working together. Feedback can be provided to a single member or a number of people within the group.

360° Feedback

Recipients ask for feedback from all of the people around them. This includes professional superiors, peers, subordinates, clients, the community and so on. This kind of feedback features many points of view and can help paint a complete picture.

Consultative Feedback

A person or a group of people act as formal or informal consultants to another. Depending on the expertise and position of the consultants, the group or person may be more open to accepting their suggestions. However, there is no obligation to follow the advice given.

Empathetic Communication

- To communicate in an empathetic way, the social worker has to establish rapport and trust with the client. This bridges the initial gap that exists between the social worker and the client.
- The client's nonverbal messages and body language are looked at when empathetic communication is concerned. This approach also centers the client in the process and stays attuned to the needs of the client during the encounter.
- Empathetic communication encourages both parties to keep the discussion more rational and constructive, clearing a path that leads to proper problem-solving in the future. Empathetic communication is especially helpful for those who choose anger and violence as a coping mechanism against helplessness or frustration.

Understanding Acceptance

A primary tenet of social work is that clients can make changes to better their situations only if they wish to do so. Social workers try to provide lots of constructive assistance, and this is possible only when clients start to take on responsibility and autonomy. Helping is not the same as giving advice, doling out punishments, etc. These are superficial and do absolutely nothing to increase the client's strength and willingness. By making use of **objective feedback**, a social worker can demonstrate acceptance and begin to help the client in a proper way.

Interactions are also very important, since they form the core background of any relationship between a social worker and a client. Interaction usually occurs through conversations and **verbal communication**, since talking it out is very helpful. At the same time, **nonverbal communication** is also very important and can provide a lot of insight. Posture, facial expression, gestures, etc., can express feelings more clearly than words in many situations.

The Principles of Building Relationships

All humans experience difficulties when they try to meet their needs, and social workers need to accept this fact. Every person holds the potential to exhibit the weaknesses and strengths that make up the human race. Clients become better at dealing with their problems when they start to develop feelings of adequacy. Social workers also need to recognize clients' positive and negative aspects and help them to achieve their goals.

To start the helping process, the social worker needs to take into account the fact that most humans act in terms of their feelings and attitudes. The interaction and extent of the work between the social worker and the client will be affected by the relationship between them. In the end, it is important to cultivate a good relationship with clients if you want to help them properly.

The Social Worker-Client Relationship

The bond between the client and the social worker is an emotional and connective one. The communication between the social worker and the client actually depends on the nature of their relationship. If the emotional connection and alliance are strong, then the bond is made with more ease. It is very important to cultivate a warm, accepting and positive relationship with the client.

The social worker also has to respect the client's individuality and uniqueness. Most of all, it is very important for the social worker to impress upon clients how vital their **self-determination** is. Once clients are fully involved in their own helping process, things will move much smoother and faster.

The Social Worker-Client Relationship in Treatment

A proper therapeutic process requires some basic conditions in order to be effective:

Both social workers and clients must listen to each other. However, the social worker has a responsibility to listen more than the client does. If the client just sits there and listens to the social worker, there will be no effect at all. Social workers need to work on listening and accepting what is said in a nonjudgmental manner.

Clients must trust social workers. Unless there is a basic and preliminary form of trust, the clients will not participate properly in the helping process. They will withhold all kinds of information, and their problems will not be explored properly. Unless there is trust in the relationship, the treatment process will not begin. However, social workers need to be patient here. **Trust does NOT come quickly**.

Last, social workers must always respect clients' confidentiality and privacy. None of the information that is shared between them should be told to anyone else. This is very important. The social worker is obligated to **keep all information private and 100% confidential**.

Chapter Nine: The Intervention Process

Biopsychosocial Models of Intervention

Social workers need to take an ecological perspective of intervention, since they know that all problems are rooted in systems. The problems persist because of an imbalance between one system and another. By examining client issues through a multifaceted lens, the interplay among all the different elements can be understood properly. The different dimensions are:

Biological, where the role of biological and physiological systems within the body and outside the body is concerned. For example, genetic makeup is a factor that plays a role inside the body, while pathogens that impair functioning are exterior factors.

Psychological, where the role of emotions, thoughts and behavior on the individual's functioning is concerned. This is a very important connection, as it fully acknowledges the link that exists between the mind and body.

Social, where the social worker examines how the client is able to relate with all of the different moving parts of society. This includes peers, societal institutions, families, etc. The social worker is responsible for individual clients, as well as others affected by similar issues.

Spiritual, where the role of spirituality or religious belief is taken into account as an element of well-being. At the same time, social workers also need to take the **cultural** sphere into account, as that provides context concerning traditions, customs, rules, values, rituals, etc.

Systems Theory Terminology

- **Closed system:** A system that uses up all of its energy and then dies
- **Differentiation:** When a system becomes specialized in function and overall structure
- **Homeostasis:** A steady state, where all the values of the system grow at a constant rate
- **Entropy:** A state of chaos or disorder that uses up all the available energy
- **Open system:** A system that can exchange with others across boundaries

- **Input/output:** Each respectively refers to the resources required from the environment and the products exported to the environment
- **Throughput:** Energy integrated into the system to attain the goals

Understanding the Problem-Solving Model

This is an approach that states that a person's inability to cope with any problem is due to a lack of motivation or opportunity. The client's problem-solving capacity has been impaired, and it can also be referred to as *maladaptive*. The goal of this process is to help enhance clients' mental, cognitive and emotional capacities so that they can access the resources they need to solve all of their problems. Here are all of the steps involved in problem-solving:

- Engagement
- Assessment
- Plan generation
- Intervention
- Evaluation
- Termination

Cognitive Approaches to Crisis Intervention

Social workers can apply a cognitive approach to crisis intervention by using the learning theory conceptual framework. This describes how humans retain, absorb and process information when they learn. Here are the four distinct types of learning theories:

- **Cognitive:** Developed by Piaget, this orientation views learning as an internal mental process that is reinforced with the help of internal cognitive structures. Social workers aim to develop chances to foster clients' capacities and skills.
- **Behaviorist:** Developed by Skinner and Pavlov, this theory posits that learning can be viewed through a change in behavior and external stimuli. The locus of learning and social workers can bring about change by making changes to the total external environment.
- **Social:** This is an orientation developed by Albert Bandura that posits that learning can be done by looking at the way clients interact with their

environments in a social context. Social workers can help by taking advantage of conversation and participation.

- **Humanistic:** Developed by Maslow, the humanistic perspective views learning as the culmination of the client's wishes to fulfill their true potential. It states that the locus of learning is to meet the different needs of the individual as a whole.

Cognitive-behavioral therapy (CBT) is a practical and hands-on approach to problem-solving. The goal of CBT is to change the thinking and behavioral patterns that are causing a client's difficulties. The goal of CBT is to change clients' attitudes and behavior by focusing on thoughts and images. A combination of psychotherapy and behavioral therapy, it is an active, collaborative, structured, time-limited, goal-oriented and problem-focused approach.

Psychodynamic Approaches to Crisis Intervention

A psychodynamic approach can help clients come to terms with emotions, thoughts, life experiences, etc. This allows them to gain insight into their lives and allows them to address their present-day problems. By understanding the recurring patterns, clients can avoid distress and develop healthy defense mechanisms. Social workers can use the psychodynamic approach to encourage clients to speak freely and discover the roots of their problems. This is a very powerful approach that empowers clients by providing them with insight and information about their dysfunctional dynamics and behaviors.

Behavioral Approaches to Crisis Intervention

Personality is the culmination of all interactions between the individual and the environment, which is why behavioral approaches analyze and treat dysfunctional behaviors directly. Social workers need to focus on **observable behavior** to bring about change. Here are the two fundamental types of human behavior:

- Operant: This is voluntary behavior that is usually controlled by its consequences in the environment. Examples include walking, talking, etc.
- Respondent: This refers to involuntary behavior that comes about as a response to a certain behavior. There is a stimulus, and this results in a

response. Examples include anxiety, fight or flight, sexual responses and more.

Behavioral modification can be best applied to the problems of sexual dysfunction and phobic disorders. There has also been some success using this approach in obsessive-compulsive behaviors, such as smoking, binge eating, etc. It can, however, be impractical to use this kind of therapy on clients who are not in residential 24-hour settings or under self-monitoring programs.

Different Types of Social Work Interventions

Macro

This is the broadest level of intervention that a social worker can undertake. The importance of social, economic and historical influences on the client's well-being is taken into account while considering macro interventions. Social workers decide how these factors can help clients grow. Social workers are responsible for making changes at the systemic level, leading to more opportunities and reducing barriers and hurdles. Macro interventions are basically changes in policies, laws, etc.

Meso

The second level of intervention is meso. This kind of intervention process usually applies to large groups and communities as a whole.

Micro

The narrowest level of intervention is the micro level, where the social worker directly helps clients solve any problems that they are having. Problems are of various types, including problems with family members, spouses, children, romantic partners and even neighbors. At the micro level, it is the social worker's job to provide support and help clients access resources from other agencies. This kind of social work is core to clinical practice and can extend to entire families.

Functional Roles in Family Dynamics

In family functioning, roles are extremely important. The establishment of clear roles is directly connected to a family's well-being and their ability to come to terms with crises. Here are the roles that exist in any healthy family, also called healthy family dynamics:

- **Resource Provision:** It is the job of some family members to provide the family with essential resources, such as shelter, financial security, food and clothing.
- **Emotional Support:** It is the job of family members to provide comfort and emotional support to other members at times.
- **Family Management:** It is the job of certain family members to make decisions about finances, boundaries, behaviors, etc. This is a very important task and is critical to healthy families.
- **Life Skills Development:** It is the job of adult family members to contribute to the children's physical, emotional, educational and social development.
- **Intimate Relationship:** Lastly, it is the job of spouses and romantic partners to maintain a healthy intimate relationship between them and their significant other. A healthy sexual and emotional relationship is very important. Emotional needs must be met.

There are various roles in dysfunctional families, such as the **family hero**, the **scapegoat**, the **mascot** and the **lost child**. The family hero tries to make up for dysfunction at home by overachieving and being successful at life. The scapegoat turns away from dysfunction within the family by displaying defiant, hostile and angry behavior. The **mascot** tries to distract members from dysfunction by being funny and improving the atmosphere. The **lost child** becomes invisible in an effort to escape the family dysfunction.

Working with Traumatized Clients

Most professionals agree that it is better to divide trauma treatment into set phases. While working with clients who have undergone serious traumatic experiences, it is important to understand all of the different phases of treatment. Usually, the three-phase model is best suited for choosing and implementing the appropriate treatment plans.

Phase #1 – Safety and Stabilization

For trauma treatment to proceed, a social worker needs to establish a safe and stable environment for the client. The basic needs described by Maslow's hierarchy are largely absent for many trauma survivors. The very basic needs of housing, food, medicine, etc., can help provide a safe environment. In this kind of situation, the social worker should use case management to provide housing, food, transportation and other systems of support. Stabilization is the replacement of unhealthy coping mechanisms with constructive ones. Developing compassion is paramount.

Phase #2 – Mourning and Remembrance

In the next stage, trauma survivors will start to acknowledge and recount the serious trauma that they have been through. They will also be ready to integrate all of their experiences into a larger context. Psychoeducation is a very important part of this phase, as it allows survivors to address the events that they went through. Some kind of loss is experienced as a result of trauma, and social workers need to help clients cope with grief to the best of their ability.

Phase #3 – Reconnection and Reintegration

The third stage of trauma intervention is when clients resolve to move forward in life and rise above their trauma. This is a stage of empowerment, where survivors use their trauma as a tool to empower and better themselves. They focus on new activities, new relationships, etc. and start to develop new identities. Social workers help survivors by teaching them how to integrate healthy self-care strategies into their lives and increase resilience.

Conflict Management and Resolution

Social workers may also be called upon to resolve conflicts between clients. Conflict management and resolution usually consist of four steps:

- The parties in the conflict have to recognize and acknowledge that there is a conflict in their interests.
- The social worker conducts a thorough assessment of the conflict in question.

- The social worker selects the right strategy to manage this specific issue.
- The social worker implements an intervention strategy.

Here are some of the powerful interaction structuring techniques that can help resolve conflicts between parties:

- Decreasing the amount of time between sessions of problem-solving
- Decreasing the formality and rules of the problem-solving sessions
- Limiting the scope of the issues being discussed and focusing only on the important points
- Making use of third-party mediators
- Decreasing the amount of contact between the parties during the early stages of the conflict-resolution process

Prevention Strategies

There are three different kinds of prevention strategies, all of which are required to come up with a comprehensive strategy for prevention and protection.

Primary Prevention Strategy

Primary prevention is the first line of defense. Its goal is to protect the client from developing a preventable disease, experiencing a preventable injury or engaging in a certain form of behavior. Here are some concrete examples:

- Providing proper immunization and vaccinations against communicable but preventable diseases like measles, influenza, etc.
- Educating clients on road safety responsibilities, such as seat belts and helmets
- Helping control hazards at work and home
- Providing the means to a nutritious and balanced diet and engaging in regular and frequent exercise.
- Counseling about the risks of harmful substances, such as tobacco

Primary prevention strategies are the most cost-effective and successful methods of prevention, since they help clients avoid an unwanted situation in the first place. The associated costs, suffering and burdens of the injury, illness or behavior are avoided from the start.

Secondary Prevention Strategy

This kind of prevention strategy is implemented after a disease, injury or behavior has already occurred. The goal of secondary prevention is to limit the long-term impacts of the event on the client's life. This kind of strategy should be put in place even if the client is asymptomatic. Preventing re-injury is the main focus of this kind of prevention strategy. Here are some examples:

- People who have developed heart conditions are told to take small doses of aspirin on a daily basis to mitigate the risk of heart attacks.
- Screenings and tests are conducted for people who may possess risk factors for certain illnesses.
- Injured employees have their work assignments modified.

Tertiary Prevention Strategy

Tertiary prevention strategies focus entirely on individuals who have been diagnosed with chronic, incurable and complicated injuries or illnesses. The goal of this strategy is to provide long-term care and prevent further deterioration of quality of life. Early detection through secondary prevention strategies, like screening, can minimize the impact of the disease later on. Examples include:

- Participating in rehabilitation programs to ensure the best possible quality of life
- Participating in support groups to assist one another with the disease
- Participating in pain management groups to deal with chronic pain

Important Elements of Behavioral Objectives

It is a good idea to break a large primary goal into smaller observable and measurable objectives. These are called **behavioral objectives,** and they can help a social worker understand if the interventions are helping. It can also help clients understand if they are making progress. Here are the important elements:

- The right behavioral objectives are clear and easily understandable, especially on behalf of the client. They come with a focus verb that describes a particular desirable action or behavior.

- These objectives are observable and can be easily noted down by the client and the social worker. These behaviors have a constructive effect on the client's life.
- These objectives always contain the behavior that the client is aiming toward or some of its components. The social worker and the client need to develop these together.
- Good behavioral objectives are always **client oriented**. The emphasis is always placed on the client in order for changes to occur.

The Various Phases of Intervention

Social workers need to prioritize the different needs of clients, depending on their specific situations. Maslow's hierarchy of needs is a very good reference when working with clients, as this hierarchy requires that the client's "deficiency needs" be addressed first. Once all of these needs have been fulfilled, the social worker can move on to "growth needs" and help clients reach their self-actualization goals. Social workers need to assess and fix physical problems by providing medical attention. Social workers also need to be wary of interventions that have a one-size-fits-all approach.

The aim of social work is to institute change at the micro and macro levels and enhance the well-being of clients and entire communities. No matter what kind of intervention, the phases of intervention are as follows:

Step #1 – Engagement with Clients

Social workers' first step is to engage with the client, the group and the community at large. It is also a good idea to establish the boundaries and parameters of the social worker-client relationship.

Step #2 – S&W Assessment

The next course of action is to assess the client's strengths and weaknesses. During this phase, the social worker collects data and determines the client's urgent needs.

Step #3 – Designing the Intervention

During the design and planning stage, the problem is understood properly. After this, the social worker and the client come up with their end goal and the measurable objectives that they will use to accomplish it. During this phase of intervention, a specific plan of action is developed.

Step #4 – Applying the Intervention

During this phase, the social worker applies the intervention plan and tracks its progress.

Step #5 – Evaluation of Intervention

Evaluation continues throughout the whole process and in conjunction with the entire intervention process. This stage determines when goals have been met and when new goals are required.

Stage #6 – Termination and Anticipation

Lastly, the intervention is terminated when the main goal has been reached. All of the progress that has been made needs to be reviewed. All the future needs and supports that will be required also need to be anticipated.

Common Motivational Approaches

Social workers need to motivate reticent clients and make them aware that their situation is not acceptable. The clients need to be urged to make changes to their lives and behaviors. This can be accomplished with the help of a motivational approach. Not all clients can look at things with an optimistic outlook, especially if they are struggling with mental health issues. In these cases, a social worker's job is to help create an atmosphere that is conducive to change and self-improvement. Here are some techniques that can help motivate clients:

- Elaborating on how the change is important and how it will help the client grow
- Identifying the barriers in the client's path and working on how to remove them
- Setting clear and measurable goals that can be attained

- Making the first steps toward change and growth
- Advocating and standing up for specific kinds of needed change
- Identifying risk areas and problem areas
- Preventing a relapse of past dysfunctional, toxic and harmful behaviors

Apart from motivating clients, social workers also need to provide them with a way to self-motivate. Clients can use these techniques while working toward a goal. Here are some of the most successful self-motivation techniques:

- Visualization – Through an image on a refrigerator or in the bedroom
- Rewards – When progress is made regarding the individual's goals
- Peers – Being around positive and empathetic people who will help
- Reminding – Constantly reminding oneself why a change is needed
- Forgiving – Forgiving oneself and being less self-critical of making mistakes

How to Engage with Mandated/Involuntary Clients

Social workers often have to work with people who did not actively seek them out. This is the case when appointments are mandated by courts and law enforcement. People in the child protection system, criminal justice system, etc., make regular appointments. Working with such clients is difficult because they usually view these appointments as some sort of punishment. Here are some approaches that work well with involuntary clients:

- Listening to clients' experiences and using that information to assess how disposed they are toward intervention
- Elaborating to clients what the purpose of the intervention is and clarifying the aspects of the intervention that they have control over; focusing on the consequences of nonparticipation
- Engaging in clear communication with clients and trying to establish a relationship that is based on mutual trust and transparency
- Giving clients the practical assistance they might need and helping them fight for their rights
- Viewing clients as more than the problems that brought them into the services and showing empathy and respect

Techniques for Stress Management

Stress is a physiological and psychological reaction to life events, and most people experience it on a regular basis. If an event is particularly traumatic or stressful, it is perceived as a threat. The body goes into fight-or-flight mode, and the hormones responsible for these feelings are released. At times, the body refuses to return to normal and stays in a heightened state of anxiety and visible stress.

Stress management is extremely important and provides individuals with the tools they need to deal with events that the mind perceives as threats. Proper stress management can deal with all kinds of threats and minimizes the impact of the traumatic event by a large margin. To achieve this, social workers need to monitor their clients and identify triggers.

Once the stress triggers have been identified, social workers need to help clients identify aspects of the trigger situations that are within their control. Clients can then make changes and benefit from stress-reduction techniques. Research shows that yoga, tai chi, music, exercise, massage, art, etc., can have a large positive effect on stress management. Having a healthy lifestyle is also very important.

Techniques for Anger Management

Almost everyone feels anger once in a while. Some people may have explosive reactions when they are angry, which can result in violence or manifest as a kind of physical problem. Social workers can help their clients develop a treatment plan so that they can change the behaviors that exacerbate their rage. Here are some of the main techniques for anger management:

The Cognitive Approach

- Teaches clients to use logic and rationality to reach a balanced approach
- Teaches clients not to jump to an all-or-nothing perspective
- Teaches clients to use empathy and different points of view to put different situations into perspective
- Teaches clients to focus on goals and try to solve problems
- Teaches clients to replace rage-inducing destructive thoughts with healthy ones

The Relaxation Approach

- Deep breathing and other meditative practices
- Guided imagery and yoga
- Physical exercise

The Communication Approach

- Teaches clients to slow their speech when angry in an effort to avoid saying things that they will regret later
- Teaches clients how to stop and listen to other people
- Teaches clients to avoid getting defensive during a tense situation
- Teaches clients to use humor and avoid heavy situations
- Teaches clients to think about their words before uttering them

The Environmental-Change Approach

- Teaches clients to walk away or leave if there is a tense situation
- Teaches clients to actively avoid people and situations that evoke anger
- Teaches clients to avoid engaging in conversations and situations that are very likely to cause anger if they are tired

Approaches to Family Therapy

Working with children and families is one of a social worker's major responsibilities. Family therapy is a form of therapeutic exercise in which the family is treated as a whole, along with the set of interacting parts. Social roles and interpersonal interactions need to be focused on, as well as real behaviors and lapses in communication. Proper therapy can remove dysfunctional dynamics and replace them with healthy and sustainable ones. Here are some different kinds of family therapy:

Strategic Family Therapy

This is built on communication theory and is based on the assumption that families are flexible units that can modify solutions and adjust according to their needs. Here are some of the main concepts of strategic therapy:

- Pretend technique – Family members are encouraged to pretend voluntary control.
- Family homeostasis – Families are resistant to change and preserve their old communication and organization patterns.
- First-order changes – These are superficial behavioral changes that do not change the system's structure.
- Second-order changes – These are systematic and structural changes made in an effort to reorganize the family as a whole.

Structural Family Therapy

The social worker engages the family and helps them restructure the existing system. Old and dysfunctional dynamics are cast aside, and healthy new ones are introduced. A good way to do this is to use the concept of interpersonal boundaries and rules. This is one of the most effective methods of basic family therapy.

Bowenian Family Therapy

The goal of Bowenian family therapy is to improve and enhance the transmission process that exists between family members of different generations. The focus is not on reducing symptoms. Instead, it is the enhancement of family functions. Here are the eight constructs needed to understand Bowenian therapy:

- Differentiation
- Emotional Fusion
- Multigenerational Transmission
- Emotional Triangle
- Nuclear Family
- Sibling Position
- Societal Regression
- Family Projection Process

A social worker trained in Bowenian therapy can improve family dynamics by attacking the root cause of dysfunction—faulty multigenerational transmissions.

Couples Intervention and Treatment Approaches

Couples experience problems frequently, and these problems usually occur due to the following reasons:

- An inability to bond and connect with one's significant other after some form of damage has been inflicted
- A lack of skill or knowledge in this area
- Instances where one partner triggers the other's emotional trauma, then takes no steps to repair the trauma

Here are some treatment and intervention techniques that social workers use when working with couples:

- Insight-oriented psychotherapy – Social workers spend time studying the interactions between two partners. In doing so, they develop a hypothesis.
- Behavior modification – Dysfunctional behavior and unhealthy tendencies are isolated, addressed and modified. The goal is to change the way that partners interact with each other.
- Gottman method – This therapy method is based on the principle that in healthy relationships, partners know each other's worries and stresses, share a mutual fondness and admiration, manage any conflicts, trust one another and are committed to one another. This method also focuses on removing any conflicting verbal communication.

Approaches to Social Group Work

Social workers can also make use of group work, in which individuals choose to improve their social functioning in the form of a meaningful group experience. In social group work, individuals come together to help each other and address all kinds of personal, group, organizational or community issues. The social worker's goal is to help members change their behavior by calling on interpersonal experiences. Members help better each other.

How to Manage Group Processes

Here are the various stages of group development that a social worker needs to be familiar with:

- Pre-affiliation – This is the forming of the group, when the members begin to develop trust with each other. This stage is also referred to as the "forming" stage.
- Power and Control – This is when individual members struggle for autonomy. This affects the identification of the group. It is also known as "storming."
- Intimacy – This is when the members utilize the self in service of the group at large. This is also called "norming."
- Differentiation – This is when the group members realize that each member is a distinct individual, and both aspects are taken into consideration. This stage is also called "performing."
- Separation – This is when the members act separately from one another, also known as "adjourning."

Groups are helpful because:

- They provide a sense of universality to the individual members.
- They allow the members to engage in acts of altruism.
- They instill a sense of hope in the individual members.
- Groups can allow members to learn efficiently via interpersonal learning.
- They help the members gain insight and significant self-understanding.

Here are some factors that can affect group cohesion:

- The size of the group
- The homogeneity of the group or the similarity of the members to each other
- The interdependence of the group; how dependent the members are on each other in an effort to achieve common goals
- The level of participation in the group's goal or norm setting
- The stability of the members; if members change frequently, the group's cohesion is negatively affected

Key Concepts

Groupthink – One of the disadvantages of group approaches is **groupthink**, where a group makes bad decisions due to faulty collective thinking. When there is homogeneity in the group, groupthink is a distinct possibility since outside opinions are scarce. Here are its main causes:

- Self-censorship – Doubts and deviations from the perceived consensus are not expressed or explained for fear of harsh criticism.
- "Mindguards" – Members of the group decide to protect the group and its leaders from critical information that is contradictory to their cohesion and point of view.
- Collective rationalization – Members of the group do not take warnings into account and fail to reconsider any assumptions they make.
- Excessive optimism – Members suffer from a delusion of invulnerability that leads to extreme risk-taking.
- Illusion of unanimity – Majority opinions are assumed to be unanimous, and the fringe or minority voices are silenced.
- Inherent morality – Group members believe that their cause is right and everyone else is assigned the role of the "other," leading them to ignore the ethical consequences of their actions.

Group Polarization – This is a phenomenon that usually occurs during the group decision-making stage. There is an adoption of a dominant perspective, and the entire group adopts an extreme position that is not in line with the individual points of view of the group members. This leads to extreme risk-taking and other bad decisions that can cause harm to the members of the group.

Integrative Case Management

Case management has always been a focus of social work, and it has been defined in many ways. All models have one common element: clients need support and assistance in accessing services in today's complex bureaucratic systems. Social workers also have a responsibility to monitor duplication and address any gaps in clients' treatment and care. There are serious service gaps despite the presence of support programs at the local and federal levels. Today's existing social work systems are highly uncoordinated, complicated, fragmented and duplicative.

The main objective of social work case management is to improve the client's functioning and well-being. This can be done by providing high-quality services in the most effective manner possible. Individuals can have multiple complex needs, and the social worker needs to address all of them properly. Social workers also need to abide by the *NASW Standards for Social Work Case Management*. There are five case management activities:

a. Assessment
b. Planning
c. Linking
d. Monitoring
e. Advocacy

Indicators of Readiness to Change

Clients do not change their behaviors all at once. There are various stages involved in the process. For most people, changes in behavior can occur only over a period of time. In this continuum, the client progresses from being uninterested, unaware or unwilling (also known as **pre-contemplation**) to considering a change, known as **contemplation**. This usually leads to **preparation** for making a change, followed by definitive actions toward the change. Attempts to maintain the behavior follow this, called **maintenance**. Social workers should know that taking part in the problem-solving process and showing up punctually are good indicators of a client's willingness to change.

Chapter Ten: Management of Cases

Case Recording for Practice Evaluation

To evaluate the impact of services, social workers can use available case records. These are existing secondary sources of data, and they can be easily accessed. However, social workers have to be prepared to deal with inconsistencies in the data that can arise due to multiple individuals working with the same client. Also, the client's perspective on the practice evaluation needs to be recorded if the social worker wants a complete picture of the entire situation. The social worker has a basic responsibility to collect all aspects of available information.

Social workers have a responsibility to obtain written consent from their clients regarding the use and examination of their records. This is especially important if the social worker is engaged in a level of formal evaluation not fully captured by the already existing records. Supervisors need to review available case records from time to time, which will ensure that all documentation is being done properly and in an unbiased manner. It is a supervisor's responsibility to stand by the same standards of confidentiality as social workers. As usual, the client's needs are always most important.

Performance Appraisal and Evaluation Methods

The social worker's performance needs to be appraised and evaluated on a regular basis to ensure that clients receive the most effective services. These reviews are a part of the supervisor's regular duty and are part of daily administrative responsibilities. The most important aim of performance evaluation is to improve the overall outcome of service delivery and client and public accountability. Some areas that need to be included in social work appraisals include:

- The cultural competence of the social worker in question
- The staff and community relationships that the social worker has forged
- The social worker's professional attributes and attitudes, including adherence to the *Code of Ethics*
- The social worker's use of supervision
- The social worker's knowledge and skills in regard to data gathering, analysis, diagnostics, treatment planning, interventions, interviewing, etc.

- The social worker's ability to adhere to the policies, procedures and objectives of the parent agency in question
- The social worker's ability to establish meaningful and professional relationships with clients

There are various formats and methods for evaluation. Ordinal rating scales and evaluation outlines can be used. However, the supervisors need to be aware of biases (such as central tendency bias, halo effect, leniency bias, etc.), which can impact the client's overall ratings.

Effects of Legislation on Practice

The client is a person in the environment, and the individual's needs are paramount. The rules and laws that govern human societies have a tremendous effect on the client's life. The client's environment is governed by these rules, and they can enhance or hamper the client's functioning over time. The influence of these laws is dynamic, as the change in one of the rules will affect the others. Social workers need to be aware of the dynamics and impacts of legislation on clients and existing work practices.

Client Education About Service Policies

Helping clients achieve self-determination and independence is one of the social worker's primary goals. Clients must be able to make informed decisions regarding their own treatment, and they must also have proper information available about the benefits that they are entitled to. They should be aware of their rights, such as the right to be referred to professionals and the right to refuse services. Clients need to be taught the limitations of the service policies and benefits.

How Agency Functioning Affects Service Delivery

Social work takes place in many different settings, ranging from single-family homes to public-sector schools, hospitals, universities and even correctional facilities. Social workers need to establish a safe environment where they can practice ethically and focus on the clients' needs. When agency policies and procedures reinforce the social worker's values and individual principles, a safe environment is created. Examples of this include supervision, workload management, professional development, etc.

The standards of ethical practice also need to be considered. The agencies and the umbrella organizations need to make ethical rules transparent and clear. Social workers have a responsibility to abide by a code of ethics, especially when clients are concerned. They need to focus on the areas of informed and written consent, risk management, client safety and confidentiality. Policies should also protect social workers and their clients from discrimination, exploitative behavior, harm, etc.

It is the agency's responsibility to provide social workers with continuing professional development. This will allow social workers to develop and enhance their skills so that they can deal with clients effectively and efficiently. Newly hired social workers also need to be provided with orientations, training, etc., so that they can easily acclimatize to their new setting. Work needs to be regularly supervised by social workers with relevant experience and qualifications. Finally, social workers need to receive proper pay while keeping client services affordable.

The Concept of Client Advocacy

Social workers are in a position to advocate for change both at the micro and macro levels. They can initiate changes on behalf of the individual clients or even the group or community of clients at large.

   a. They can obtain services or resources for the client or group that would otherwise be impossible or very difficult for them to procure on their own.
   b. They can modify or lobby against policies that would directly hamper the growth and advancement of certain groups and communities.
   c. They can promote and lobby for laws and policies that would result in the growth and provision of resources for clients, certain groups and communities.

Social workers are on-the-ground individuals who fight for client rights on a regular and daily basis. In fact, social workers are the voice for the voiceless and most vulnerable members of society: immigrants, marginalized groups, battered women and children, among others. Advocacy does not need to be done from within the agency. It can also be done from outside. The goal of advocacy is to obtain public support for a certain kind of policy or regulation so that resources such as power, finances, etc., can be redistributed more equitably.

Some Important Federal Social Welfare Regulations and Impact

Many federal laws have been instituted to make the jobs of social workers easier. Social workers need to understand and appreciate these. These laws are listed in chronological order below.

Title VI, Civil Rights Act (1964)

This states that no person can be excluded from federal financial assistance on the grounds of race, color and national origin. This act desegregated schools and public works, and all governmental and private agencies were prohibited from discriminatory hiring practices. It is the social worker's responsibility to uphold equal rights for every person.

Older Americans Act, OAA of 1965

This policy protects the rights of senior citizens and older Americans. This law established the Administration on Aging, which allows the federal government to provide supportive services and funds to individuals over the age of 60. Local Area Agencies on Aging (AAA) look out for vulnerable senior citizens by providing support.

Child Abuse Prevention and Treatment Act (1974)

This was one of the first pieces of US legislation to address child abuse and neglect on a federal level. It has been amended many times, and it provides large-scale funding to states to support the prevention, assessment, investigation, treatment and prosecution of all child abuse. It also provides grants and support to nonprofit nongovernmental organizations.

Family Educational Rights & Privacy Act (FERPA), of 1974

This law protects the privacy of all educational records. It applies to all schools that receive funds from the U.S. Department of Education. FERPA gives parents a lot of rights with respect to their children's educational records. These rights then transfer to students when they turn 18. Schools need written permission from parents and students before releasing information about their records.

Education for Handicapped Children Act (1975)

This law guarantees proper public educational services to all children with disabilities between the ages of three and 21. Also, children enrolled under this are eligible for Individual Educational Plans (IEPs), which are revised on an annual basis. Support services, such as speech therapy, cognitive therapy, etc., are provided at no cost to the family.

Indian Child Welfare Act (1978)

This law was put in place to directly support one of the most marginalized groups in the United States—Native American children. This law specifies a procedure for an Indian child's placement:

a. Verify the child's ethnic and tribal identity.
b. Allow for tribal jurisdiction over the child in question.
c. If the tribe rejects the jurisdiction, then the child must be placed with a family member.
d. If placement with a family member is impossible, then the child will be placed in a family belonging to the same native tribe.
e. If this is impossible, the child must be placed in the home of a family that is not Native American or indigenous.

Adoption Assistance & Child Welfare Act (1980)

This law focuses on family preservation by keeping families and children together and out of foster care if possible. This act mandates courts to look at child welfare cases with more regularity and requires them to make reasonable efforts to keep families together. This law also empowers and requires state-level agencies to play a direct role.

Americans with Disabilities Act (1990)

The ADA is a key civil rights legislation that prohibits all forms of discrimination on the basis of disability. It acts as one of the follow-ups to the Civil Rights Act of 1964. Furthermore, the ADA also includes physical and mental disabilities while maintaining that disabilities need not be severe or permanent to qualify.

Patient Self-Determination Act (1991)

This is a set of federal requirements that implement directive policies in all health-care facilities that receive some sort of federal funding. This act specifies that clients have to be informed of all matters regarding their health, and clients are the only ones who have the right to determine what their treatment will be.

Family & Medical Leave Act (1993)

All employers have to provide employees with at least 12 weeks of job-protected leave if employees have certain family or medical reasons. Health coverage should be continuously provided to employees as if they were not on leave.

Multiethnic Placement Act (1994)

MEPA and its amendments prohibit agencies from refusing or delaying foster care or adoptive placements because of a child's race, color or national origin. It also prohibits agencies from considering race, color or national origin as a basis for denying approval as a foster or adoptive parent.

Violence Against Women Act (1994)

VAWA improves the criminal justice response to all forms of violence against women, ranging from domestic violence to sexual violence. Penalties against sex offenders have been increased under VAWA. Also, victims are required to be kept in a safe environment, and all states, tribal areas, territorial jurisdictions, etc., must enforce protection.

Health Insurance Portability & Accountability Act (1996)

HIPAA provides all individuals with access to their medical records, along with reinforced control over the distribution and use of this information. In particular, individuals have full control over their personal health information. The law also provides federal privacy protections for individuals. State laws offering protections to individuals are not affected by HIPAA.

Patient Protection & Affordable Care Act (2010)

The ACA expands the individual's access to insurance and increases the protection of health insurance in general. It expands the health workforce and helps check rising health-care costs. ACA also institutes changes to existing medical aid policies and reduces health care fraud and abuse.

Important Written Communication Skills

In order to ensure that all communications are written in a professional manner, social workers need to ensure that:

- The purpose and language of the written communications are clear and concise.
- The matter of client confidentiality is addressed in an ethical manner and is maintained no matter the situation.
- The format of the communication is clear, and the headings are appropriately distributed.
- The content is clear, written in simple language and easy to understand; jargon should be avoided as much as possible.
- The language is culturally appropriate and includes objective descriptions that are free of values or subjective opinions.
- The social worker's assessments and recommendations are made based on data instead of assumptions or guesswork.
- The social worker's arguments and opinions are expressed in a logical manner, and recommendations are provided.

If written communications are not prepared with care and skill in a thoughtful manner, they can be harmful to clients. Social workers need to keep their audience in mind when drafting all written communications. The aim is to make information very easy to implement.

Chapter Eleven: Consultation and Interdisciplinary Collaboration

Models of Peer Supervision

Peer supervision is a paradigm in which professional social workers' performance in the field is evaluated by peers. There is no superior who is in charge of doing evaluations. Instead, everything is a cooperative arrangement in which peers work together. Increased access and frequency of supervision is a benefit of peer supervision models. There is also an opportunity for reciprocal learning and decreased dependency on expert supervisors. Here are the different models:

Developmental Model

This peer supervision model focuses on the stage nature of treatment and intervention. All interventions have a beginning, middle and end. Peer supervision in the developmental model allows the client and social workers to collaborate.

Psychodynamic Model

This is a peer supervision model in which human interactions are most important. The relationship between the client and the social worker is looked at. Supervisors can use audio or video clips to examine the interactions.

Role-Centered Model

This is a peer supervision model that takes a look at the relationship between clients and social workers through the lens of social role theory. Every member of the group is assigned a role; the members of the group discuss the case from their assigned POV, which can bring about interesting insights.

Relying on Other Specialized Professions

According to the *NASW Standards for the Practice of Clinical Social Work*, social workers have to maintain access to professional consultation. Many times, these professionals may be qualified experts in other disciplines, such as medicine, law, etc. To provide the best services and promote the clients' best interests, social workers should consult with professionals and refer their clients to them.

Interdisciplinary relationships with experts and specialized professionals might not constitute team practice, but they are very necessary elements.

Approaches to Consultation

Social workers might also be called upon to consult on a problem related to a client, service or organization. This is usually limited by time, and the consultant's advice can be very valuable. Here are some critical elements of consultation:

- The purpose of the consultation should be clearly defined.
- The role of the consultant should be clearly defined.
- The consultation process should be outlined with transparency and clarity.
- The nature of the consultation problem should be clarified.

It is important to seek advice and consultation only from colleagues when it is in the client's best interests. It is also important to only ask for advice from people who have demonstrated significant knowledge and expertise regarding the matter at hand. Social workers are also entitled to serve as consultants themselves when the need arises.

Collaboration on an Interdisciplinary Scale

In the realm of social work, interdisciplinary collaborations are extremely important. They also are challenging but rewarding tasks. Collaborative teams have a lot of potential, and they can tackle problems innovatively. Here are some guidelines that can help social workers who are part of a collaborative effort:

- Each social worker has a responsibility to clearly articulate his or her specific role in the interdisciplinary collaborative team.
- A social worker has to look for and establish common ground with all the different people and professionals on the team.
- Social workers need to understand the roles that these professionals play in the interdisciplinary collaborative effort.
- Social workers should address any underlying conflict between teams so that conflict does not interfere with the team effort.
- Social workers must establish and maintain good relationships with the team members.

- The representation of the facts should be clear, concise and unbiased.
- All of the decisions must be written down.
- The report should be free of value judgments and any personal subjective opinions of the social worker concerned.
- The reports should be timely.

In most cases, the social worker should limit the client's access to records and reports. However, the social worker can make exceptions in certain exceptional circumstances. If restricting access can cause harm to the client, then the social worker can release the information. Steps must be taken to protect the client's confidentiality at all times.

The Steps for Client Referral

Step 1 – Clarifying the Referral's Need or Purpose

Social workers should refer clients to other professionals only when the social worker believes that the services of that professional are in the client's best interests.

Step 2 – Looking up Resources

It is the social worker's responsibility to make sure that the resources recommended to the client are of the very best quality.

Step 3 – Discussing Options with a Client

The client needs to be involved in each step of the referral process. The social worker needs to discuss options with the client and select from all available options.

Step 4 – Making Initial Contact

The social worker needs to work with the client and prepare him or her for initial contact with the professional. The social worker needs to take steps to facilitate this and should make sure that responsibility is transferred in a proper way.

Step 5 – Following Up

Lastly, the social worker always needs to commit time and resources to conduct follow-ups, both with the client and the professional. This ensures that there is no break in the client's overall service.

Unit IV: Professional Ethics and Values

Chapter Twelve: Ethical Issues

Principles and Processes of Informed Consent

There may be instances where clients are not familiar with various medical or legal procedures that they are going to be involved in. In these situations, it is the social worker's task to ensure that clients understand everything they are involved in. It is the social worker's task to break down the intervention plan and explain everything simply and concisely.

If clients cannot provide informed consent due to some kind of barrier, social workers need to obtain permission from an appropriate third party. While doing so, they need to ensure that the third party acts in a way that is consistent with the client's wishes and interests. Social workers can also provide their services by making use of email, texting, etc.

Before any videotaping or audio recording or written recording, the social worker needs to obtain the client's express informed consent. If the social worker acts on behalf of a client who is unable to make informed decisions, the social worker has to ensure that he or she is acting in the client's best interests. Using clear and understandable language is very important.

Professional Boundaries

Social workers need to maintain strict professional boundaries with their clients. The *NASW Code of Ethics* is clear about this. One area is the use of physical contact with clients. Setting clear and appropriate boundaries is vital. Any kind of physical contact of a sexual nature with a client is inappropriate and absolutely not allowed.

Social workers are not supposed to engage in sexual or physical relationships with their clients. This rule extends to the people in charge of the client, such as their relatives, friends, etc. It is the social worker's responsibility—not the client's—to establish boundaries. It is a conflict of interest if a social worker works with someone with whom he or she once had a relationship.

Dual Relationships

Social workers are forbidden from engaging in dual relationships with their clients. An example of a dual relationship is when the social worker sees the client in a clinical POV and also knows the client because the client provides a service to him or her. Social workers are not allowed to take advantage of previous professional relationships. The main goal is to avoid a conflict of interest. This is especially true for social workers engaged in research.

Resolution of Ethical Issues

One situation that can crop up in social work is an **ethical dilemma**, since real life is rarely black or white. The social worker will have to choose between two solutions, both of which seem to have a similar ethical value. There may be a case where the social worker's **ethical obligations** clash with the **policies of the agency** or **relevant laws**. It is the social worker's responsibility to solve the problem in a way consistent with the *NASW Code of Ethics*.

Steps of Ethical Problem Solving

- The social worker identifies the ethical standards, which are clearly defined by the professional *Code of Ethics*, identifies which tenets are being compromised and reviews the *Code of Ethics*.
- The social worker suggests modifications based on the main ethical values that are central to the proposed dilemma; once that is done, the modifications need to be implemented.
- The social worker monitors for new ethical dilemmas.

Ethical and Legal Issues

Social workers come in contact with ethical and legal issues. In most cases, ethical and legal standards complement each other. But sometimes, the two standards can be at odds with each other. Social workers need to be aware of legal mandates, which fall under five areas: constitutional, statutory, regulatory, court-made or common and executive orders. Here are the distinct categories of ethical and legal issues:

- Actions that are neither legal nor ethical in social work, especially considering the prevailing standards – not legal and not ethical
- Actions that are fully compatible with the prevailing legal and ethical standards of social work – legal as well as ethical
- Actions that are legal but do not comply with the prevailing ethical standards of social work – legal, but not ethical
- Actions that are ethical but do not comply with the existing legal standards of social work – ethical, but not legal

If there are any conflicts between ethical and legal standards, the social worker has to identify the mandates that apply to the conflict. It is also very important to understand which groups and individuals will be directly affected by the conflict. Conflicts should not be resolved in a vacuum, and social workers should consult with colleagues, experts and their superiors. The results of the decision should be monitored.

Chapter Thirteen: Confidentiality and Its Limits

Legal and Ethical Considerations Regarding Confidentiality

Social workers have a responsibility to protect their clients' rights, especially the right to privacy. Social workers are not allowed to elicit or solicit private information from clients unless it is essential for the proper provision of services. Once information has been shared, the standards of confidentiality apply (*NASW Code of Ethics*). A social worker can disclose confidential information only when it is appropriate and only with express consent from clients.

Social workers also have a responsibility to inform the clients about the disclosure of confidential information and the consequences of doing so. This has to be done in all kinds of situations—whether there is some legal requirement for doing so or whether it is done with the client's consent. Disclosure may be necessary when there is some serious or imminent harm to the client or identifiable persons. Informed consent is very important in the realm of social work.

Even during legal proceedings, the social worker has a professional responsibility to keep clients' information confidential to the fullest extent of the law. Social workers can also take steps to limit court orders for information if they have reasons to believe that disclosure will cause serious harm to the client. It is a good idea to limit the scope of the court order. If a subpoena is served, the social worker should respond and claim privilege. Confidentiality of minors' records needs to be handled carefully.

Ethical and Legal Issues Regarding Mandatory Reporting

Social workers may be required to disclose confidential information against the client's wishes to comply with mandatory reporting laws. This is especially important in cases of child abuse. Even if physical or sexual abuse of a minor is merely suspected, it is the social worker's responsibility to reach out to local law enforcement. If social workers fail to do so, they may face civil and criminal liabilities.

This mandatory reporting law can cause severe ethical issues for social workers who have committed to protecting their clients' best interests. At the same time, they also have to fulfill their responsibilities to society at large. Most reports of abuse and neglect actually come from professionals who are usually expected to keep information private. Examples include medical personnel, law enforcement agents, educators, lawyers and social workers.

Chapter Fourteen: Value Issues

Influences of Social Workers' Values and Beliefs on the Social Worker-Client Relationship

Social workers have a responsibility to recognize personal values and beliefs that may inhibit the therapeutic relationship between them and their clients. Here are some examples of such values:

Dichotomous Thinking

Many people think in terms of "either/or," and this can lead to a misconception that any differences are inferior, wrong or just bad. It is important to recognize that sometimes, differences can arise and peacefully coexist.

Universalism

This is a flawed way of thinking that considers that there is only one acceptable and universal norm of behavior for all people. Social workers need to understand that there are multiple valid standards of behavior.

Valuation of Control and Restraint

Social workers can highly value personal values of control, restraint and even constraints. This can clash with clients who place more importance on expressiveness, emotions and spirituality. It is important for a social worker not to give into these prejudices just to satisfy the assumption of objectivity.

Measure of Self Comes From Outside

Many people think that a measure of self comes only from what other people have to say. This value is in contrast with the fact that value comes from within. People have to understand and realize that they are worthwhile just because they were born and that they have to live in harmony with other people and the larger environment.

Power Is "Power Over" Others

Many people think that power can be defined as the mastery of one's environment. This can clash with the value that power can also be defined as "power through" harmony with others in the environment. Sharing power leads to expansion.

The Effects of Culture, Race and Ethnicity on Values

Individuals' culture, race and ethnicity are strongly linked to their values. Social workers need to be highly self-aware of their own attitudes, values and beliefs. They also need to be willing to acknowledge differences that arise due to different races and cultures. Here are some things that social workers should do:

- Be culturally aware of their own heritage and the heritage and values of others
- Be aware of their personal values and biases and acknowledge how they can affect client relationships
- Value and celebrate the differences they have with people of other cultures instead of maintaining ethnocentricity
- Be comfortable operating in an environment where there are significant cultural and racial differences between them and all their clients
- Be socially aware and accepting of their professional and personal limitations
- Acknowledge and accept their own attitudes, beliefs and feelings about race

Professional Values and Ethics of the Social Worker

Social workers have to abide by a core set of values, which serve as the foundation of social work practice in general:

- Dignity and worth of the person
- Importance of human relationships
- Integrity
- Competence
- Social justice
- Service

All of the professional ethics that social workers abide by are based upon these core and foundational values of social work. Professional standards and ethics can be a great tool for guiding new social workers who may be confused.

ASWB Clinical Exam 1

(1) Which of the following drugs is typically prescribed for the treatment of attention deficit hyperactivity disorder?

(A)   Adderall

(B)   Dextromethorphan

(C)   Tofranil

(D)   Acetaminophen

(2) Which of the following is a primary prevention strategy?

(A)   Taking low doses of aspirin daily after a certain age

(B)   Engaging in a healthy lifestyle with a balanced diet and exercise

(C)   Getting yearly health checkups

(D)   Modifying work assignments for injured individuals

(3) Which of the following options is not an indicator of resistance?

(A)   A client who is largely silent and uncooperative during appointments

(B)   A client who behaves in a rude and hostile manner

(C)   A client who has been referred by another professional

(D)   A client who delves into irrelevant small talk during appointments

(4) If a social worker learns of a colleague's specific impairment that will affect the person's practice, what is the social worker's responsibility?

(A)   Submit an anonymous report to the social work licensing board in the area

(B)   Consult with the colleague and help him or her pursue remedial action

(C)   Notify the superior so that he or she can make decisions

(D)   Come up with a short-term intervention plan with other colleagues

(5) A client has just been laid off from his company and is currently very worried about the financial duress that he and his family will be facing. How will unemployment affect other areas of this person's life, according to the systems approach?

(A)   It will affect his physical and mental health, as well as his family.

(B)   It will affect his financial well-being and savings.

(C)   It will cause his mental health to decline and cause him to be worried about finding a job.

(D)   It will teach him to be resilient about other impending life crises.

(6) Which of the following is a symptom of Wernicke's encephalopathy?

(A)   Confusion and disorientation

(B)   Hypertension

(C)   Consistent pain in the chest and abdomen

(D)   Loss in senses of taste and smell

(7) A client is feeling very distressed because her 15-year-old daughter has not been pulling her weight around the house. She has also been doing her homework on her own and is doing fine at school. The daughter complains that her mother is too involved and does not give her any privacy. What is the problem here?

(A)   Some sort of developmental disorder

(B)   Some sort of communication problem

(C)   Some sort of insecurity on the part of the mother

(D)   Some sort of role discomplementarity

(8) A client suddenly stops coming to sessions after two months and refuses to answer emails, phone calls or text messages. After four weeks, the client calls the social worker and asks for a copy of his records. There is no harmful information in the report, but the social worker refuses to give it to the client. How would you categorize the social worker's actions?

(A)   Ethical, because such a request has to be made in writing

(B)   Unethical, because the social worker has a duty to provide records to the client

(C)   Ethical, because the client voluntarily disengaged from the social worker

(D)   Unethical, because the records belong to the client only

(9) The client has reddish eyes, displays a little bit of paranoia and displays some delayed reaction times. Which of the following drugs has the client probably consumed?

(A)   Heroin

(B)   Amphetamines

(C)   Marijuana

(D)   Vicodin

(10) Which of the following is true about most personality disorders?

(A)   They can cause interpersonal relationship difficulties for the client.

(B)   They are usually diagnosed in childhood.

(C)   Anyone with personality disorders needs to be institutionalized.

(D)   Personality disorders can easily be treated with medication alone.

(11) Which of the following is associated with low ego strength?

(A)   Treating challenges as a puzzle to solve

(B)   A strong sense of self and uniqueness

(C)   Growth due to facing struggles and challenges

(D)   Substance abuse and avoidance

(12) What is the duty of the social worker according to the Tarasoff decision?

(A)   Only intended victims need to be warned of imminent danger.

(B)   Both authorities and intended victims should be notified in case of imminent danger.

(C)   Only the authorities need to be notified of imminent danger.

(D)   None of the above.

(13) Which of these is a therapeutic advantage of Prozac (fluoxetine)?

(A)   Prozac inhibits serotonin absorption and results in improved mood.

(B)   Prozac increases the amount of noradrenaline in the synaptic cleft.

(C)   Prozac prohibits the reabsorption of norepinephrine by the brain.

(D)   None of the above.

(14) Which is the primary criterion that needs to be considered when making level-of-care determinations in a behavioral health setting?

(A)   The patient's psychiatric history

(B)   The patient's criminal history

(C)   The patient's medical necessity

(D)   The patient's risk

(15) A client has made substantial progress and has managed to achieve all his goals. When the social worker speaks to the client about termination, the client says that he wants to keep visiting the social worker. The social worker gives the client one month of pro bono visits. The social worker's actions are _____.

(A)   Ethical, because the client is not yet ready to end treatment

(B)   Unethical, because termination and autonomy are central to the treatment

(C)   Ethical, because the worker is not charging any fees

(D)   Unethical, because there are no treatment goals

(16) Which trait is associated with someone with borderline personality disorder?

(A)   Extreme apathy

(B)   Non-dichotomous thinking

(C)   Repressed anger

(D)   Unstable relationships

(17) Which of the following is an objective associated with the foster care program?

(A)   The perceived safety and happiness of children

(B)   The proportion of children reunited with their parents

(C)   The average high school diploma rate

(D)   None of the above

(18) What is the first goal of a client who has undergone a major life crisis?

(A)   A sense of equilibrium and stability

(B)   Strong coping skills

(C)   A support network

(D)   Delving into the nature and causes of the life crisis

(19) A social worker suspects that a child under the care of her agency is being neglected and subjected to psychological abuse. She discusses the situation with her superior, but the supervisor does not agree. What should the social worker do?

(A)   Contact Child Protective Services (CPS) while informing the superior that she is doing so.

(B)   Monitor the child for a while before going ahead.

(C)   Not do anything and drop the subject.

(D)   Get in touch with primary caregivers who are in charge of the child.

(20) A social worker is seeing a family and conducting family therapy. The 16-year-old daughter reveals that her father molested her twice when she was six years old. The father is present at the meeting. He confirms the account and appears remorseful. What should the social worker do?

(A)   Not contact any agency because 10 years have passed

(B)   Contact Child Protective Services without telling the family

(C)   Contact Child Protective Services after telling the family

(D)   Do nothing and continue therapy

(21) At which stage of development do imaginary friends come into the picture?

(A)   Preoperational stage

(B)   Sensorimotor stage

(C)   Formal operational stage

(D)   Concrete operational stage

(22) Which is not a clinical scale in the Minnesota Multiphasic Personality Inventory?

(A)   Psychopathic behavior

(B)   Indication of gender identity

(C)   Schizophrenic behavior

(D)   Sleepiness and tiredness

(23) Which of the following elements contains thoughts, feelings, etc., that the client has no awareness of?

(A)   Superego

(B)   Conscious

(C)   Unconscious

(D)   Preconscious

(24) Which of the following is a level of awareness according to Sigmund Freud's theory?

(A)   Preconscious

(B)   Subconscious

(C)   Superego

(D)   Anal-retentive behavior

(25) According to the basic problem-solving process used by social workers, what is the next step after the client assessment has been completed?

(A)   Intervention planning

(B)   Further evaluation

(C)   Direct intervention

(D)   Engagement

(26) A client's mother recently passed away, and the client and his mother had a very close bond. To memorialize his mother, the client has gotten a tattoo on his arm depicting his mother and her name. While showing the social worker the tattoo, the client tears up and states that the tattoo always reminds him of his mother and makes him cry. What can the tattoo be a form of?

(A)   Splitting the form

(B)   Hallucination

(C)   Idealization

(D)   Symbolization

(27) Which of the following does not fall into the category of a deficiency need as defined by Maslow in his hierarchy of needs?

(A)   Esteem – Love, affection and care

(B)   Self-actualization and growth

(C)   Safety – A safe environment to stay in

(D)   Physiological – Medical care, food, water, etc.

(28) What is the main reason behind the practice of peer supervision in the field of social work?

(A)   It is a learning relationship based on reciprocity and skill sharing.

(B)   It is more cost effective than one-on-one supervision.

(C)   It is easy to implement and enforce.

(D)   It ensures that clients always receive the best services.

(29) Which of the following is true about racial and ethnic identities?

(A)   They are invented and reinvented by each generation.

(B)   They are myopic and reticent to integrate other people.

(C)   They are linked to a feeling of total belonging.

(D)   They remain stable for decades at a time.

(30) Which of the following is not a core value in the social work field, according to the *Code of Ethics*?

(A)   The importance of relationships

(B)   Minimizing harm to self and others

(C)   Dignity and worth of the person

(D)   Social justice and service

(31) When designing an intervention or treatment strategy, which of the following is not an important consideration?

(A)   The biopsychosocial-spiritual-cultural assessment of the client

(B)   The government agency assessment of the client

(C)   The medical doctor's assessment of the client

(D)   The social worker's assessment of environmental conditions

(32) Which of the following is not an element of or task in the family life cycle of young children?

(A)   Adopting and developing the parenting roles of new parents

(B)   Helping young children develop peer relationships

(C)   Adjusting to children taking a central role in family maintenance

(D)   Providing children with safe environments

(33) What is meant by a co-occurring disorder?

(A)   Presence of a mental health and substance abuse disorder

(B)   Presence of a mental health and physical health disorder

(C)   Presence of a pain disorder and substance abuse disorder

(D)   None of the above

(34) A social worker is reviewing the list of medications currently taken by a 70-year-old client. She discovers that the client is taking Paxil after being switched from Zoloft. What condition is the client most likely diagnosed with?

(A)   Insomnia and general fatigue

(B)   Attention deficit hyperactivity disorder

(C)   Bipolar disorder

(D)   Major depressive disorder

(35) Which of the following is false about risk factors for violence?

(A)   The risk factors predict with 100% certainty who will participate in violence.

(B)   The risk factors increase the likelihood that the client will engage in violence.

(C)   The risk factors can be present at the community level as well.

(D)   The risk factors are not positively associated with protective and other predictive factors.

(36) If a client sues a social worker for malpractice, the social worker needs to fulfill his ethical obligations by _____.

(A)   Not responding to the court

(B)   Providing all the information obtained during treatment so that the court can see

(C)   Releasing only information related to the lawsuit

(D)   Refusing to cooperate with the court or client by releasing no information

(37) A social worker receives a frantic call from an ex-boyfriend who is now married. The ex-boyfriend is having trouble dealing with the loss of his father and mother, who passed away in an accident. He would like to see the social worker for some counseling. The social worker has not had any contact with the ex-boyfriend in over five years. What should the worker do?

(A)   Set up an appointment and start treatment immediately.

(B)   Contact the local licensing board to gain permission.

(C)   Inform the ex-boyfriend that she cannot provide counseling services.

(D)   Comfort the ex-boyfriend personally.

(38) With respect to the diagnosis of conduct disorder, how have *DSM-IV* and *DSM-V* changed?

(A)   At least a single symptom has to be exhibited in the last month.

(B)   Symptoms must impair academic, social and/or occupational functioning.

(C)   Conduct disorder occurs prior to adulthood.

(D)   A descriptive features specifier is used for those meeting criteria.

(39) Which of the following is not a diagnostic used in the *DSM-V* for gambling disorder?

(A)   A preoccupation with gambling games and strategies

(B)   Lying to family and friends to conceal gambling

(C)   A loss of relationships, jobs, grades, etc. due to gambling

(D)   Facing legal problems as a consequence of gambling

(40) When are social workers permitted to terminate their services?

(A)   When they are owed money and have not been paid

(B)   When they are leaving employment to pursue other opportunities

(C)   When they do not want to maintain social relationships with clients

(D)   When they believe clients are being uncooperative and overly hostile

(41) What is the framework used to assess a client's global functioning?

(A)   Myers-Briggs Type Indicator (MBTI)

(B)   Thematic Apperception Test

(C)   World Health Organization Disability Assessment Schedule

(D)   Rorschach Inkblot Psychological Test

(42) A social worker who is associated with a hospital makes use of the SOAP documentation format. Which of the following elements is not recorded in the SOAP record?

(A)   Subjective opinions regarding the client's well-being

(B)   Clear assessment of the client's current needs

(C)   A well-defined plan of client intervention and care

(D)   The client's insurance and financial coverage limits

(43) Which of the following diagnoses is most likely to be assigned as a result of a mental status examination?

(A)   Avoidant personality disorder

(B)   Schizophrenia

(C)   Delirium

(D)   Oppositional defiant disorder

(44) When a social worker makes use of multiple sources to collect data on a client and the client's situation, that method is called _____.

(A)   Twinning

(B)   Triangulation

(C)   Social exchange

(D)   None of the above

(45) During a family therapy assessment, the social worker learns that the parents set very strict rules. If the children fail to follow the rules, the parents dole out very severe punishments. The children do not know the reasoning behind the rules. Which is the most likely parenting style being used here?

(A)   Corporal

(B)   Authoritarian

(C)   Authoritative

(D)   Punitive

(46) A social worker is treating a 65-year-old client who is a former smoker. The man also suffers from chronic obstructive pulmonary disease (COPD). He takes many medicines, one of which helps regulate chronic hypertension. What is this client's primary prevention need?

(A)   Regular influenza immunizations

(B)   Participation in a support group for other people with COPD

(C)   Reduction of any activity that would cause heavy breathing and exacerbate issues

(D)   Monitoring of blood pressure and modifying medications as required

(47) Which of the following is not a key concept in the field of individual psychology?

(A) Perfection

(B) Psychosexual urges

(C) Inferiority

(D) Compensation

(48) What is the most important role of a social worker who is currently engaged in a client's crisis intervention?

(A) Being highly involved and focused on meeting the client's basic needs

(B) Being passively involved and acting only as a resource in case of any concerns

(C) Providing short-term, intensive support focused on the client's psychological needs

(D) Providing long-term support that encompasses all aspects of the client's trauma and needs

(49) A social worker is seeing a group of clients, all of whom are suffering from anorexia nervosa. Over the course of a month, all the clients talk about their diverse backgrounds and different childhood experiences. The social worker then comments that the condition can arise due to many factors. This statement is based on what concept?

(A)   Subsystems

(B)   Equifinality

(C)   Diagnostic-related groups

(D)   Complete homeostasis

(50) Why is self-monitoring used in the realm of social work?

(A)   It is based on the principle of self-determination.

(B)   It prevents clients from escapism and allows them to understand their problems.

(C)   Clients are the most reliable sources of information.

(D)   It saves time and money for the social worker and the agency.

(51) Which of the following is the most common side effect of antipsychotic drugs?

(A)   Akathisia

(B)   Persistent cough

(C)   Blurred vision

(D)   Hypertension

(52) There is a specific medication that makes clients feel ill if they consume alcohol while taking the drug. What is this medicine, used to treat alcoholism, called?

(A)   Paracetamol

(B)   Ranitidine

(C)   Clozaril

(D)   Antabuse

(53) A social worker has been asked to provide case management to a family that has recently immigrated to the United States from another country. The parents do not speak English, but their 13-year-old daughter is fluent in English and their native language. The social worker can speak only English, but she accepts the case anyway. This action is _____.

(A)   Unethical, because the social worker is unable to understand and communicate with all of the family members

(B)   Ethical, because the services are not clinical in nature and are limited by time

(C)   Unethical, because the social worker does not know if the daughter will translate

(D)   Ethical, because the need is very urgent

(54) A social worker has a client who says that he feels that his wife does not care about him, which has been causing a lot of problems in his marriage. The social worker discovers that the man thinks this because his wife appears to be distracted whenever he talks to her. The social worker tells him, "She cares about you; she is just distracted by other pressing matters." What approach is being used here?

(A)   Ego psychology

(B)   Psychosexual analysis

(C)   Cognitive-behavioral therapy

(D)   Operant conditioning and retraining

(55) What is generally true about self-image during a person's life cycle?

(A)   Young children have relatively low self-image, which gradually increases over time.

(B)   Self-image almost always declines during the teenage years due to concerns about body image, academic challenges, social challenges, puberty, etc.

(C)   Self-image increases in older adulthood because individuals have fewer demands.

(D)   Self-image gradually declines during adulthood and levels off around 55 to 60 years.

(56) A social worker sees a couple for counseling because they are having relationship problems. They have very little intimacy and a disconnect. The husband admits that he has started to drink, which has led him to get fired from his job. The wife is fearful of her husband because he is loud when he drinks and spends a lot of time out of the house. What is the first issue to be addressed?

(A)   The husband's alcohol issues

(B)   The couple's intimacy and sexual issues

(C)   The wife's general fear

(D)   The couple's financial issues

(57)   A man visits a social worker because he is "struggling to find himself" and is feeling "bored" with his life now that his children have become adults and left the house. What is his current stage of psychosocial development?

(A)   Intimacy versus isolation

(B)   Industry versus inferiority

(C)   Generativity versus stagnation

(D)   Initiative versus guilt

(58) A couple is having problems, and the wife is unable to communicate with her husband. Instead, she starts to increasingly confide in her sister-in-law. What is this situation called?

(A)   Differentiation

(B)   Familial regression

(C)   Triangulation

(D)   Growth

(59)   A client is taking Nardil. What is an important part of being on this medication?

(A)   Watching calorie intake

(B)   Taking aspirin on a preventive basis

(C)   Getting regular blood work done

(D)   Consuming foods with low levels of tyramine

(60)   Which phase of development has rapprochement as a subphase?

(A)   Normal symbiotic

(B)   Separation-individuation

(C)   Normal autistic

(D)   Object constancy

(61) A social worker is working on the biopsychosocial-spiritual-cultural assessment of a client who has been admitted to the hospital. The social worker lists weight, height, blood pressure, current medications, subjective assessments, etc. Then the social worker moves on to the psychological and spiritual sections of the report. What parts are missing?

(A)   Objective information regarding the client's spiritual needs

(B)   The client's medical history, developmental milestones and spiritual needs

(C)   Current medical assessment by the presiding physician in charge

(D)   Nothing

(62) A social worker has been seeing a client privately. The client has not paid the social worker for many weeks, despite knowing the payment policy. The social worker has reminded the client repeatedly that services will be terminated if the bill remains unpaid. At the last session, the client breaks down and says he does not think he can go on without receiving the social worker's services. The social worker is acting _____.

(A)   Unethical, because the client may be a danger to himself or others

(B)   Ethical, because the social worker has given the client notice of nonpayment

(C)   Unethical, because the *Code of Ethics* does not permit social workers to terminate services because of nonpayment

(D)   None of the above

(63) When does the period of latency occur in Freud's psychosexual stages of development?

(A)   From the age of five until adolescence

(B)   During infancy

(C)   Between three and five years old

(D)   From late adolescence to adulthood

(64) Which of the following techniques is the best way to understand and diagnose the reasons behind a family's dysfunctional structures while doing structural family therapy?

(A)   Confrontation between members

(B)   Enactments of events

(C)   Journaling and record-keeping

(D)   Collateral

(65) What is the most effective method of engagement when working with an involuntary client?

(A)   Telling the client how social work will help his or her problem

(B)   Forcing the client to cooperate by threatening a court order

(C)   Listening to the client to understand his or her feelings and current situation

(D)   Talking about the *Code of Ethics*

(66) A school social worker also freelances with a mental health agency. A mother whose child is a regular visitor with the social worker at school asks the social worker to provide mental health counseling to her child. The social worker and the child already have a very good bond, and the mother thinks that the social worker can provide quality services. What should the social worker do in this situation?

(A)   Contact the school and liaise directly with the mental health agency

(B)   Refuse to counsel the child, as this is a conflict of interest

(C)   Refer the child to another social worker at the same mental health agency

(D)   Begin to serve the child in both school and counseling settings

(67) Which of the following is a neurotransmitter chemical that is responsible for providing mood balance and is one of the key elements of depression?

(A)   Dopamine

(B)   Noradrenaline

(C)   Histamine

(D)   Serotonin

(68) A social worker has taken a position on the board of directors for an agency that provides support to victims of domestic violence and abuse. Previously, she worked as a volunteer for the same agency. Which of the following actions is unethical for her to take?

(A)   Conferring with philanthropists directly to raise money for the agency

(B)   Educating the public by conducting seminars about domestic violence

(C)   Providing referrals for private practice to clients leaving the domestic violence shelter

(D)   Working with the clients directly

(69) Which of the following situations is an example of an ethical application of identifying client information?

(A)   Notifying Child Protective Services about suspected abuse or neglect

(B)   Using client information in a grant application for emergency funding

(C)   Using client information to advertise the successes of the private practice

(D)   Using client information to provide estranged family members with information about the client

(70) A client behaves in a very hostile manner during his first session, during which he yells and blames others for his situation. How should the social worker approach the problem-solving process in this case?

(A)   Ask the client why he is so upset and loud.

(B)   Listen to the client and understand his concerns.

(C)   Develop an intervention plan with the client.

(D)   Tell the client to calm down.

(71) A man makes an appointment with a social worker and says that he has finally "had enough" after indulging in years of heroin abuse. He gave up the drug two days ago. He appears anxious and agitated. He tells the social worker that he has been vomiting and is also suffering from insomnia. He needs _____.

(A)   Immediate medical attention to treat his heroin withdrawal symptoms

(B)   A long-term treatment program to prevent a relapse

(C)   Contact with loved ones to stage a relapse prevention plan

(D)   None of the above

(72) Social work intervention with violent offenders is most effective when the area of focus is on which of the following?

(A)   Arrest record and past legal involvement

(B)   Static risk factors

(C)   Genetic risk factors

(D)   Dynamic risk factors

(73) What is the typical mental functioning of older adults?

(A)   They are unable to acquire new skills.

(B)   Their cognitive skills continue to fall.

(C)   They learn well, but their memory starts to decline.

(D)   They are at the peak of their cognitive skills.

(74) A couple, both of whom are blind, come to visit a social worker because they feel discriminated against and are distraught. They would like to adopt a child, but child adoption agencies have declined their application because of their visual impairments. How should the social worker best assist this couple?

(A)   Provide them with other ways to become parents.

(B)   Help them fight the bias displayed by agencies.

(C)   Introduce them to support groups.

(D)   Help them cope with disappointment.

(75) A single mother comes to a social worker and confesses that she binge drinks frequently during the weekends. She also states that she does not want to stop binge drinking. What should the social worker do according to the harm reduction approach?

(A) Inform the mother of the potential risks and consequences of her alcoholism.

(B) Refer the mother to a drug and alcohol abuse evaluation to determine the extent of her problem.

(C) Take the mother to a physician immediately.

(D) Provide the mother with alternative childcare options during the weekends when she drinks.

(76) If there is an ethical dilemma in a social worker's agency, what or whom should he turn to first?

(A) His supervisor

(B) The *Code of Ethics*

(C) The agency policies and rules

(D) A more experienced colleague

(77) Which of the following is not an example of a role reversal?

(A)   A 12-year-old girl physically and emotionally caring for her father, who was permanently disabled in an accident

(B)   A 10-year-old boy yelling at his mother for not contributing to chores

(C)   A 14-year-old boy working to support the household while his parents stay home voluntarily

(D)   A 15-year-old girl cooking and being in charge of all chores while her parents do not make any contributions

(78) A social worker evaluates a mental health outpatient program by constructing a focus group to collect information about the client. He also makes use of information kept by the agency to analyze which proportion of clients have been re-hospitalized. What kind of evaluation is the social worker conducting?

(A)   Mixed evaluation method

(B)   Qualitative evaluation

(C)   Quantitative evaluation

(D)   Experimental evaluation

(79) Which of the following is a protective factor that can contribute to violence toward others?

(A)   Exposure to violence in childhood

(B)   Exposure to drugs and/or alcohol from an early age

(C)   Acts of violence at an early age

(D)   Clinical services for physical and/or behavioral care

(80) A client says that she was often criticized by her mother when she was growing up, which has affected her self-esteem. She often doubts her abilities and is afraid to take chances in employment. Which stage of psychosocial development did she have a crisis in?

(A)   Integrity vs. despair

(B)   Generativity vs. stagnation

(C)   Industry vs. inferiority

(D)   Identity vs. role confusion

(81) A social worker finds that she has a lot in common with a client, and she refers her to another social worker because the client says she "would be a better friend than a client." The social worker agrees to this but persuades the client to remain no-contact for a month to prevent conflicts of interest. The social worker's actions are _____.

(A)   Unethical, because services cannot be terminated for this reason

(B)   Ethical, because the client's self-determination is being respected

(C)   Unethical, because a month is not long enough to prevent conflicts

(D)   Ethical, because interpersonal relationships are being fostered

(82) At a social work agency, the therapy sessions are frequently audiotaped so that supervisors can review them. When clients are terminated, the tapes are deleted. The agency uses a standard consent form. However, consent is taken only from the social worker conducting the therapy. Is this ethical practice?

(A)   Yes, because supervisory review is extremely important.

(B)   No, because the client's informed consent has not been obtained.

(C)   Yes, because the tapes are deleted after client termination.

(D)   No, because clients do not receive access to the tapes.

(83) A social worker breaks down the treatment objective into smaller and more easily achievable steps. The client is given a reward after she accomplishes each step. What kind of behavioral technique is being used here?

(A)   Flooding

(B)   Shaping

(C)   Biofeedback

(D)   Modeling

(84)   After several months of therapy sessions, a social worker and client discover that they go to the same mosque. They both continue to visit the same mosque and interact with each other informally. This situation may be classified as _____.

(A)   Ethical, because neither knew about this prior to treatment

(B)   Unethical, because there is a conflict of interest

(C)   Ethical, because religious bonding helps develop a therapeutic relationship

(D)   Unethical, because the social worker and the client interact while they are at the mosque

(85) Which of the following techniques should not be used to address resistance during engagement?

(A)   Dividing the main goals into steps and doling out rewards so that the client can gradually make incremental progress

(B)   Providing hope and optimism with regards to a change

(C)   Explaining the limits of the confidentiality the social worker maintains with the client

(D)   Clarifying all the steps that the social worker will take during treatment

(86) A social worker has a colleague who specializes in child abuse and neglect cases and has more than a decade of extensive experience. The social worker regularly refers clients to this colleague, and the colleague is very thankful. As a form of thanks, the colleague offers the social worker vouchers to a well-known restaurant in their area. The social worker takes the vouchers so as to not "hurt his feelings" but donates them to clients instead. How can these actions be classified?

(A)   Ethical, because the vouchers are being used by clients

(B)   Unethical, because the social worker makes multiple referrals to the same person

(C)   Ethical, because the social worker and the colleague are old friends

(D)   Unethical, because the social worker should not accept the vouchers

(87) A man receives a court order to be evaluated by a social worker. Although he agreed initially, he states toward the end of the interview that he has changed his mind. He wishes that he had never agreed to be interviewed at all. He asks the social worker not to provide any information to the court. What should the social worker do?

(A)   Release the notes from the meetings but not the formal evaluation.

(B)   Complete the formal evaluation based on the notes.

(C)   Agree with the client and withhold all information from the court.

(D)   Inform the court about the client rescinding consent and ask them to suggest the next steps.

(88) Which of the following can be said to be true of young people who are non-gender- conforming or not heterosexual?

(A)   They have different stages of development.

(B)   They receive more support from loved ones, peers and supervisors.

(C)   They struggle to develop identities because they have fewer role models.

(D)   They struggle to develop physically on par with peers.

(89) A 16-year-old girl comes to visit a social worker. She tells him that she has often been the subject of bullying and public ridicule from a group of students at her school. The social worker advises the girl to simply walk away whenever something similar occurs in the future instead of crying and being laughed at as a result. What kind of strategy is the social worker using to reduce bullying?

(A)   Time out

(B)   Extinction

(C)   Negative reinforcement

(D)   None of the above

(90) Which of the following body systems is Hodgkin's disease associated with?

(A)   Lymphatic

(B)   Neurological

(C)   Endocrine

(D)   Musculoskeletal

(91) Which of the following best defines *acculturation*?

(A)   One culture dominating other cultures to reap some associated social rewards

(B)   One culture trying to work with another despite differences

(C)   One culture trying to individualize itself and its identity

(D)   One culture importing elements from another culture into its own

(92) A company CEO realizes that extensive modifications have to be made to his new company's HR policies. The new company's financial health is very unsound, and they realize they cannot afford an HR professional. However, the company employs a social worker whose spouse is a professional HR manager at a very large company. The spouse agrees to take on the task at a discounted rate to meet the requirements. This situation can be classified as which of the following?

(A)   Ethical, because the spouse is being hired in a consulting capacity

(B)   Unethical, because there is a conflict of interests

(C)   Ethical, because the spouse's discounted services are the last resort for the agency

(D)   Unethical, because the spouse is not doing pro bono work

(93) A social worker's client becomes upset when the social worker asks him about his family and relationships. When the social worker says that it is clear that the client is unhappy about his situation, the client remarks that "everything is fine." What is the client exhibiting?

(A)   Denial of any underlying problems with the family

(B)   Lack of trust in the social worker

(C)   Lack of congruence in communication

(D)   Signs of a psychiatric issue

(94) Which of the following tasks is not an element of the process of termination?

(A)   Showing a client how to address any recurrences of the problem

(B)   Reviewing all the accomplishments achieved during treatment

(C)   Recognizing and coping with loss faced by the client

(D)   Identifying issues that may need to be addressed later

(95) A social worker is assigned to a family that has recently immigrated from another country. The family needs basic resources, such as access to nutrition and affordable rental space. The children appear healthy, neat and clean. The social worker sees that the mother mixes a very small amount of alcohol with milk because she says it soothes the teething child. The family also says that they do not believe in Western medicine and prefer to pray if one of them falls ill. What should the social worker do?

(A)   Inform them that CPS needs to be involved and contact the agency immediately

(B)   Respect the family's cultural traditions and work with the family's immediate needs

(C)   Try to learn more about the family's culture

(D)   Provide the family with rent and nutrition without interfering

(96) A social worker working at a mental health facility is very upset with the passage of a new piece of legislation that will detrimentally affect his clients. He joins a protest in his own time and without doing anything that would identify his employer. His agency director is upset at his participation because the mental health facility directors supported the passage of the legislation. The actions of the worker are _____.

(A)   Unethical, because the social worker is an employee of the mental health facility

(B)   Ethical, because it is his responsibility to protest policies that can negatively affect his clients

(C)   Unethical, because he required the permission of the director

(D)   Ethical, because he acted as a private individual

(97) A social worker has been assigned to a family that is temporarily homeless due to their home burning down. They have an 11-year-old son who starts to use baby talk and clings to the mother all the time—behaviors that were absent before the fire. The child also sucks on his thumb at times. He wants to sit in his mother's lap a lot. What kind of defense mechanism is the child using?

(A)   Regression

(B)   Denial

(C)   Projection

(D)   Reaction formation

(98) A social worker receives an email from a client's insurance company. The email asks the social worker to provide information regarding detailed treatment summaries. It also states that the insurance company will cease payments unless this is provided. What should the social worker do in this situation?

(A)   Report the insurance company for unethical behavior.

(B)   Prepare the treatment summaries, but send them only if the client gives written consent.

(C)   Refuse to send the summaries, citing confidentiality mandates.

(D)   Send the summaries to preserve the continuity of the treatment.

(99) A man comes to a social worker and explains that he is sexually attracted to men and is feeling very distressed by the fact that he could be homosexual or bisexual. The feelings experienced by the client can be categorized under which of the following?

(A)　Ego-syntonic

(B)　Obsessive denial

(C)　Anal retention

(D)　Ego-dystonic

(100) What is the primary objective when it comes to planning for permanency?

(A)　Ensuring that all treatment decisions are based on individual needs

(B)　Enhancing the individual's educational and skill training outcomes

(C)　Providing residence in a stable and long-term home environment

(D)　Including all of the parties in the case conferencing

(101) Which of the following side effects is not exhibited after the ingestion of Xanax?

(A)　Insomnia

(B)　Polyuria

(C)　Vertigo and presyncope

(D)　Dysarthria

(102) Which of the following is a life-threatening side effect of Clozaril, a drug that can be used to treat the symptoms of schizophrenia?

(A)   Agranulocytosis, a lowering of the neutrophil count

(B)   Cerebrovascular ischemic attack (stroke)

(C)   Myocardial infarction

(D)   Deep vein thrombosis (DVT)

(103) Which of the following factors is not used to evaluate a client in the person-in- environment classification system?

(A)   Mental and physical health

(B)   Psychiatric pathology

(C)   Social role functioning

(D)   Any problems in the individual's environment

(104) A social worker in a mental health facility is attracted to one of her supervisors and asks her out on a date. They date for around two years and end up getting married. After they get married, the supervisee finds a job at a substance abuse facility. The supervisee's behavior is _____.

(A)   Ethical, because she took another job after getting married

(B)   Unethical, because she was engaged in a dual relationship with her superior

(C)   Ethical, because their relationship eventually resulted in marriage

(D)   Unethical, because she used her relationship to get a new job

(105) Which of the following can be classified along with the antisocial personality disorder grouping, which is characterized by dramatic and erratic tendencies?

(A)   Schizophrenia

(B)   Attention deficit hyperactivity disorder

(C)   Narcissistic personality disorder

(D)   Obsessive compulsive personality disorder

(106) Which of the following statements is false when it comes to a task-centered approach in the realm of social work practice?

(A)   The client has a firsthand role in bringing about change.

(B)   There is no formal assessment phase.

(C)   The first session is concerned with termination.

(D)   Usually, task-centered approaches are highly time-limited.

(107) A client reports that she is very upset with the behavior of her 16-year-old daughter. Apparently, the daughter's grades have been slipping, and she is becoming very irregular with her homework. The client says that she took away the daughter's cell phone as a punishment. What technique is she using?

(A)   Negative punishment

(B)   Positive punishment

(C)   Negative reinforcement

(D)   Positive reinforcement

(108) Which of the following statements is false about social work interviews?

(A)   They exist to serve the client's best interests.

(B)   They can be therapeutic or simply informational.

(C)   They are focused on information collection to aid the therapeutic process.

(D)   They are uniform and are only intended to collect basic, consistent information.

(109) A client tells the social worker that she has been feeling like a failure because she cannot seem to juggle being a single parent and working. The social worker tells her that many people in similar situations experience something similar. What technique is she using?

(A)   Clarification

(B)   Validation

(C)   Reflection

(D)   Paraphrasing

(110) A client in treatment has made substantial progress, but she loses her job and no longer has the means to pay for therapy. She wants to continue therapy, and the social worker agrees that continued treatment would be helpful. What is an ethical way for the social worker to help this client?

(A)   Provide pro bono services to the client until she finds new employment.

(B)   Continue treatment and tell the client that all services will be billed to her new place of employment.

(C)   Terminate services until a new insurer is found.

(D)   Figure out work that the client can do to pay her back.

(111) Which of the following practices is acceptable under the *Code of Ethics* with regard to confidentiality in group work?

(A)   Group members are legally bound to not disclose any information that is shared by members of the group.

(B)   Group members are provided the same confidentiality that they would have received in an individual setting.

(C)   Social workers cannot provide the group members with reassurances that their information will be kept confidential.

(D)   Social workers can freely utilize and discuss information from the group with other people because it is not confidential.

(112) What is the best definition of positive regard?

(A) Clients are accepted and supported without any judgment about their actions or beliefs.

(B) Clients are supported, and their protective factors are explored at length.

(C) Intervention plans and goals are established to enhance clients' quality of life.

(D) Clients are provided with constant support with regard to all of their basic needs.

(113) A client is extremely dejected and tells his social worker that he "cannot take this anymore" and that he "just can't" make any changes to his life. He constantly talks about how different his life would be if he did not have any problem behaviors. What stage of change is he at right now?

(A) Precontemplation

(B) Contemplation

(C) Preparation

(D) Maintenance

(114) A brand-new client brings a coworker to her social work session. What is the best response on the part of the social worker?

(A)   Ask the coworker to look over the intake paperwork because he will also be regarded as a client from now on.

(B)   Do a preliminary assessment in the waiting area to determine if the coworker should be present.

(C)   Allow the client to determine the extent of the coworker's presence.

(D)   Prohibit the coworker from attending sessions on the grounds of confidentiality.

(115) Which of the following cannot be characterized as an indicator of ego strength?

(A)   Blaming others

(B)   Accepting one's own limitations and showing accountability

(C)   Taking responsibility for one's actions

(D)   Dealing with moods

(116) Which of the following is not a respondent behavior on the part of the client?

(A)   Tapping a foot when nervous

(B)   Crying when feeling sad

(C)   Sexual arousal while with a spouse or romantic partner

(D)   Walking away from someone when angry

(117) Which of the following best defines empowerment?

(A)   Placing importance on self-determination and helping clients realize that they have the will and skills to solve all of their own problems

(B)   Providing clients with the easiest ways to retrieve resources and solve all their problems

(C)   Developing a strong therapeutic relationship with clients that is based on trust and mutual respect

(D)   Providing clients with funds so that they can resume their education

(118) An agency providing support to drug addicts is concerned with clients relapsing. To look into the matter, it hires an outside consultant to provide advice and recommendations about the services offered. The consultant has extensive experience and possesses a doctorate and a medical degree. He provides a report with many suggested changes, but the social worker thinks that these would be detrimental to the clients. What should the social worker do?

(A)   Leave it up to the agency director, but inform the director of these concerns.

(B)   Engage another consultant to look into the issue and get a second opinion.

(C)   Not implement the changes after making the reasons clear to the consultant.

(D)   Implement the changes, as the consultant is an obvious expert.

(119) A social worker is seeing a client who is the single mother of a seven-year-old boy. The mother tells the social worker that she has the urge to slap her child when he angers her. Lately, she has been saying that she has trouble moving her arm. What defense mechanism is she exhibiting here?

(A)   Reaction formation

(B)   Introspection

(C)   Conversion

(D)   None of the above

(120) In the *DSM-V* categorization, which of the following statements is true about transvestic disorder?

(A)   This disorder causes significant distress in social and interpersonal relationships.

(B)   This disorder causes significant distress to a client's job or occupation.

(C)   This disorder is restricted to heterosexual males.

(D)   This disorder causes someone to be sexually aroused only when cross-dressing.

(121) Which of the following is the best definition of *delirium tremens*?

(A)   Mental symptoms that manifest as a result of drug abuse

(B)   Mental symptoms that manifest as a result of alcohol withdrawal

(C)   Severe physical symptoms associated with alcohol withdrawal

(D)   Neurological symptoms that are associated with COVID-19

(122) What is the role of the enabler or martyr in a dysfunctional family dynamic?

(A)   Makes everybody laugh to distract them from the dysfunction

(B)   Denies issues to keep everyone in the family happy

(C)   Does very well at academics or work to feed the delusion that everything is fine

(D)   Tries to blend into the background to stay safe

(123) Which of the following needs does not need to be met by caregivers under the aegis of self-psychology?

(A)   Idealization

(B)   Twinship needs

(C)   Mirroring needs

(D)   Biological needs

(124) A client tells the social worker that his boss screams at him on a daily basis. He does not respond despite his anger because he cannot afford to lose his job. He has also been unhappy at home for the past few weeks because he cannot control his temper around his husband and children. What defense mechanism is being exhibited?

(A)   Displacement

(B)   Incorporation

(C)   Compensation

(D)   Denial

(125) Which of the following is not a violation of the rules set in the *Code of Ethics* in the context of social work?

(A)   Engaging in a business transaction with a current adult client

(B)   Writing a professional recommendation letter for a current adult client

(C)   Engaging in a romantic or sexual relationship with a current adult client

(D)   Lending money to a current adult client for rent, medicines and groceries

(126) A client tells the social worker that she is having a lot of issues at her job and needs her help. She mentions how she "can't wait for advice on how to fix" her issues. What should the social worker do?

(A)   Ignore the comment

(B)   Clarify what will happen during treatment and outline the social worker and client's responsibilities

(C)   Clarify the treatment responsibilities later, after rapport has been achieved

(D)   Ask the client why she feels like the social worker's advice will solve all of the client's problems

(127) Which of the following is false about addictive disorders and substance-related disorders outlined in the *DSM-5*?

(A)   Caffeine use disorder is included as a new addictive disorder.

(B)   Legal problems have been removed from the diagnostic criteria.

(C)   Substance use and abuse have been combined into a single continuum.

(D)   Gambling is the only non-substance-related addiction disorder.

(128) Which of the following best defines *entropy*?

(A)   A system that is open and informationally transparent

(B)   A system that is random and disorderly, heading toward decline

(C)   A system that is progressing forward toward goal achievement

(D)   A system that is specialized in its purpose

(129) During the first session after intake, a client says that she wants to hurt herself but will be fine later. She assures the social worker that she will not hurt herself even if she wants to. What should the social worker do first?

(A)   Take the client to the hospital for a medical checkup.

(B)   Take the client for a proper psychiatric evaluation.

(C)   Conduct a proper safety assessment.

(D)   Ask the client why she is feeling like hurting herself.

(130) When two or more people are suffering under the same delusional system, what is it called?

(A)   Codependency

(B)   Stockholm syndrome

(C)   Munchausen's by proxy

(D)   Folie á deux

(131) A social worker developed an innovative program that has drastically reduced the recidivism rate of juvenile offenders. She approaches her director about using the same approach for adult offenders, but the latter is skeptical about this. What concerns are being expressed?

(A)   External validity

(B)   Internal validity

(C)   Autoregression

(D)   Heteroskedasticity

(132) Which of the following is false about the relationship between race and ethnicity?

(A)   *Ethnicity* and *race* are synonyms for each other.

(B)   Individuals who are of the same race might be in different ethnic groups.

(C)   Individuals who are of the same ethnic group might be of different races.

(D)   None of the above.

(133) After a family therapy session with a family of four, the social worker says, "During the last 90 minutes, each of you has had a chance to discuss your frustrations with one another. You have also seen how sometimes your actions have been hurtful, even if that wasn't the intention behind them." What is the reason behind this statement?

(A)   The social worker is asking the family members not to be mad at each other.

(B)   The social worker is doling out praise to the family members for doing well during the session.

(C)   The social worker is being objective and clarifying doubts for the family members' benefit.

(D)   The social worker is summarizing the events of the session so that the family members walk away with a new understanding of their actions.

(134) A social worker is working with a client who is currently staying at a group home. The social worker asks two staff members at the home to independently record the frequency of a particular set of client behaviors and submit the reports to him weekly. He asks them to not share reports with one another. What approach is the social worker using?

(A)   Interrater reliability

(B)   Parallel external validation

(C)   Test and retest

(D)   Internal consistency validation

(135) What should a social worker do first if she receives a subpoena for a former client's record?

(A)   Provide the record immediately because the client has been terminated

(B)   Ignore the subpoena because the information is privileged

(C)   Respond to the court and claim privilege

(D)   Send the subpoena directly to the former client

(136) Which of the following topics has been discussed in theories of human development in social work?

(A)   Focus on prevention of mental deficiency

(B)   Systems approach to clients

(C)   Abiding with law enforcement and legal directives

(D)   Mandated reporting

(137) A social worker employed at a school asks the parents of an Indian student to come in for a discussion. The child has been experiencing problems in school by not following the rules and showing no interest in academics, etc., despite being a promising student. During the meeting, the boy's grandparents also show up. What is this most likely an indication of?

(A)   The child will listen only to his grandparents.

(B)   The child is spoiled by his grandparents, which is why he is behaving badly.

(C)   The grandparents are an important part of the child's support system and should play an important role in the discussions.

(D)   The parents rely on the grandparents to control the child.

(138) Which of the following statements is false with regard to attachment and bonding?

(A)   Insecure attachment systems can be linked to psychiatric and personality disorders.

(B)   Attachment is a set of learned behaviors linked to classic and operant conditioning.

(C)   Attachment and bonding should be viewed from the point of view of the client's culture because the theoretical process is universal.

(D)   Attachment can be best understood through an evolutionary context.

(139) What is the role of the mascot in a dysfunctional family setting?

(A)   To make others laugh and distract them from the problems they are facing

(B)   To blend into the background and attempt to be invisible

(C)   To do extremely well in academics or work to help family image

(D)   None of the above

(140) Which of the following is the best description of Munchausen by proxy syndrome?

(A)   A person pretends to be sick or induces symptoms of sickness to receive care and attention from others.

(B)   A person invents or causes an illness or symptoms of illness in someone in his or her care in order to receive attention as a caregiver

(C)   A person forms a bond with hostages or victims of abuse after being involved with those people for a long time.

(D)   A person develops an abnormal interpretation of reality, resulting in hallucinations or delusions.

(141) What's the sequence of relationship formation followed by the theory of psychosocial development?

(A)   Intimacy – Autonomy – Attachment

(B)   Autonomy – Attachment – Intimacy

(C)   Attachment – Autonomy – Intimacy

(D)   Intimacy – Attachment – Autonomy

(142) A client tells a social worker that she is unhappy and wants to end her marriage. But first, she would like to talk to a priest and get guidance. What should the social worker do first?

(A)   Advise the client not to talk to the priest because religious support is not required.

(B)   Ask the client why the advice of a priest would be helpful.

(C)   Ask the client to talk to a marriage counselor first.

(D)   Determine how to prepare the client for her meeting with the priest.

(143) Which of the following statements is true about transference in the realm of social work?

(A)   It is mostly sexual in nature.

(B)   It can be seen mostly in clients with specific personality features.

(C)   It is a very conscious and willful process.

(D)   It has no therapeutic value.

(144) Which of the following options contains the stages of group development in sequential order?

(A)   Preaffiliation -> Power and Control -> Intimacy -> Differentiation -> Separation

(B)   Preaffiliation -> Power and Control -> Separation -> Intimacy -> Differentiation

(C)   Preaffiliation -> Differentiation -> Power and Control -> Intimacy -> Separation

(D)   None of the above

(145) What perspective of human behavior is characterized by the belief that people have an innate ability to change themselves, as well as a drive to grow and care about personal meaning and competence?

(A)   Developmental

(B)   Humanistic

(C)   Rational choice

(D)   Psychodynamic

(146) Which of the following is not a *DSM-5* criterion for a client to be diagnosed with schizophrenia?

(A)   The presence of two or more of the following: delusions, hallucinations, very disorganized or catatonic behavior and disorganized speech

(B)   Major disturbances to academics, work, self-care and interpersonal relationships

(C)   Disturbances attributable to the physiological effects of a substance

(D)   History of schizoid disorders in the family

(147) Which of the following is not a drawback of using existing case records as the basis for client evaluations in the present?

(A)   Clients' opinions about service are not considered.

(B)   Evaluations are limited to topics covered in the old case records.

(C)   Existing case records may not be consistent or even complete.

(D)   No additional cost or time is associated with the use of old case records.

(148) Which of the following is not a type of blood cancer?

(A)   Myeloma

(B)   Myelodysplastic syndromes (MDS)

(C)   Ewing sarcoma (also known as Ewing tumor)

(D)   Waldenstrom's macroglobulinemia

(149) Which of the following drugs is not used to control the tics associated with Tourette's syndrome?

(A)   Haloperidol (Haldol)

(B)   Amphetamine salts (Adderall)

(C)   Pimozide (Orap)

(D)   Risperidone (Risperdal)

(150) Assent and consent are _____ in the context of social work.

(A)   Distinct because consent is defined as the legal authorization to participate in treatment

(B)   Identical because *consent* and *assent* are synonyms

(C)   Distinct because consent is required of everyone, and assent is required only from voluntary clients

(D)   Sequential because consent is required first, followed by assent

(151) Which of the following statements is false about feedback in social work?

(A)   Clients should be told why the feedback is needed and what will be done with the information.

(B)   Feedback is extremely important during the key decision nodes of service development and implementation.

(C)   Client consent is unnecessary if the consultation is not related to client care.

(D)   The best insights are often obtained from critics.

(152) What should the social worker do when he and a client belong to different ethnic groups?

(A)   Ask the client if it is a problem before starting with the treatment.

(B)   Understand the differences and their impact on the treatment process.

(C)   Recognize that customs and beliefs are universal to a specific ethnic or racial group.

(D)   Get supervision or consultation from someone from the same ethnic group.

(153) Which parenting style usually has the most positive outcomes for children?

(A)   Permissive

(B)   Authoritative

(C)   Authoritarian

(D)   Uninvolved

(154) Which of the following disorders is currently being studied further, according to the *DSM-5* manual?

(A)   Caffeine use disorder

(B)   Pica disorder

(C)   Sexual masochism disorder

(D)   COVID-19 paranoia

(155) A social worker is currently working with a client suffering from pica. The social worker is struggling with the client because pica is not commonly served by her agency. Whom should the social worker bring on as a consultant—a coworker who she has known since graduation or an external consultant with relevant experience?

(A)   Both, since the coworker can provide valuable insight while the external consultant can provide specific guidance

(B)   The coworker, because she has known this person for a longer time

(C)   Neither

(D)   An external expert because this person is an expert on treating people who have pica

(156) Which of the following options is not a change to the set of neurodevelopmental disorders listed in the *DSM-5*?

(A)   Autism spectrum disorder now contains autistic disorder, Asperger's syndrome, childhood disintegrative disorder and pervasive developmental disorder.

(B)   Mental retardation has been renamed intellectual disability.

(C)   Disruptive mood dysregulation disorder has been added as a new diagnosis for people aged 18 and younger.

(D)   Stuttering has been renamed childhood-onset fluency disorder.

(157) Until what age does the normal symbiotic phase of development last, according to the context of object relations theory?

(A)   2 weeks

(B)   10 years

(C)   Lifelong

(D)   5 months

(158) A social worker has started seeing a couple for couples counseling because of their destructive pattern of fighting. The husband complains that his wife always nags him to do his chores. He says that he will do all his chores the moment she stops complaining. What behavioral technique is the husband referring to?

(A)   Positive reinforcement

(B)   Negative reinforcement

(C)   Positive punishment

(D)   Negative punishment

(159) Which of the following statements is true about a client who is transgender?

(A)   The client is likely to experience stigma, bias and discrimination on the basis of gender identity.

(B)   The client is likely to be homosexual.

(C)   The client is likely to opt for sex reassignment surgery in the future.

(D)   The client is likely to cross-dress.

(160) A client contacts a social worker and reports that he has been under the surveillance of the police and the FBI. He says that they have been following him for the past week and are tapping his cell phone. He does not have any other evidence to support this claim. The client's report is most likely due to _____.

(A)   Delusion

(B)   Schizophrenic hallucination

(C)   Manic state

(D)   Depression

(161) Which of the following groups is not appropriate for any form of genetic counseling?

(A)   Men who are sexually active and have a family history of birth defects and dangerous diseases

(B)   New mothers who are undergoing postpartum depression (PPD) or anxiety (PPA)

(C)   Couples who have a child with an inherited genetic disorder

(D)   Women who have had suffered multiple miscarriages or whose babies died in infancy

(162) What is dysthymia now called in the *DSM-5*?

(A)   Major depressive disorder

(B)   Disruptive mood dysregulation disorder

(C)   Bipolar disorder

(D)   Persistent depressive disorder

(163) A client was admitted to the hospital. While there, he was very depressed, felt hopeless and spent most of the day sleeping. After being discharged, he appeared very energetic, was fidgeting a lot and was rambling during his appointment with the social worker. What medication is he most likely going to be prescribed?

(A)   Imipramine or Tofranil

(B)   Carbamazepine or Carbatrol

(C)   Haldol or Haloperidol

(D)   Sertraline or Zoloft

(164) A client tells the social worker that she wants to be more assertive at work. What should the social worker do to help her achieve her goal?

(A)   Identify the outcomes that will result from this behavioral change.

(B)   Provide communication strategies for better self-expression.

(C)   Help the client enroll in classes aimed at increasing assertiveness.

(D)   Gather information about the communication barriers for the client.

(165) Which of the following disorders usually has hypomania as a symptom?

(A)   Schizophrenia

(B)   Persistent depressive disorder

(C)   Bipolar disorder

(D)   Narcissistic personality disorder

(166) A client has been diagnosed with late-stage thyroid cancer, and her oncologist has referred her to a pain management support group. This will help minimize the pain and discomfort associated with cancer. Which type of prevention does this support group fall under?

(A)   Hospice care

(B)   Primary prevention

(C)   Secondary prevention

(D)   Tertiary prevention

(167) Which of the following best describes the "Not Otherwise Specified" diagnostic categories in the *DSM-5*?

(A)   They are expanded to include new diagnostic criteria.

(B)   They are eliminated completely, with no alternative options.

(C)   They are unchanged and can still be used in the same way.

(D)   They are replaced with "Other Specified" and "Unspecified."

(168) A client is very upset because she feels that her four-year-old daughter is selfish. She goes on to state that her daughter does not understand how her behavior impacts other people in the family. However, the child has no problems in preschool and gets along very well with her peers. What is the best way to assist this client?

(A)   Explain the development process of young children.

(B)   Assess the child for a serious behavioral disorder.

(C)   Work with the child to get her to behave properly.

(D)   Gather more information on the child from other people.

(169) Which of the following rules must not be present in the boundaries that govern how social workers engage in physical contact with their clients?

(A)   The contact should be culturally sensitive and in line with the client's beliefs and traditions.

(B)   The use of contact should be clearly articulated to clients and social workers.

(C)   Contact should not occur if it can cause psychological damage.

(D)   Contact should occur only with adults, not children.

(170) A client starts to miss appointments with her social worker after she has achieved her set goals. Prior to this, she had very good attendance and made very good progress. What are these missed appointments a likely indicator of?

(A)   Codependency

(B)   Dissatisfaction with outcomes

(C)   Readiness to terminate

(D)   Emergence of a new problem

Answers to Exam 1

(1)   (A) Adderall.

Adderall is a combination drug containing four salts of amphetamine. It treats ADHD by enhancing the individual's focus and attention and reducing impulsivity.

(2)   (B) Engaging in a healthy lifestyle with a balanced diet and exercise.

A healthy lifestyle, consisting of a balanced diet and plenty of exercise, is regarded as a primary prevention strategy. It helps people avoid developing diseases and health conditions in the first place.

(3)   (C) A client who has been referred by another professional.

Only this action is not an indicator of resistance on the part of the client.

(4)   (B) Consult with the colleague and help him or her pursue remedial action.

According to the *Code of Ethics*, you first have to consult with the social work colleague who you think is suffering from some kind of impairment. Going to a superior is the right choice, but only after talking to the colleague.

(5)   (A) It will affect his physical and mental health, as well as his family.

According to the systems approach, the loss of unemployment will result in a worsening of physical and mental health. Stress about financial insecurity can have a negative effect on a client's physical or mental well-being.

(6)   (A) Confusion and disorientation.

Wernicke's encephalopathy is a disease associated with the chronic abuse of alcohol over a long period of time. Disorientation and confusion are its classic symptoms, along with ataxia and ophthalmoplegia.

(7)   (D) Some sort of role discomplementarity.

This is a classic example of role discomplementarity. The mother believes that her daughter is not fulfilling the responsibilities attached to her role. This is untrue, because the daughter is doing all of her tasks. This is why the daughter is unhappy with the fulfillment of her own role expectations.

(8)   (B) Unethical, because the social worker has a duty to provide records to the client.

According to the *Code of Ethics*, the social worker has to provide this client with reasonable access to his records. Unless the information can do serious harm to the client, the worker should provide the requested records.

(9)   (C) Marijuana.

The symptoms listed are all indicators of marijuana use, especially red eyes and paranoia.

(10)　(A) They can cause interpersonal relationship difficulties for the client.

Personality disorders can cause severe mood swings, explosive outbursts, abandonment fears, etc., which can effectively hamper a person's interpersonal relationships.

(11)　(D) Substance abuse and avoidance.

People who have low ego strength avoid problems altogether because they seem overwhelming. They also have a tendency to escape through substance abuse, wishful thinking and fantasizing.

(12)　(B) Both authorities and intended victims should be notified in case of imminent danger.

Ever since the Tarasoff decision of 1974, it has been social workers' duty to protect intended victims from serious threats. To do so, they have to reach out to the proper authorities and the intended victims of harm.

(13)　(A) Prozac inhibits serotonin absorption and results in improved mood.

Prozac is an example of a Selective Serotonin Reuptake Inhibitor (SSRI), which improves mood by inhibiting the absorption of serotonin by the brain.

(14)　(C) The patient's medical necessity.

When making level-of-care determinations in a behavioral health setting, the patient's medical necessity is the one and only criterion used. The evidence-based standards of clinical care are used for this.

(15) (D) Unethical, because there are no treatment goals.

Even though visits are offered pro bono, the social worker's actions are unethical because the client does not have any treatment goals left. It is in the client's best interests to assess his future needs and come back only if necessary.

(16) (D) Unstable relationships.

People who have BPD constantly have to deal with unstable relationships, which are a consequence of their disorder. The disorder leads to difficulty managing any interpersonal relationships.

(17) (B) Proportion of children reunited with their parents.

The proportion of children served by the foster care program who are reunited with their parents is an objective that can be used to measure the system's effectiveness.

(18) (A) A sense of equilibrium and stability.

The social worker's very first goal is to relieve and comfort the person who has undergone a major life crisis. The client must first be returned to a state of equilibrium and safety. Only after this can the other answer options be considered.

(19)   (A) Contact Child Protective Services (CPS) while informing the superior that she is doing so.

Social workers are mandated reporters, and it is their responsibility to get in contact with CPS if they have even a reasonable suspicion of abuse or neglect. Irrespective of what the supervisor says, the social worker has to faithfully fulfill the duties of this mandate.

(20)   (C) Contact Child Protective Services after telling the family.

A social worker is a mandated reporter and needs to report all instances of abuse, suspected or confirmed, to the relevant authorities. Social workers also need to keep in line with the *Code of Ethics*, which means that they have to be transparent with the client family.

(21)   (A) Preoperational stage.

The preoperational stage (between two and seven years old) is when the child engages in magical thinking. It is during this stage that imaginary friends come into the picture and can stay for a while.

(22)   (D) Sleepiness and tiredness.

In the Minnesota Multiphasic Personality Inventory, there are various items listed, such as hypochondriasis, indicating stress over physical health; depression, indicating depression and hopelessness; hysteria, indicating anxiety and tension; psychopathic, etc. However, sleepiness and tiredness are not listed in the MMPI scale.

(23)   (C) Unconscious.

The unconscious element contains all of the information, such as thoughts, feelings, desires, etc., that the client has no awareness of. However, these very much influence every aspect of clients' lives.

(24)   (A) Preconscious.

The preconscious contains all of the information required by the client. All of this information is within reach and can be easily retrieved. As a result, it is a level of awareness according to Freud's theories.

(25)   (A) Intervention planning.

Once the client assessment has been completed, the social worker needs to come up with a formal plan of action and intervention based on data and evidence and supported by theory.

(26)   (D) Symbolization.

The client has symbolized and memorialized his mother in the form of a tattoo. That is why it evokes an emotional response from him every time he looks at it and devotes some thought to it.

(27)   (B) Self-actualization and growth.

Maslow's needs can be divided into deficiency needs and growth needs. The base needs—such as physiological needs, safety and esteem (such as love, affection, etc.)—are deficiency needs. Self-actualization and growth are not deficient needs. They are referred to as growth needs by Maslow.

(28)   (A) It is a learning relationship based on reciprocity and skill sharing.

Peers interact and share their experiences and knowledge with one another. This establishes a learning relationship in which social workers get to reciprocate and learn skills from each other. Using feedback from peers to improve one's own skills and learning is the objective of peer supervision.

(29)   (C) They are linked to a feeling of total belonging.

Cultural and ethnic identities are very important considerations, especially for clients who belong to marginalized groups and minorities. Cultural and ethnic identities are primarily born out of a feeling of belonging. The tribe's sentiment is built into human society.

(30)   (B) Minimizing harm to self and others.

According to the *Code of Ethics* and its preamble, this is not one of the core values in the social work field.

(31)   (B) The government agency assessment of the client.

Any social work intervention or treatment plans are based on a complete assessment of the client across all aspects—biological, psychological, social, spiritual and cultural. The government agency assessment of the client is not very important when treatment planning is concerned.

(32) (C) Adjusting to children taking a central role in family maintenance.

In the life cycle of a family with young children, there is no requirement for parents to adjust to children taking on central roles in family maintenance. Young children are heavily dependent and cannot fulfill any such responsibilities.

(33) (A) Presence of a mental health and substance abuse disorder.

A co-occurring disorder usually refers to a situation in which a client has a mental health disorder as well as a substance abuse disorder. Co-occurring disorders may be severe or mild, but it depends on the specific case.

(34) (D) Major depressive disorder.

Paxil and Zoloft are examples of selective serotonin reuptake inhibitors or SSRIs. These are antidepressant drugs, and the client is most likely suffering from major depressive disorder.

(35) (A) The risk factors predict with 100% certainty who will participate in violence.

Risk factors for violence can indicate a likelihood of violence, but they can never predict impending violence with 100% certainty. As a result, Option (A) is false.

(36) (C) Releasing only information related to the lawsuit.

According to the *Code of Ethics*, the social worker is permitted to defend himself if he is sued for malpractice. He can fulfill his ethical obligations by divulging specific information related to the lawsuit in court.

(37) (C) Inform the ex-boyfriend that she cannot provide counseling services.

Social workers cannot provide clinical care and services to intimate partners, even if five years have passed since the relationship. This is a conflict of interest, and the social worker needs to inform her ex-boyfriend that she cannot help him. However, she can refer him to another social worker.

(38) (D) A descriptive features specifier is used for those meeting criteria.

The descriptive features specifier clause is absent in the *DSM-IV*, but it has been added in the *DSM-V*. Limited pre-social emotions have also been included.

(39) (D) Facing legal problems as a consequence.

According to the *DSM-V*, legal problems as a consequence of gambling are not viewed as a diagnostic criterion for gambling addiction. However, lying to families and letting gambling affect relationships, academics, jobs, etc., are major red flags.

(40) (B) When they are leaving employment to pursue other opportunities.

If social workers are leaving their position to explore other career avenues or opportunities, they are allowed to terminate their services. However, they need to gain clearance before stopping their client services completely.

(41)   (C) World Health Organization Disability Assessment Schedule.

Social workers use the World Health Organization Disability Assessment Schedule (WHODAS) to conduct a client's global functioning assessment. Under the *DSM-V* framework, multiaxial tests have been omitted, and WHODAS is singularly used for assessment.

(42)   (D) The client's insurance and financial coverage limits.

The client's insurance and financial coverage limits are not included in the SOAP report prepared by the social worker. The report contains Subjective, Objective, Assessment and Plan. Costs and insurance coverage are not included in it.

(43)   (C) Delirium.

Delirium is defined as a quick change between mental states. A mental status examination is an objective and subjective examination used to gauge a client's mental status. It is not a test of psychiatric health, which is why delirium is the only possible diagnosis here.

(44)   (B) Triangulation.

In the realm of social work, triangulation is a process wherein the social worker makes use of multiple sources to collect and verify information about the client. The accuracy of the information that has been collected can be increased if it is collected and collated across various sources.

(45) (B) Authoritarian.

In this kind of parenting style, the children are supposed to blindly follow the rules set by the parents. Failure to do so usually results in strict punishment, which may be corporal in some cases. Unlike authoritative parenting, no explanation is provided.

(46) (A) Regular influenza immunizations.

Influenza can have a massively detrimental effect on the client's overall health and well-being. The client's primary prevention need is regular immunizations against influenza, which can be done quite easily. It is the first line of defense for his COPD.

(47) (B) Psychosexual urges.

This is not a key concept in the field of individual psychology. According to Adler's theory of individual psychology, individuals' behavior is driven by the quest for perfection. Instead of basing behavior on psychosexual urges, Adler's theory states that individuals try to compensate for their feelings of inferiority by trying to achieve perfection in their careers and lives.

(48) (A) Being highly involved and focused on meeting the client's basic needs.

Social workers who are engaged in crisis interventions are responsible for providing all of a client's basic needs, as defined by Maslow's hierarchy of needs. They have to be very involved.

(49)   (B) Equifinality.

Equifinality is a concept in social work that states that different experiences can sometimes lead to similar outcomes. There are many experiences that can lead to a similar type of disorder, behavior, etc., as the outcome. Even eating disorders can have varying points of origin.

(50)   (B) It prevents clients from escapism and allows them to understand their problems.

Self-monitoring allows clients to better understand the causes and frequency of their own behaviors. This, in turn, prevents any escapism on the part of the client.

(51)   (A) Akathisia.

Uncomfortable restlessness or akathisia is one of the most common side effects of most antipsychotic drugs. Not all antipsychotic drugs will result in these symptoms, but there is a high chance of akathisia. Tardive dyskinesia is also a common side effect.

(52)   (D) Antabuse.

Normally, the body converts alcohol into acetaldehyde, which is then converted into acetic acid. Antabuse prevents the body from converting acetaldehyde to acetic acid, leading to a buildup of the former in the blood. High levels of acetaldehyde can cause a variety of unpleasant symptoms, such as low blood pressure, chest pain, palpitations and vertigo.

(53)   (A) Unethical, because the social worker is unable to understand and communicate with all of the family members.

The social worker has a responsibility to arrange for a translator or interpreter because she needs to communicate with all of the family members in order to provide proper treatment. The daughter is a minor and cannot assume the responsibility of being the sole point of contact between the social worker and the family.

(54)   (C) Cognitive-behavioral therapy.

The social worker and the client are making use of cognitive-behavioral therapy, which aims to challenge the thinking patterns responsible for the client's problems. The client's cognitive processes are examined, and the toxic ones are replaced with healthy ones (cognitive restructuring).

(55)   (B) Self-image almost always declines during the teenage years due to concerns about body image, academic challenges, social challenges, puberty, etc.

Self-image is almost always expected to drop during the teenage years, as children start to navigate complex social structures and come to terms with their developing bodies.

(56)   (A) The husband's alcohol issues.

From a cursory glance, it is clear that most of the couple's issues are a direct result of the husband's drinking issues. This problem has cost him his job and is now causing him problems with his wife. The social worker will focus on developing intervention plans related to alcohol abuse.

(57)   (C) Generativity versus stagnation.

During middle adulthood, the individual goes through a period marked by a conflict between stagnation and generativity. This usually happens when grown children move out.

(58)   (C) Triangulation.

Anxiety and tension between two individuals can hamper their communication, and a third party may unwillingly get involved. This is commonly referred to as triangulation.

(59)   (D) Consuming foods with low levels of tyramine.

Nardil is a monoamine oxidase inhibitor antidepressant, and it can cause unwanted reactions if coupled with tyramine. The client needs to limit the consumption of foods that are rich in tyramine, such as cheese, pepperoni, etc.

(60)   (B) Separation-individuation.

Rapprochement occurs during the phase of separation-individuation, which occurs from the ages of 15 to 24 months. This is when the child develops closeness with the mother.

(61)   (B) The client's medical history, developmental milestones and spiritual needs.

In order to provide a complete picture of the client's current state of well-being, the social worker needs to include the client's medical history, developmental milestones and spiritual needs and information to create a report.

(62) (A) Unethical, because the client may be a danger to himself or others.

The social worker's actions are unethical because a lack of services can exacerbate the client's problems. There is a chance that he may end up harming himself or others due to his problems.

(63) (A) From the age of five until adolescence.

According to Freud's psychosexual stages of development, the period of latency immediately follows the child's phallic stage. This starts around the age of five and continues until the child reaches puberty.

(64) (B) Enactments of events.

Social workers can use enactments of events to view the root causes of dysfunction in the family. This is the first step in restructuring the family, which would then solve the existing problems.

(65) (C) Listening to the client to understand his or her feelings and current situation.

The first step in building a therapeutic alliance with involuntary clients is to engage them in cursory conversation. To do that, the social worker needs to listen to them and understand their feelings and current situation.

(66)   (B) Refuse to counsel the child, as this is a conflict of interest.

According to the *Code of Ethics*, the social worker needs to minimize any conflicts of interest that may arise. Treating the same child in both settings is a conflict of interest, and the social worker should clearly inform the parent of why he or she cannot go ahead and provide counseling.

(67)   (D) Serotonin.

Serotonin is a monoamine transmitter that is responsible for stabilizing moods. All the antidepressant medications try to leverage its malleability, and it is one of the most powerful neurotransmitters in the body.

(68)   (C) Providing referrals for private practice to clients leaving the domestic violence shelter.

Apart from Option (C), all the other options are responsibilities routinely expected from someone who is a director of a domestic violence shelter. Providing referrals to one's private practice is an abuse of power and would be a highly unethical action.

(69)   (A) Notifying Child Protective Services about suspected abuse or neglect.

Out of all the given options, Option A is the only one in which the social worker's actions would be ethical. A social worker is a mandated reporter, and it is a legal mandate to report even the slightest suspicion of child abuse or neglect.

(70)   (B) Listen to the client and understand his concerns.

The social worker's goal is to establish a therapeutic bond with the client. The only way to do that is to listen to the client, however irate he may be, and understand what his concerns are. Then, a treatment plan can be developed.

(71)   (A) Immediate medical attention to treat his heroin withdrawal symptoms.

According to Maslow's hierarchy of needs, the social worker needs to address the client's health and safety needs. The man is clearly exhibiting the symptoms of heroin withdrawal, which can be very painful. He needs immediate medical attention.

(72)   (D) Dynamic risk factors.

Dynamic risk factors are those that can be modified by bringing about a change in environment. Each client has a set of unique dynamic risk factors, and the social worker should focus on them.

(73)   (C) They learn well, but their memory starts to decline.

Older adults are active learners, and their cognitive skills remain largely unaffected by the onset of age. In fact, many senior citizens are very enthusiastic when approached with new skills. However, their memory skills may start to decline slowly.

(74)   (B) Help them fight the bias displayed by agencies.

Refusing adoption rights to couples because of visual impairments is a form of ableism and agency bias. The social worker's responsibility is to assist clients in coming up with changes at the grassroots level, which can be done by helping them fight agency bias. This is especially true for someone who has experienced discrimination.

(75)   (D) Provide the mother with alternative childcare options during the weekends when she drinks.

The social worker's main responsibility is to reduce the risk of harm that may fall on the child when in the mother's care. The first thing is to help the mother arrange alternative sources of proper childcare.

(76)   (B) The *Code of Ethics*.

To address any ethical issues, the proper ethical standards need to be looked at. Information on what behavior is permissible and what behavior is not permissible can be found in the *Code of Ethics* of social work.

(77)   (B) A 10-year-old boy yelling at his mother for not contributing to chores.

When people switch roles, it is a case of role reversal. When the boy yells at his mother for not contributing to chores, that is *not* an example of roles being switched. In the other case examples, a clear case of role reversal is visible.

(78)   (A) Mixed evaluation method.

The social worker is combining qualitative data received from the outpatients with a list of quantitative data maintained by the agency. He is basically using patient opinions and combining them with independent statistical inferences from the agency data. This is a mixed evaluation method.

(79)   (D) Clinical services for physical and/or behavioral care.

A protective factor is something that is not associated with actual acts of violence. Clinical services for behavioral or physical care can actually reduce violence.

(80)   (C) Industry vs. inferiority.

From the age of six until puberty, children develop a sense of pride in their accomplishments. When they do not receive praise and get only criticism, it can result in feelings of inferiority. This is what has happened with this client.

(81)   (A) Unethical, because services cannot be terminated for this reason.

The social worker is not permitted to terminate services with a client just for the sake of friendship. Social workers may not terminate services to pursue a financial, personal or sexual relationship with one of their clients.

(82)   (B) No, because the client's informed consent has not been obtained.

The social work agency does not take into account the wishes of the clients, and their consent is not obtained at all. This is an extremely unethical practice, and even deletion of tapes does not solve it.

(83)   (B) Shaping.

Shaping is a behavioral technique in which the main goal is achieved in steps, and each step is rewarded. This is called positive reinforcement. It is one of the most effective ways to motivate clients to modify behaviors.

(84)   (D) Unethical, because the social worker and the client interact while they are at the mosque.

It would have been fine if the social worker and client had minimized contact after learning that they visit the same mosque. However, the actions are unethical because they casually interact with each other while they are there.

(85)   (A) Dividing the main goals into steps and doling out rewards so that the client can gradually make incremental progress.

Breaking main goals into small steps is a good idea for solving the original problem, but it is not a recommended course of action while addressing resistance during engagement. Clients should be reassured, and hope should be given instead.

(86)   (D) Unethical, because the social worker should not accept the vouchers.

Accepting the vouchers is a form of fee splitting, and the social worker should not accept the vouchers in the first place. If the social worker and the colleague interacted socially, then it would not have been an unethical practice.

(87)   (B) Complete the formal evaluation based on the notes.

The evaluation has been ordered by the court, which means that the social worker does not need to respect the client's wishes. The social worker has to complete the formal evaluation based on the information collected.

(88) (C) They struggle to develop identities because they have fewer role models.

Young people who are non-gender-conforming or not heterosexual have to face the same set of challenges as any other adolescents. However, they struggle to develop their identities because of the lack of role models. In recent times, however, this situation has begun to change.

(89) (B) Extinction.

Extinction is a strategy in which a reinforcer who normally follows a specific kind of behavior withholds that behavior. In this case, the girl crying as a result of the bullying is a reinforcer. If she simply walks away when she gets teased again, this response is removed, and there is a chance that the bullying might stop altogether.

(90) (A) Lymphatic.

Hodgkin's disease is a form of lymphoma. It is a cancer that originates from white blood cells called lymphocytes, which originate in the body's lymphatic system.

(91) (D) One culture importing elements from another culture into its own.

Acculturation is a process in which one culture adopts the behaviors, values and beliefs of another.

(92) (B) Unethical, because there is a conflict of interest.

Hiring an outside consultant at a discounted rate is fine, but it's concerning that the consultant happens to be the spouse of a social worker employed at the company. The HR policies that she designs will directly affect her husband, so her working there will be a major conflict of interest.

(93) (C) Lack of congruence in communication.

Congruence is a process in which awareness and experiences are matched with the person's communication. In this case, the client is exhibiting a lack of congruence. He is insisting that everything is fine even though his physical symptoms show that it is not.

(94) (D) Identifying issues that may need to be addressed later.

Termination should be done only when all the issues have been addressed and treated. Identifying issues that may need to be addressed later is not a part of termination.

(95) (A) Inform them that CPS needs to be involved and contact the agency immediately.

While the social worker should always respect traditions and cultural practices, it is important not to let that conflict with the welfare of the child. Mixing alcohol with food and denying medical attention is a serious case of neglect, which needs to be handled by CPS. They can provide additional resources.

(96) (D) Ethical, because he acted as a private individual.

The social worker acted as a private individual and not as a representative of the mental health facility at large. He attended the protest on his own time and was, for all intents and purposes, representing only himself.

(97) (A) Regression.

In this case, the child has clearly regressed to a younger mental state, mainly due to the trauma of losing his childhood home and belongings. To cope with the trauma, he has started to display infantile behavior—using baby talk, clinging to his mom increasingly, etc.

(98) (B) Prepare the treatment summaries, but send them only if the client gives written consent.

It is not ethical for the insurance company to request detailed treatment summaries before getting in touch with the client first. The social worker should send the summaries only after receiving consent from the client so that the funding does not stop. Only after this should a complaint be lodged with the insurer.

(99) (D) Ego-dystonic.

Ego-syntonic describes a condition in which the client's ego is comfortable with feelings and behaviors. The opposite of such a situation is called ego alien or ego-dystonic, feelings, as exhibited by the client in this case.

(100) (C) Providing residence in a stable and long-term home environment.

When someone is engaging in permanency planning for a child who has undergone abuse or trauma, the primary goal is to provide a stable and long-term home environment. Children need permanence to thrive.

(101) (B) Polyuria.

Polyuria or an increase in the frequency and volume of urination is not an associated side effect of Xanax. However, Xanax can sometimes lead to dizziness (vertigo), slurred speech (dysarthria), presyncope (lightheadedness) and insomnia.

(102) (A) Agranulocytosis, a lowering of the neutrophil count.

Clozaril is one of the many drugs associated with agranulocytosis, which is a life-threatening condition wherein neutrophils stop being synthesized. This can increase the risk for infection and can appear in the form of fever, chills, pain, etc.

(103) (B) Psychiatric pathology.

According to the PIE classification system, psychiatric pathology need not be used while evaluating an individual. PIE was established as an alternative to the *DSM* system and consists of four elements: social role functioning, health and environmental issues.

(104) (B) Unethical, because she was engaged in a dual relationship with her superior.

The *Code of Ethics* prohibits social workers from forming dual relationships of a sexual nature with each other, since there arises a major conflict of interest. It is prohibited for two social workers who work together in the same agency in the capacity of supervisor-supervisee to engage in a sexual or romantic relationship.

(105) (C) Narcissistic personality disorder.

Narcissistic personality disorder can be classified as a personality disorder in which a person behaves in a dramatic, emotional and erratic way. This particular grouping contains borderline personality disorder and histrionic personality disorder as well.

(106) (B) There is no formal assessment phase.

This is false. Task-centered approaches in social work are extremely structured and time-limited, and they involve a lot of participation on the client's part. Termination is also discussed from the first session onward. A formal assessment phase is also key.

(107) (A) Negative punishment.

The client is making use of the negative punishment technique because she is taking away the stimulus until the child produces the desired behavior. In this case, the client is taking away the cell phone (the stimulus) to decrease her daughter's academic nonchalance (behavior).

(108) (D) They are uniform and only intended to collect basic, consistent information.

This is false. A social work interview does not necessarily have to be uniform. A social worker can use all kinds of interviews to collect information, diagnose issues, engage in problem-solving and provide clients with therapeutic value.

(109) (B) Validation.

The social worker is validating the client's feelings by telling her that many people in the same situation have similar reactions and feelings.

(110) (A) Provide pro bono services to the client until she finds new employment.

An ethical way for the social worker to help this client is to provide her with pro bono or cheaper services until she gets another job.

(111) (C) Social workers cannot provide the group members with reassurances that their information will be kept confidential.

In a group setting, it is impossible to provide group members with confidentiality assurances. The members of the group are not bound to keep their insights private.

(112) (A) Clients are accepted and supported without any judgment about their actions or beliefs.

As a technique in the humanistic therapeutic setting, positive regard is a practice in which clients are accepted and supported without any judgments being made with regard to their actions, beliefs, statements, etc.

(113) (B) Contemplation.

In this case, the client is considering a change even though he is saying that he cannot make any changes. His conversations with the social worker indicate that he is actively contemplating making a change, even though it is passive at the moment.

(114) (C) Allow the client to determine the extent of the coworker's presence.

In this setting, self-determination is key. The social worker needs to leave all decisions to the client. The coworker might be a valuable member of the client's support system.

(115) (A) Blaming others.

Ego strength is the ego's ability to deal with the demands placed by the superego and the id. Blaming others for anything that goes wrong is not an indicator of ego strength. In fact, it is the opposite.

(116) (D) Walking away from someone when angry.

A respondent behavior is involuntary and not conscious. Walking away from someone when angry is a healthy coping mechanism used to deal with anger. This is a behavior that has to be learned and cultivated and is therefore not respondent.

(117) (A) Placing importance on self-determination and helping clients realize that they have the will and skills to solve all of their own problems.

The goal of any social worker is to empower clients, which involves directed assistance so that the clients can see that they have it in themselves to deal with all of their problems.

(118) (C) Not implement the changes after making the reasons clear to the consultant.

If the social worker thinks that the changes will be detrimental to clients, then he or she is not obligated to implement them. However, the social worker does need to make the reasons clear to both his or her superiors and the consultant.

(119) (C) Conversion.

Conversion is a defense mechanism in which the client's conflicts manifest as some kind of physical problem. In this case, the client's urge to slap her child is showing itself as a temporary paralysis of the arm.

(120) (D) This disorder causes someone to be sexually aroused only when cross-dressing.

According to the *DSM-V*, transvestic disorder is a specific disorder in which a person is sexually aroused only when dressing as the opposite sex. The *DSM-V* does not limit this disorder to heterosexual males.

(121) (C) Severe physical symptoms associated with alcohol withdrawal.

Delirium tremens is one of the most severe physical symptoms of alcohol withdrawal. It is characterized by anxiety, nausea, insomnia, tremors, etc., and can even result in total cardiovascular collapse.

(122) (B) Denies issues to keep everyone in the family happy.

In a dysfunctional family dynamic, the enabler or the martyr is the person who willfully chooses to ignore the real issues at hand. The enabler does this to deny any problems that might be present in the family.

(123) (D) Biological needs.

According to Kohut, caregivers do not need to meet the biological needs of any children in their care. However, they do need to meet mirroring needs, twinship needs and basic idealization.

(124) (A) Displacement.

The client is displaying symptoms of displacement. He is directing his anger and frustration toward less-threatening objects, namely his husband and children, instead of his boss.

(125) (B) Writing a professional recommendation letter for a current adult client.

It is completely acceptable for a social worker to write a current adult client an honest letter of recommendation. If this helps the client gain employment, then he or she can take another step forward in the journey toward self-sufficiency.

(126) (B) Clarify what will happen during treatment and outline the social worker and client's responsibilities.

It is not the social worker's job to solve all the client's problems. At the outset, the social worker should set clear expectations and responsibilities by outlining the treatment process and explaining the roles of social worker and client.

(127) (A) Caffeine use disorder is included as a new addictive disorder.

This is false. Caffeine use disorder is not a part of the disorders listed under the *DSM-5*. It is not a clinically significant disorder, although the symptoms of caffeine withdrawal have been thoroughly looked into.

(128) (B) A system that is random and disorderly, heading toward decline.

In systems theory, entropy can be best defined as a system that is random and disorderly. Over time, this chaos will push the system into a state of decline. This concept first came into being in thermodynamics and then found a place in the study of psychology.

(129) (C) Conduct a proper safety assessment.

It is clear that the client is a danger to herself and to others. Despite the client's reassurances, the social worker should conduct a safety assessment to measure the extent of the client's self-harm tendencies before any further steps.

(130) (D) Folie á deux.

Also known as shared psychosis, folie á deux is an extremely rare psychiatric disorder in which two or more people share the same psychosis. In most cases, the people involved have a very close relationship.

(131) (A) External validity.

The agency supervisor is concerned about generalizing the results because similar methods cannot be applied to both children and adults. This is an external validity issue.

(132) (A) *Ethnicity* and *race* are synonyms for each other.

This is false. Although they are closely related to each other, *ethnicity* and *race* are not synonyms or interchangeable terms. Each has a specific connotation and stands for something specific.

(133) (D) The social worker is summarizing the events of the session so that the family members walk away with a new understanding of their actions.

By discussing and summarizing the important points made during the session, the client and the social worker can walk away with a better understanding of their actions. This helps provide the client family with a sense of closure.

(134) (A) Interrater reliability.

The social worker is conducting an interrater reliability test so that the estimates of behavior are consistent across different reporters. This technique eliminates any bias that might come into play during data collection.

(135) (C) Respond to the court and claim privilege.

Even if client records are subpoenaed, the social worker is not obligated to provide them to the court. Confidentiality is extremely important, and the social worker needs to respond to the court and immediately claim privilege.

(136) (B) Systems approach to clients.

In the theories of human development in the context of social work, the systems approach is the most widely used technique. This is stressed by various different theories.

(137) (C) The grandparents are an important part of the child's support system and should play an important role in the discussions.

In Indian culture, the entire family is very involved with one another, especially when it concerns children. The grandparents are valuable members of the child's support system and need to be included while formulating any treatment plans.

(138) (C) Attachment and bonding should be viewed from the point of view of the client's culture because the theoretical process is universal.

This is false. The theoretical process is not universal. Many studies have shown that bonding can be evolutionary, can consist of learned behaviors and is linked to disorders.

(139) (A) To make others laugh and distract them from the problems they are facing.

In a dysfunctional family setting, the mascot's role is to be the class clown. The mascot tries to distract everyone from all the underlying issues by making others laugh and resorting to humor.

(140) (B) A person invents or causes an illness or symptoms of illness in someone in his or her care in order to receive attention as a caregiver.

Munchausen by proxy syndrome is a serious psychological disorder in which someone deliberately causes issues or symptoms in people in their care (usually small children) to garner attention as a caregiver.

(141) (C) Attachment – Autonomy – Intimacy.

According to Erikson, psychosocial development includes attachment, which is then followed by a stage of autonomy and finally a stage of intimacy.

(142) (D) Determine how to prepare the client for her meeting with the priest.

Asking religious figureheads for advice during tumultuous events is common to many people. If the client finds solace by talking to a priest, the social worker should enable and support her by preparing her for the meeting.

(143) (B) It can be seen mostly in clients with specific personality features.

Research has shown that transference is more common with clients who have certain specific personality features. For example, people with borderline personality disorder are more likely to engage in transference. It is totally unconscious.

(144) (A) Preaffiliation -> Power and Control -> Intimacy -> Differentiation -> Separation.

Group development always follows the sequential process of preaffiliation (also known as forming), followed by power and control (storming), intimacy (norming), differentiation (performing) and separation (also known as adjourning).

(145) (B) Humanistic.

According to the humanistic perspective of human behavior, all individuals have the capacity to change and grow. It also states that all people have the drive to grow, find personal meaning and gain competence.

(146) (C) Disturbance attributable to the physiological effects of a substance.

Schizophrenia is a mental disorder that may not be attributable to the physiological effects of any drug or substance.

(147) (D) No additional cost or time is associated with the use of old case records.

Option D is actually an advantage (not a drawback) of using old case records. The social worker does not have to spend time or money to access old case records.

(148) (C) Ewing sarcoma (also known as Ewing tumor).

A Ewing tumor, also known as Ewing sarcoma, is an extremely rare form of cancer that occurs in the bones (not the blood). Most often, it occurs in children and young adults.

(149) (B) Amphetamine salts (Adderall).

Adderall is not used to control the tics associated with Tourette's syndrome. It is a combination drug containing the salts of amphetamine, which is used to treat the symptoms of ADHD or narcolepsy. It is a stimulant that directly affects the central nervous system (CNS).

(150) (A) Distinct because consent is defined as the legal authorization to participate in treatment.

Consent is defined as the legal authorization provided by a client to participate in treatment, divulge information about treatment, etc. *Assent,* on the other hand, describes someone's willingness to pursue treatment. The terms are distinct in the context of social work.

(151) (C) Client consent is unnecessary if the consultation is not related to client care.

This is false. Even if the consultation is unrelated to client care, getting the client's consent is paramount. If outside parties are to be involved in the treatment process, the client must always give total consent.

(152) (B) Understand the differences and their impact on the treatment process.

When working with someone from a different ethnic group, it is imperative for a social worker to recognize that there may be cultural differences. The impact of such differences on the treatment process is also important to understand.

(153) (B) Authoritative.

Authoritative parenting styles usually produce the best results in children. The children understand and follow the rules set by their parents, and they have a voice in the setting of the rules. They grow up to become balanced, capable and well-adjusted.

(154) (A) Caffeine use disorder.

According to the *DSM-5*, experts and researchers are studying the effects of caffeine and are deciding whether withdrawal symptoms from caffeine can be categorized as a separate disorder.

(155) (D) An external expert because this person is an expert on treating people who have pica.

The social worker's duty is to provide the best quality of service to the client. She should engage the expert as a consultant because the person has experience working with those suffering from pica.

(156) (C) Disruptive mood dysregulation disorder has been added as a new diagnosis for people aged 18 and younger.

DMDD has been added to the list of depressive disorders in the *DSM-5,* not the list of neurodevelopmental disorders.

(157) (D) 5 months.

According to the object relations theory, the normal symbiotic phase of development lasts until five to six months of age.

(158) (B) Negative reinforcement.

The husband is referring to negative reinforcement. This is the removal of the negative stimulus (his wife's nagging) so that the target behavior (doing his chores) can be increased.

(159) (A) The client is likely to experience stigma, bias and discrimination on the basis of gender identity.

The other options are all harmful stereotypes that actually contribute to the stigma against people who are transgender. Transgender individuals are more likely to experience overt discrimination and bias.

(160) (A) Delusion.

A delusion is an erroneous belief or impression that will remain even after being contradicted by reality, evidence or argument. In this case, the client maintains that he is being surveilled by police and the FBI despite being unable to provide any evidence about this claim.

(161) (B) New mothers who are undergoing postpartum depression (PPD) or anxiety (PPA).

New mothers undergoing PPD or PPA would not benefit at all from genetic counseling. On the other hand, the other options would benefit greatly by engaging in proper genetic counseling.

(162) (D) Persistent depressive disorder.

According to the *DSM-5*, dysthymia is now referred to as persistent depressive disorder. This is related to depression that lasts for two years.

(163) (B) Carbamazepine or Carbatrol.

It is clear that the client has the symptoms of bipolar disorder. He is depressed in one situation and exhibiting manic symptoms in the other. As a result, he will be prescribed Carbatrol, which is a very powerful mood stabilizer.

(164) (A) Identify the outcomes that will result from this behavioral change.

This is the planning stage, during which the social worker and the client chart out the needed intervention plan. The social worker needs to identify the outcomes of this particular behavioral change.

(165) (C) Bipolar disorder.

Hypomania is an abnormally active state of mind that can cause an abnormally upbeat mood, a sudden increase in activity and energy, unusual talkativeness and racing thoughts. This is one of the classic symptoms of bipolar disorder, characterized by lows and highs.

(166) (D) Tertiary prevention.

The goal of tertiary prevention is to provide care to people suffering from painful and chronic diseases, injuries and illnesses. As the cancer is not terminal, hospice is not associated with this patient.

(167) (D) They are replaced with "Other Specified" and "Unspecified."

In the *DSM-5*, "Not Otherwise Specified" disorders have been grouped into "Other Specified" and "Unspecified" classes. This gives social workers more flexibility.

(168) (A) Explain the development process of young children.

The best way to comfort and assist the client is to explain the development process of young children. At this age, children are egocentric and cannot easily take on others' perspectives.

(169) (D) Contact should occur only with adults, not children.

There are no rules that prohibit social workers from engaging in appropriate physical contact with children. The *Code of Ethics* does not limit physical contact to adult clients.

(170) (C) Readiness to terminate.

Missing appointments after achieving goals is a clear indicator of the client's readiness to terminate. She is most likely ready to stop making appointments.

ASWB Clinical Exam 2

(1) A social worker takes on a new client—a teenage girl—only to discover that her physician has switched her from Adderall to Ritalin. Which disorder does the girl most likely have?

(A)   Obsessive-compulsive disorder

(B)   Attention deficit hyperactivity disorder

(C)   Oppositional defiant disorder

(D)   None of the above

(2) A social worker meets a client who suffered a debilitating back injury a couple of months ago. During the appointment, the client is yawning, appears anxious and tells the social worker that she has cramps. What kind of withdrawal is the client most likely suffering from?

(A)   Heroin

(B)   Cocaine

(C)   Methamphetamine or amphetamine

(D)   Vicodin

(3) At what age do children experience the anal psychosexual stage of development?

(A)   0 to 12 months

(B)   1 to 2 years

(C)   Adolescence

(D)   Above 18

(4) Which of the following statements best describes the unconscious?

(A)   Thoughts not present in the client's attention that can be retrieved

(B)   All of the thoughts that the client is conscious about

(C)   Thoughts and feelings that the client is unaware of

(D)   None of the above

(5) Which of the following is not a self-object need in self-psychology?

(A)   Twinship

(B)   Idealization

(C)   Mirroring

(D)   Dystonicity

(6) During which stage of Erikson's psychosocial development does the individual make the transition from childhood to adulthood?

(A)   Identity vs. role confusion

(B)   Industry vs. inferiority

(C)   Intimacy vs. isolation

(D)   Ego identity vs. despair

(7) At the age of 24 to 38 months, children reach which stage, during which they start to view themselves as separate, unique individuals?

(A)   Normal autism

(B)   Rapprochement

(C)   Object constancy

(D)   Practicing

(8) Which of these is an interpersonal change that elders have to face?

(A)   They have to take on new roles of grandparents.

(B)   They have to stay productive and care for children.

(C)   They have to focus on education and growth.

(D)   They have to accept personal losses and live as independently as possible.

(9) Which of these is not a stage of cognitive theory as proposed by Jean Piaget?

(A)   Sensorimotor

(B)   Object constancy

(C)   Concrete operations

(D)   Formal operations

(10) A client comes in because she is worried about her five-year-old boy. He has an imaginary friend, a boy he calls Tony. The client finds this behavior very concerning. What is the best thing to tell her to calm her?

(A)   Imaginary friends are very common between two and seven years of age.

(B)   This behavior is the result of abuse.

(C)   A psychological assessment is required for the boy.

(D)   The treatment for this is easy.

(11) Which of these is not an indicator of physical growth in young children?

(A)   Move slowly

(B)   Enjoy listening to stories

(C)   Are toilet trained

(D)   Have better motor skills

(12) Which of the following is not a deficiency need according to Maslow's hierarchy of needs?

(A)   Esteem needs

(B)   Physiological needs

(C)   Self-actualization needs

(D)   Safety needs

(13) Which of the following is one of the five stages of grief proposed by Elizabeth Kubler-Ross?

(A)   Emotional dependency

(B)   Bargaining

(C)   Breakdown

(D)   Memorialization

(14) Which of the following is not an element of the family life cycle stage, also called "Launching the children"?

(A)   Dealing with deaths in the family

(B)   Adjusting to life with the spouse only

(C)   Establishing healthy adult relationships with the children

(D)   Coping with one's own physical decline

(15) A social worker is assigned to an 11-year-old boy who complains about his parents. He says that his mother and father are largely absent from his life, do not show up to school events and do not pay attention to him at home. What kind of parenting style is most likely being used by this child's parents?

(A)   Authoritarian parenting

(B)   Autopilot parenting

(C)   Uninvolved parenting

(D)   Self-dependent parenting

(16) Which of the following is not a physical manifestation of a major traumatic event?

(A)   Pain and fatigue

(B)   Insomnia, nightmares and/or sleep disorders

(C)   Hypersexuality

(D)   Anxiety

(17) Which of the following is not a term used for the summarization of risk factors in the realm of social work?

(A)   Poor skills – low IQ, poor at communication, religiously or politically bigoted

(B)   Genetic factors – chronic diseases, genetic conditions, etc.

(C)   Stressors – low income, sustained financial problems, low self-esteem, etc.

(D)   Family issues – domestic violence, substance abuse, infidelity, etc.

(18) Which of the following can be classified as one of the long-term effects of discrimination due to race or ethnicity?

(A)   A sense of hostility and anger toward the perpetrators

(B)   Depression and a marked increase in behavioral issues

(C)   A thirst for vengeance bordering on physical harm

(D)   A desire to flee the country and delve into illegal substances

(19) Which of the following is not a risk factor for substance abuse?

(A)   The client is married to a recovering alcoholic.

(B)   There is a history of substance abuse in the family.

(C)   The client lives under cultural norms that allow easy access to drugs.

(D)   The client has low self-esteem and depression.

(20) Which of the following is not an accepted model used to view and diagnose addiction to substances, behaviors, etc., in the realm of social work?

(A)   The family and environmental model

(B)   The biopsychosocial model

(C)   The genetic matrix model

(D)   The self-medication model

(21) Which of the following is not a primary risk factor that a social worker can use to identify someone who may abuse another person?

(A)   A documented and diagnosed mental disorder, such as bipolar disorder, psychosis, etc.

(B)   A history of owning, collecting and using weapons against others

(C)   A very low IQ and traits of very low empathy

(D)   A well-documented substance abuse issue

(22) Which of the following is one of the most commonly seen aftereffects of sexual abuse, especially in the case of children or preadolescent survivors?

(A)   Clients develop an aversion to sex in general. In some cases, they may also develop hypersexual behavior in an effort to compensate.

(B)   Clients develop antisocial personality elements and a tendency to resort to violence at the slightest provocation.

(C)   Clients are extremely bad with matters of finance and money.

(D)   Clients trust in others very willingly and can be said to be extremely naive and gullible.

(23) Which of the following is not a psychological defense mechanism?

(A)   Splitting of mental state to express desires without having to take responsibility

(B)   Development of online personas different from real-life ones

(C)   Adopting behaviors to compensate for any perceived deficiencies

(D)   Partial, symbolic or entire return to childlike patterns of thinking and behaving

(24) What is the best definition of *sublimation*?

(A)   People try to explain their irrational beliefs and behaviors by coming up with an explanation that is ridiculous.

(B)   People turn on themselves and subject themselves to extraordinary levels of harm, violence and criticism.

(C)   People channel their maladaptive impulses into an activity that is constructive and good.

(D)   People admire others, overestimate their good qualities and put them on a pedestal.

(25) Which theory of human behavior posits that humans are cogent beings and that all of their behavior is target oriented and measured?

(A)   Systems theory

(B)   Psychodynamic theory

(C)   Economic action theory

(D)   Rational choice theory

(26) Which of the following can be said to be the best advantage of using person-in-environment (PIE) theory?

(A)   The client is the center of attention in PIE theory.

(B)   The social worker is the main focus in PIE theory.

(C)   The statistical benefits are very large in PIE theory.

(D)   The treatment process is transactional in the context of PIE theory.

(27) Which of the following is not a characteristic followed by a family with young children?

(A)   The couple adopts and perfects the role of parents.

(B)   The young children are encouraged to form successful peer relationships.

(C)   The couple learns to live together practically and emotionally.

(D)   The family is realigned to allow space for the young kids.

(28) Who was the original developer of the popular object relations theory, which states that behavior and individual personality are affected by relationships developed with other people?

(A)   Sigmund Freud

(B)   Margaret Mahler

(C)   Jean Piaget

(D)   Ivan Pavlov

(29) Which of the following is the best definition of the reality principle, which forms the underlying drive for the ego, according to Freud?

(A)   The knowledge that reality is more important than fantasy

(B)   The knowledge that fantasy is more important than reality

(C)   The knowledge that impulses and desires have to be delayed to meet the needs of the real world

(D)   The knowledge that reality drives behavior

(30) A social worker sees a client who has a toddler. The client is very upset because the toddler no longer wants to be fed by her. During meals, the toddler insists on sitting at the table and eating her own food, even if she makes a mess. Which stage of psychosocial development is the toddler at?

(A)   Autonomy vs. shame

(B)   Industry vs. inferiority

(C)   Identity vs. role confusion

(D)   Initiative vs. guilt

(31) Which of the following options is not a role usually found in any dysfunctional family dynamics?

(A)   The lost child

(B)   The caretaker

(C)   The hero

(D)   The instigator

(32) Who is responsible for the development of the theory of attachment and bonding, which states that the caregiver-infant relationship can affect the child's personality?

(A)   Erik Erikson

(B)   John Bowlby

(C)   Jean Piaget

(D)   Margaret Mahler

(33) Which of the following options is not a sign of mental growth in older children (between ages seven and 12)?

(A)   An understanding of cause and effect

(B)   An ability to read and do simple mathematics

(C)   An eagerness to learn

(D)   A willingness to conduct experiments

(34) A social worker takes on a new client who is a rebellious 15-year-old boy. Which of the following approaches is not appropriate for this client?

(A)   Provide information to make positive choices.

(B)   Avoid treating him as a child; try to treat him as an adult.

(C)   Encourage him to stay secretive and avoid open communication.

(D)   Provide him with the information to make positive choices.

(35) Which of the following statements is true?

(A)   During the teenage years, individual self-esteem continues to rise.

(B)   Small children have a remarkably low amount of confidence.

(C)   Females have lower levels of self-esteem during adolescence.

(D)   Health problems usually do not affect self-image.

(36) A social worker takes on a 34-year-old man as a client. The man has a blank expression and gets extremely defensive at the slightest questioning. The social worker notices that the man has scratch marks on his neck. During the session, the man divulges that his wife tracks his movements by using a mobile app. What should the social worker do first?

(A)   Encourage the client to speak openly about his home life.

(B)   Inform the client that the social worker will be getting in touch with law enforcement with a report of domestic violence.

(C)   Tell the client that he is being abused and that the social worker is mandated to report this instance to the police.

(D)   Berate the client for bowing to his wife's demands.

(37) A social worker sees a client who almost always gets flatulent whenever he starts talking about his anxiety in social spaces. Which defense mechanism is being used here?

(A)   Conversion

(B)   Projection

(C)   Compensation

(D)   None of the above

(38) Which of the following factors does not affect the life and family dynamics of those who have been sexually abused?

(A)   How other people react to the news of the abuse

(B)   The existing relationship between the abuser and victim

(C)   The victim's age during abuse

(D)   The abuser's occupation at the time of abuse

(39) Which of the following is an observed effect of trauma on behavior?

(A)   Development of an eating disorder

(B)   Development of academic rigor and stress

(C)   Development of meticulous behavior with regards to cleaning

(D)   Development of compulsive lying behavior

(40) A social worker working in a school treats a nine-year-old child who is having problems with her academics. The child is Indian-American; her parents and family emigrated to the United States before her birth. The social worker schedules a meeting with the child's parents, only to see that the grandparents show up as well. What should the social worker do?

(A)   Understand that the grandparents are an integral part of the child's support system and incorporate them into the treatment plan.

(B)   Ask the parents if the child wants the grandparents to attend the meeting.

(C)   Forbid the grandparents from attending because only the parents have a say in their child's treatment.

(D)   None of the above.

(41) Which of these is not a communication trait exhibited by African Americans?

(A)   Individuals tend to speak up in an effort to make themselves heard.

(B)   A history of racism and prejudice impacts all of their interactions.

(C)   Physical touch and direct communication are valued.

(D)   Expletives are often used to demonstrate affection.

(42) Which of the following statements is false?

(A)   LGBTQ+ youth suffer from poor self-image as a result of bullying.

(B)   LGBTQ+ youth have a lot of advantages growing up.

(C)   LGBTQ+ youth go through social isolation.

(D)   LGBTQ+ youth can internalize the abuse they face and develop self-hatred.

(43) Which of the following is not something that a social worker should do to communicate with people of different cultures and ethnicities?

(A)   Come up with a large set of verbal and nonverbal responses as a part of strategies that can be used in multiple situations

(B)   Try to speak with people of different cultures by developing a set of stereotypical responses.

(C)   Understand and recognize direct and indirect communication styles

(D)   Understand and remove barriers to communication

(44) Which of the following is not a technique that a social worker can use while interviewing a client?

(A)   Confrontation

(B)   Universalization

(C)   Reframing and relabeling

(D)   Humorous quips

(45) A social worker is working with a client who recently had a child. The client cries during the session and says that she feels like she is a horrible mother. She also says that she cannot bond with the baby. The social worker tells her that this is a normal feeling and that almost every new mother experiences this. The best way to treat this is to reassure the new mother. What technique did the social worker use?

(A)   Clarification

(B)   Universalization

(C)   Reframing or relabeling

(D)   Interpretation

(46) Which of the following is not a part of the social section of a client's biopsychosocial history?

(A)   Sexual identity issues or concerns

(B)   Marital and relationship status

(C)   Academic record

(D)   Summary of all risks

(47) How many total personality types exist under the Myers-Briggs Personality Type Indicator?

(A)   16

(B)   24

(C)   20

(D)   22

(48) Which of the following is not a temperamental factor included in client assessments?

(A)   A belief in justice

(B)   An ability to stay happy

(C)   A lack of hostility and anger

(D)   An immense mistrust of other people

(49) Which of the following is not an indicator of resistance?

(A)   Engaging in banal chitchat with the social worker instead of talking openly

(B)   Being reticent or cagey about feelings and thoughts

(C)   Being completely transparent and forthcoming with feelings

(D)   Flattering the social worker in an effort to soften him or her up

(50) Which of the following is not a primary component of the mental status exam?

(A)   Orientation and intellectual function

(B)   Injuries and pain

(C)   Thought processes

(D)   Physical appearance

(51) A social worker takes on a client who has recently been switched from Moban to Clozaril. What condition is most likely being treated with the help of these drugs?

(A)   Depressive disorder

(B)   Bipolar disorder

(C)   Psychosis

(D)   Anxiety

(52) Which of the following drugs is commonly abused and can be very dangerous if taken with alcohol?

(A)   Remeron

(B)   Paracetamol or acetaminophen

(C)   Elavil

(D)   Klonopin

(53) Which of the following medications needs to be dispensed in highly controlled quantities, since the line between therapeutic and toxic amounts is very thin?

(A)   Topamax

(B)   Lithium

(C)   Zyprexa

(D)   Xanax

(54) What is the difference between a typical psychotropic drug and an atypical psychotropic drug?

(A)   Typical drugs are prescribed under less serious conditions.

(B)   Typical drugs are prescribed under the typical symptoms of psychosis.

(C)   Typical drugs work on the dopaminergic system, and atypical drugs work on the serotonergic system.

(D)   Typical drugs are prescribed to patients whose symptoms are severe enough to warrant institutionalization.

(55) Which of the following is not an indicator of psychological abuse?

(A)   Very little empathy for other people

(B)   Dangerous and self-destructive behavior patterns

(C)   A tendency to experience manic and depressive episodes

(D)   Disruptive or aggressive behavior toward other people

(56) What is the full form of the SOAP framework?

(A)   Subjective – Objective – Assessment – Plan

(B)   Statistical – Objective – Assessment – Penance

(C)   Subjective – Objective – Assignment – Plan

(D)   Statistical – Observed – Allopathy – Penetration

(57) A social worker takes on a 20-year-old female client who is addicted to impulsive spending and shopping. She also routinely displays a dichotomous thinking pattern and has poor eating habits. What are these most likely indicators of?

(A)   Bipolar disorder

(B)   Major depressive disorder

(C)   Traumatic stress

(D)   Anxiety regarding the future

(58) Which of the following is not a risk factor relating to suicide?

(A)   The client has attempted suicide in the past.

(B)   The client has a history of substance abuse.

(C)   The client lives alone and has little or no social support.

(D)   The client is part of a criminal gang in the city.

(59) Which of the following is an example of a monoamine oxidase inhibitor (MAOI) antidepressant?

(A)   Luvox

(B)   Parnate

(C)   Elavil

(D)   Prozac

(60) Which of the following elements is not a part of a client's appearance component during a mental status examination?

(A)   Grooming: haircut, shave, makeup, cleanliness of appearance, etc.

(B)   Dressing style

(C)   Intellectual function

(D)   Facial expressions

(61) Which of the following intelligence scales measures a child's intelligence and cognitive skills using four index scales and a full-scale score?

(A)   Stanford-Binet Intelligence Scale (SBIS)

(B)   Wechsler Intelligence Scale for Children (WISC)

(C)   Differential Ability Scale (DAS)

(D)   Universal Nonverbal Intelligence (UNVI)

(62) Which of the following would not be a part of the psychological section of a client's biopsychosocial history?

(A)   History of past psychiatric illnesses or symptoms

(B)   Current mental status exam results

(C)   Sexual identity issues or concerns

(D)   A list of all past and current medications

(63) A social worker is working with a client who tells the social worker about his anxiety issues, especially in social situations. The social worker listens to the client, then repeats what she has heard and puts it into a context with a different point of view. Which technique is she using?

(A)   Universalization

(B)   Reframing or relabeling

(C)   Clarification

(D)   Confrontation

(64) Which of the following is not the purpose of a social work interview?

(A)   Informational

(B)   Diagnostic

(C)   Punitive

(D)   Therapeutic

(65) How many items are present in the standard Beck Depression Inventory (BDI) test?

(A)   21

(B)   22

(C)   23

(D)   24

(66) Which of the following personality tests consists of a verbal objective inventory with 550 statements? Keep in mind that 16 of these are repeated.

(A)   Thematic Apperception Test (TAT)

(B)   Wechsler Intelligence Scale for Children (WISC)

(C)   Minnesota Multiphasic Personality Inventory (MMPI)

(D)   Stanford-Binet Intelligence Scale

(67) Which of the following is not a variant of the role a social worker can take in the professional capacity of an observer?

(A)   Observer as a participant

(B)   Complete observer

(C)   Participant as an observer

(D)   Participant with the role of evaluator

(68) Which of the following statements best describes the role of complete observers?

(A)   They are completely removed from the activity and are only allowed to observe the participants' actions and interviews remotely.

(B)   All interviews and medication lists are mailed to them, and they observe these and provide their own inputs.

(C)   Complete observers act as assistants to the primary interviewer and social worker, working with all the participants.

(D)   Their job is to observe the participants' activities while pretending to be participants themselves.

(69) Which of the following elements is not a good sign of a client's healthy defense and coping mechanisms used in the strength and weakness analysis?

(A)   The ability to regulate impulses

(B)   The ability to make good investments

(C)   The ability to respond well to stressors

(D)   The ability to soothe themselves

(70) A social worker is working with a client who has a compulsive eating habit. During the first few meetings, the client denies that he has a problem. He even misses the next few meetings and appears very sullen during the consequent meetings. Which stage of motivation is the client most likely to be in?

(A)   Contemplation

(B)   Ego syntonic

(C)   Denial

(D)   Precontemplation

(71) The social worker asks her client the date during the meeting while she takes notes. She also asks the client his opinion regarding the NBA basketball game that happened the previous day. She writes down the client's responses. Which component of the mental status examination is the social worker checking?

(A)   Intellectual function

(B)   Awareness and orientation

(C)   Insight

(D)   Knowledge of sports

(72) Which of the following options is not a typical antipsychotic drug?

(A)   Thorazine

(B)   Abilify

(C)   Haldol

(D)   Moban

(73) How does lithium work as a mood stabilizer?

(A)   It's unclear, but it affects the central nervous system.

(B)   It balances the mood by initiating the flush of dopamine.

(C)   It balances the mood by initiating an adrenaline rush.

(D)   It's unclear, but it works by affecting the lymphatic system.

(74) Which of the following categories of antidepressants does Remeron belong to?

(A)   Monoamine oxidase inhibitors

(B)   Tricyclics

(C)   Selective serotonin reuptake inhibitors

(D)   None of the above

(75) Which of the following options is not a reliable indicator of sexual abuse in children?

(A)   Injuries in the genital or rectal areas

(B)   An unusual interest in sex that is inappropriate for their age

(C)   Recurring nightmares and sleep disorders

(D)   Intense gastrointestinal pain

(76) Which of the following persons is not the most vulnerable to violence?

(A)   A 18-year-old male whose brother is a drug dealer and who has already been in juvenile detention for assault when he was 15 years old

(B)   A 21-year-old female who is in rehabilitation with a cocaine addiction issue and was involved with delinquent peers

(C)   A 20-year-old male who was bullied as a child and therefore has a lot of anxiety that he channels into aggression

(D)   A 14-year-old who routinely engages in precocious sexual intercourse and has unfettered access to guns, drugs, etc.

(77) Which of the following elements is not a part of the Objective (O) section of a SOAP format treatment plan?

(A)   Clients' opinions regarding their well-being

(B)   Pulse and blood pressure readings

(C)   Temperature

(D)   Intelligence and psychoanalytic test scores

(78) Which of the following can be used as the best definition of *reliability* in the context of experimental research findings in social work?

(A)   The level of confidence in the cause-and-effect relationship defined by the social worker

(B)   Whether the same results or answers can be reproduced by another social worker or researcher in a similar setting

(C)   Whether the scientific findings and hypothesis tests hold up under statistical scrutiny, such as a t-test or a p-test

(D)   Whether the social worker's research and data were obtained in an ethical way

(79) A social worker works with a client and collects a lot of subjective and objective information. He then proceeds to consolidate the information and facts into a short and descriptive report. Which stage of the SOAP framework is the social worker in?

(A)   Plan

(B)   Subjective

(C)   Objective

(D)   Assessment

(80) Which of the following is not a component of the criteria component that social workers use while setting measurable objectives for their clients?

(A)   The healthy behavior that the client needs to exhibit

(B)   The unhealthy behavior that the client needs to eliminate

(C)   How often the client must do this and under what conditions

(D)   How long the client has to do this

(81) Which of the following is not an example of self-destructive behavior?

(A)   Never wearing a seat belt while driving and driving very recklessly

(B)   Using dangerous drugs on a regular basis

(C)   Engaging in self-harm and self-mutilation

(D)   Playing football very aggressively and injuring others

(82) Which of the following medications is used to treat anxiety disorders and can also be used to treat status epilepticus?

(A)   Remeron

(B)   Anafranil

(C)   Ativan or Lorazepam

(D)   Desyrel

(83) Which of the following is the most appropriate channel of communication while working with a client who is 30 years old or younger?

(A)   Emails or texting

(B)   In-person surprise visits

(C)   Visits to a coffee shop

(D)   Family interviews

(84) Which of the following options is not a valid method of feedback that can be used in the realm of social work?

(A)   Group-to-group feedback

(B)   One-to-one feedback

(C)   Client-to-superior feedback

(D)   360° feedback

(85) Which of the following is not a term that can be frequently seen in the prevailing terminology of systems theory?

(A)   Homeostasis or entropy

(B)   Closed system

(C)   Adiabatic system

(D)   Input, output and throughput

(86) Which of the following drugs should be prescribed to a person who is suffering from anxiety or panic disorders?

(A)   Rohypnol

(B)   Buspar

(C)   Nardil

(D)   Bismuth subsalicylate (Pepto Bismol)

(87) A social worker is seeing a 29-year-old woman for the very first time. The client has moderate kleptomania, and the social worker asks her if she is aware of the consequences of theft. The woman answers quite clearly, and she appears well informed. What element of the mental status examination is being scrutinized?

(A)   Orientation

(B)   Thought process

(C)   Intellectual function

(D)   Insight

(88) A social worker is working with an 18-year-old woman. The client usually engages in banal small talk and refuses to discuss the problem she is seeing the social worker for. She often compliments the social worker's clothes, makeup, etc. What is the client trying to do?

(A)   The client is demonstrating resistance. She is using flattery in an effort to manipulate the social worker.

(B)   The client is scared and does not trust the social worker yet. Engaging in small talk allows her to do so.

(C)   The client trusts the social worker implicitly and sees her as a friend, which is why she is engaging her in casual conversation.

(D)   The client is unsure whether this social worker is good enough, which is why she is testing the waters by making casual conversation.

(89) Which of these is not a factor that needs to be taken into consideration while conducting a strength and weakness analysis of a client?

(A)   The state of physical health

(B)   Whether the client prefers to use a car or public transportation

(C)   Whether the client is part of institutions like churches, clubs, etc.

(D)   Whether the client has a stable source of legal income

(90) Which of the following is a cognitive skill?

(A)   Patience

(B)   An ability to confide in other people and friends

(C)   An ability to take responsibility for one's actions

(D)   An ability to construct, develop and maintain healthy relationships

(91) A social worker has a client who is extremely distrustful of everyone around him. He refuses to take responsibility for his actions and finds a way to blame others for his own shortcomings. In what area does the client have a weakness?

(A)   Defenses and coping mechanisms

(B)   Temperamental factors

(C)   Genetic factors

(D)   Cognitive and intelligence skills

(92) Which of the following techniques involves calling attention to the problem and highlighting it in front of the client?

(A)   Confrontation

(B)   Universalization of behavior

(C)   Interpretation

(D)   Clarification

(93) Which of the following cognitive approaches to crisis intervention was developed by Ivan Pavlov and Burrhus Frederic Skinner?

(A)   Humanistic

(B)   Social

(C)   Behaviorist

(D)   None of the above

(94) Which of the following dysfunctional roles tries to overachieve in academics and work in order to hide dysfunctional family dynamics from the world?

(A)   The lost child

(B)   The mascot

(C)   The scapegoat

(D)   The family hero

(95) Which of the following is not a phase that social workers need to follow while they are working with clients who have undergone trauma?

(A)   Self-destruction and violence

(B)   Mourning and remembrance

(C)   Safety and stabilization

(D)   Reconnection and reintegration

(96) A social worker is working with a very difficult client who is not making a lot of progress. Is it a good idea for the social worker to ask for feedback now?

(A)   Yes, because it is important to identify feedback from someone who is critical.

(B)   No, the poor relationship will shift the feedback into a negative bias.

(C)   Yes, because it is important to the social worker's future career.

(D)   No, because the client will not be objective.

(97) Which of the following statements is the best encapsulation of first-order changes in the context of strategic family therapy?

(A)   Systematic and structural changes made in an effort to reorganize the family

(B)   Involuntary changes made to the family when an adult is incarcerated

(C)   Superficial behavioral changes that do not affect family structure

(D)   None of the above

(98) Which of the following is not a treatment and intervention technique that is used for the treatment of unhappy couples?

(A)   Behavior modification

(B)   Cognitive-behavioral therapy

(C)   Insight-oriented psychotherapy

(D)   Gottman method

(99) Which of the following is the best description for the Gottman method of couples therapy?

(A)   The social worker studies the interactions between the two partners.

(B)   The dysfunctional behaviors are isolated and addressed.

(C)   The couple addresses underlying patterns that lead to dysfunction.

(D)   The social worker encourages verbal communication and intimacy and removes barriers.

(100) Which stage of the group development is also referred to as performing?

(A)   Differentiation

(B)   Intimacy

(C)   Preaffiliation

(D)   Power and control

(101) Which of these is not a reason why groups are helpful?

(A)   They provide members with a sense of hope.

(B)   They allow members to engage in altruistic acts.

(C)   They provide a sense of universality.

(D)   They widen the members' social circles.

(102) Which of the following factors can have an effect on the group's overall cohesion level?

(A)   The members' stability

(B)   The members' income level

(C)   The members' favorite football teams

(D)   None of the above

(103) Which of the following is not one of the main causes of groupthink?

(A)   Illusion of unanimity

(B)   Mindguards

(C)   Religion

(D)   Inherent morality

(104) Which of the following is not a construct required for studying and understanding Bowenian family therapy?

(A)   Family projection process

(B)   Multigenerational transmission

(C)   Sibling position

(D)   Reproductive health

(105) Which of the following is not a technique learned under the environmental change approach to anger management?

(A)   Walking away in a tense situation

(B)   Using humor in a tense situation

(C)   Avoiding people and conversations that evoke anger

(D)   Avoiding situations that may cause anger

(106) When is not the best time for the social worker to summarize a conversation?

(A)   At the completion of the conversation

(B)   Periodically throughout the conversation

(C)   Only at the beginning of the conversation

(D)   None of the above

(107) What method of communication should a social worker use to form a bond with a client who comes to her in search of help?

(A)   Treat the client with negative regard.

(B)   Communicate with fakeness and insincerity.

(C)   Display empathy and form a bond with the client.

(D)   Use adversarial behavior.

(108) Which of the following is not a nonverbal communication method that social workers need to be adept at?

(A)   Active listening

(B)   Paraphrasing and clarifying

(C)   Silence

(D)   Hostility

(109) Which of the following is the best description of 360° feedback?

(A)   A person or group act as consultants to each other

(B)   Recipients seek feedback from everybody around them

(C)   Group seeks feedback from within itself

(D)   Group seeks feedback from another group

(110) Which of the following statements is false with regard to the social worker and client relationship during treatment?

(A)   All client information needs to be kept 100% confidential.

(B)   The social worker needs to financially support the client through treatment.

(C)   The social worker and client must trust each other.

(D)   The social worker and client must listen to each other without judgment.

(111) What should a social worker not do while using the spiritual mode of the biopsychosocial models of intervention?

(A)   Understand the role of spirituality in well-being.

(B)   Take the client's cultural background into account.

(C)   Understand the context regarding values, ethics, rituals, etc.

(D)   Do a comprehensive medical examination of the client.

(112) Which of the following is the best definition of a closed system?

(A)   A system that uses up all of its energy and then dies.

(B)   A system that is self-contained and does not permit alien elements into itself.

(C)   A system that is closed and does not allow itself to be perceived.

(D)   None of the above.

(113) Which of the following is not an acceptable definition of *throughput* in the context of systems theory?

(A)   Energy that is integrated into the system to attain its goals

(B)   Energy invested into the system to achieve certain KPIs

(C)   Energy that makes its way into a system permanently

(D)   None of the above

(114) Which of the following options is not an element of the standard problem-solving model in the context of social work?

(A) Termination

(B) Evaluation

(C) Engagement

(D) Preservation

(115) Who was responsible for developing the social approach to client crisis intervention?

(A) Sigmund Freud

(B) Albert Bandura

(C) Carl Rogers

(D) Abraham Maslow

(116) Which of the following is not an example of operant observable behavior?

(A) Sexual arousal

(B) Walking on the beach

(C) Talking

(D) Writing

(117) A social worker is working with a client who is suffering from anxiety. The client has a tendency to immediately run away when she finds herself engaged in casual conversations. What kind of behavior is she exhibiting?

(A)   Fight or flight

(B)   Response to stimulus

(C)   Avoidance

(D)   None of the above

(118) Which of the following is not a level of social work intervention?

(A)   In situ

(B)   Macro

(C)   Micro

(D)   Meso

(119) Which of the following is not a typical role that can be seen in a functional family?

(A)   Family management

(B)   Resource provision

(C)   Emotional support

(D)   Deflection of trauma through humor

(120) Which of the following is not an interaction-structuring technique that can help in conflict management and resolution?

(A)   Bringing on third-party mediators

(B)   Limiting the scope of the issues being discussed

(C)   Providing financial benefits to those involved

(D)   Decreasing the time gap that exists between resolution sessions

(121) Which of the following is not a primary prevention strategy?

(A)   Counseling about the risks of drugs

(B)   Regular medical tests and screenings

(C)   Education to spread awareness about road safety

(D)   Providing clients with vaccines against flu, COVID-19, etc.

(122) A social worker has a client who has some heart problems and is at risk of suffering a heart attack. The client's doctor has asked him to take one aspirin daily to mitigate the risk. Which kind of prevention strategy are the doctor and client using?

(A)   Primary

(B)   Secondary

(C)   Tertiary

(D)   Quaternary

(123) Which of the following is not an important element of behavioral objectives?

(A)   They are abstract and need proper specification.

(B)   They are client oriented.

(C)   They are clear and easy to understand.

(D)   They are observable and easily measurable.

(124) A social worker is working with a client who has lost his home in a huge fire. The client has managed to find safe temporary housing for the time being with close relatives. Which stage of the intervention process should the social worker undertake next?

(A)   Engagement with the client

(B)   Strength and weakness assessment

(C)   Intervention design and implementation

(D)   None of the above

(125) Which of the following items is not a common motivational approach used by social workers while conducting client interventions?

(A)   Providing clients with a hefty financial reward as a goal

(B)   Taking the first steps toward change and growth

(C)   Identifying risk and problem areas with the clients in a transparent manner

(D)   Preventing a relapse of past dysfunctional and toxic behaviors

(126) Which of the following cannot be classified as a self-motivation technique that clients can use?

(A)   Reminding themselves why they need to make a change

(B)   Surrounding themselves with positive and kind peers

(C)   Relying on medication to achieve ideal results

(D)   Forgiving themselves and being less self-critical

(127) A social worker has started to see a mandated client as a result of a court order. The client is reticent and does not want to engage in any conversation with the social worker. What is the first thing that the social worker should do to get the client to talk openly?

(A)   Threaten to report him to the court for noncooperation.

(B)   Provide cash bribes to induce some cooperation.

(C)   Include the guardian or partner in the treatment process.

(D)   Elaborate on the purpose and aspects of the intervention plan.

(128) Which of the following is not a healthy way to manage stress?

(A)   Going to a gun range and shooting targets

(B)   Engaging in risky behavior with friends

(C)   Engaging in meditation, yoga and tai chi

(D)   Finding an interest in art, music, etc.

(129) A social worker is seeing a client with anger management issues. The social worker has decided that he will take the relaxation approach to anger management with this particular client. Which of the following activities is not a part of this?

(A)   Teaching the client to force himself to use logic

(B)   Introducing the client to guided imagery and yoga

(C)   Helping the client manage anger by running, boxing, etc.

(D)   Introducing the client to meditative acts like breathing exercises

(130) Of the following options, which is the best definition of *family homeostasis*?

(A)   Families are resistant to change and tend to preserve their communication and structural patterns.

(B)   Families are malleable and can be easily changed by applying pressure and providing members with incentives.

(C)   Families are made of eight inherent constructs, and the social worker can induce change by picking the right option.

(D)   It is the internal energy of a closed system.

(131) Which of the following is the best description of the psychodynamic approach to crisis intervention?

(A)   The social worker observes shifts in behavior that affect client feelings and experiences.

(B)   The social worker helps clients come to terms with emotions, feelings and life experiences and gain insight into their problems.

(C)   The social worker helps clients change their thinking and behaviors, which are the root cause of their issues.

(D)   The social worker helps clients achieve their true wishes and fulfill their true potential.

(132) Which of the following issues is the behavioral modification approach most effective with?

(A)   Binge eating

(B)   Major depressive disorder

(C)   Psychosomatic limps

(D)   Anger and stress management issues

(133) Which level of intervention is applied to large groups and communities?

(A)   Macro

(B)   Micro

(C)   Meso

(D)   Magna

(134) A social worker is seeing a 13-year-old boy who is the son of a single father. The boy resents his father because he works a low-paying job and is unable to afford items the boy's friends take for granted, such as fast food meals, toys, sports equipment, etc. What role of the family dynamic does the boy think his father is failing to fulfill?

(A)   Family finance and behavior management

(B)   Resource provision and supply

(C)   Emotional support

(D)   Life skills development

(135) While working with a traumatized client who has lost her spouse in a road accident, the social worker encourages the woman to speak about her spouse. The social worker also encourages the client to acknowledge the accident and address her experiences. Which stage is the social worker working on?

(A)   Mourning and remembrance

(B)   Reconnection and reintegration

(C)   Safety and stabilization

(D)   Denial and grief

(136) What is the first step that parties in conflict need to take if they want to find a positive and constructive solution to their problems?

(A)   They need to limit the amount of time between problem-solving sessions.

(B)   They need to get a social worker to conduct a thorough assessment of the conflict in question.

(C)   They need to get a social worker to devise and implement an intervention plan.

(D)   They need to recognize and acknowledge that there is a conflict.

(137) Which federal law was ratified in 1978 to support the welfare of Native American children who have been displaced or abused?

(A)   Native American Adoption & Child Welfare Act

(B)   Education and Housing for Native American Children

(C)   Native American Child Abuse Prevention & Treatment Act

(D)   Indian Child Welfare Act

(138) Which federal act, enacted in 1996, provides the individual with unlimited access to and discretionary powers over their own medical information?

(A)   HIPAA

(B)   PACA

(C)   VAWA

(D)   MEPA

(139) Which of the following is not a characteristic of written communication that social workers engage in with their clients?

(A)   It should be written only in English.

(B)   It should be clear and written in simple language.

(C)   It should be worded in a culturally appropriate way.

(D)   It should be 100% transparent.

(140) Which of the following is not a factor included in the evaluation of a social worker?

(A)   The social worker's compliance with the *Code of Ethics*

(B)   The social worker's cultural competence

(C)   The social worker's knowledge and skills

(D)   The social worker's sexual orientation

(141) A social worker's child has a friend whose father is struggling with depression. The father suggests that he come to the social worker for counseling and therapy. The social worker agrees and gives him the office address. The social worker's actions here are _____.

(A)   Ethical, because he is doing his child's friend's father a favor

(B)   Unethical, because this situation constitutes a conflict of interests

(C)   Ethical, because he will be able to provide targeted and improved treatment

(D)   Unethical, because this constitutes an impermissible dual relationship

(142) Which of the following is not a step in ethical problem-solving?

(A)   The social worker identifies ethical standards according to the *Code of Ethics*.

(B)   The social worker identifies if there is an ethical issue at all.

(C)   The social worker keeps all dilemmas hidden from superiors.

(D)   The social worker monitors the issue for new ethical dilemmas.

(143) A social worker has a practice of using a lapel camera and microphone to record audio and video clips of clients. He uses the recordings to improve questioning and prepare client reports. He does not ask clients for permission because he deletes the recordings each week. These actions are _____.

(A)   Ethical, because the recordings get deleted

(B)   Unethical, because the clients' consent is not obtained

(C)   Ethical, because the social worker uses the recordings to improve his service quality

(D)   Unethical, because he uses nonstandard camera equipment

(144) A social worker and a client discover that they have a lot in common, including favorite sports teams and favorite movies. They develop a friendly rapport over the course of the treatment. The treatment is successful, and the client is terminated. After one year, the client reaches out and asks the social worker out on a date. If the social worker accepts, his actions will be _____.

(A)   Ethical, because the client has been terminated and sufficient time has passed

(B)   Unethical, because this would be a conflict of interests

(C)   Ethical, because clients and social workers can have sexual relationships

(D)   Unethical, because the client's written consent was not obtained

(145) Which of the following is not a value that can inhibit the therapeutic relationship between a social worker and a client?

(A)   Universalism

(B)   Valuation of control and restraint

(C)   Dichotomous thinking

(D)   Religion

(146) Which of the following terms best describes a flawed way of thinking, in which people consider that there is a single standard of behavior for everyone?

(A)   Measure of self comes from outside

(B)   Universalism

(C)   Concrete thinking

(D)   Dichotomy and differences

(147) Which of the following is not an acceptable behavior in social workers?

(A)   Ethnocentric point of view

(B)   Awareness and acceptance of personal and professional limitations

(C)   Understanding of dignity and worth of a person

(D)   Awareness of integrity and social justice

(148) A social worker sees a 14-year-old boy who says he was sexually abused by his aunt when he was 10 years old. He begs the social worker to keep this information private. What should the social worker do?

(A)   Contact law enforcement because social workers are mandated reporters.

(B)   Keep the information private.

(C)   Contact the boy's family immediately.

(D)   Not meddle in the family affairs.

(149) Which of the following professionals are not mandated reporters?

(A)   Social worker

(B)   Critical medical personnel

(C)   Lawyers and solicitors

(D)   Janitorial staff

(150) Which of the following is not an example of a legal mandate?

(A)   Constitutional mandate

(B)   Lawyer-served mandate

(C)   Statutory mandate

(D)   Court-made or common-law mandate

(151) A Native American child who has been abused by his family is referred to a social worker. He is picked up by CPS and sent to the social worker for further support. What should the social worker do first in this situation?

(A)   Contact the tribal jurisdiction.

(B)   Place the child with a safe member of the family.

(C)   Verify the child's ethnic or tribal identity.

(D)   None of the above.

(152) Which 1974 federal law placed the onus of mandatory reporting on the shoulders of professionals like lawyers, law enforcement officers, social workers and medical personnel?

(A)   Title VI of the Civil Rights Act

(B)   Child Abuse Prevention and Treatment Act

(C)   Family Educational Rights and Privacy Act

(D)   Adoption Assistance and Child Welfare Act

(153) Which law ensures that disabled children between the age of 3 and 21 have access to Individual Educational Plans (IEPs), along with therapy and supportive services?

(A)   U.S. Federal Education for All Act

(B)   No Child Left Behind Act

(C)   Family Educational Rights and Privacy Act

(D)   Education for Handicapped Children Act

(154) Which of the following is not a way for social workers to advocate for clients' rights?

(A)   They can lobby for policies that would be beneficial for their clients.

(B)   They can collect money for clients to encourage charity drives.

(C)   They can modify or lobby against policies that would be detrimental for their clients.

(D)   They can obtain services and resources on behalf of their clients.

(155) Which of the following should social work professionals use to assess and evaluate the work of a peer or junior employee?

(A)   The social worker's education level

(B)   The social worker's gender and sexual orientation

(C)   The social worker's ethnic or racial makeup

(D)   The social worker's use of professional supervision

(156) Which approach of power is appropriate in the realm of social work?

(A)   Power is mastery of the environment.

(B)   Power is mastery of other people.

(C)   Power is a laissez-faire approach to life.

(D)   Power is harmony gained with people in the environment.

(157) Which of the following is not an advantage of multidisciplinary collaboration among social workers and related professionals?

(A)   It can lead to an increase in remuneration and funding.

(B)   It can provide peer support and reinforce the quality of existing service delivery.

(C)   It can lead to cross-fertilization of professional skills.

(D)   It can fulfill all the aspects of client care.

(158) Which of the following is not an element of a basic case presentation in social work?

(A)   Client medical and psychiatric history

(B)   Client personal and social history

(C)   Client financial statement

(D)   A history of the problem at hand

(159) Which of the following is an important standard regarding social work case recording?

(A)   Reports should be punctual.

(B)   All decisions can only be recorded verbally.

(C)   Consent is not always required.

(D)   Subjective opinions must also be recorded.

(160) Which of the following is not an appropriate step during the client referral process?

(A)   Looking up resources appropriate to the situation

(B)   Discussing all available options with the client

(C)   Discussing payment methods and financial considerations with the client

(D)   Clarifying why the referral is needed and how it is going to help

(161) What is the objective of the initial contact phase in the context of client referrals?

(A)   The social worker and the client look up all available resources.

(B)   The social worker and the client discuss their available options.

(C)   The social worker and the client discuss finances and payment.

(D)   The social worker and the client prepare for their first meeting with the consultant.

(162) Which of the following should not be done while social workers set up a collaborative effort with an interdisciplinary team?

(A)   Establish a clear chain of command.

(B)   Establish and maintain good relationships with team members.

(C)   Set up common ground with the team members.

(D)   Understand the roles that the team members play.

(163) Which federal law provides patients with the right to the final say in all matters regarding their health?

(A)   Health Insurance Portability and Accountability Act

(B)   Patient Self-Determination Act

(C)   Family & Medical Leave Act

(D)   None of the above

(164) Which of the following is an area where a social worker will be most likely to have ethical conflicts?

(A)   Misallocation of resources

(B)   Family therapy

(C)   Therapy for depression

(D)   Treatment of minors

(165) Which of the following elements is a value that is expressed in the *Code of Ethics* for social work?

(A)   Dignity and worth of the person

(B)   Ensuring income equality

(C)   Total commitment to clients

(D)   Importance of self-determination

(166) Which of the following is not a responsibility of a social work agency?

(A)   Workload management

(B)   Professional development

(C)   Legislative groundwork

(D)   Supervision

(167) What is the main goal of advocacy in the context of social work?

(A)   Equitable redistribution of wealth

(B)   Equitable redistribution of resources

(C)   Promotion of civil rights and liberties

(D)   Ensuring constitutional rights

(168) Which federal medical insurance act was introduced by President Obama in 2010 and is known as Obamacare?

(A)   HIPAA

(B)   VAWA

(C)   PPACA

(D)   FMLA

(169) According to Freud's psychosexual stages of development, what is the consequent personality trait if a person has an uncorrected oral fixation?

(A)   Sexual promiscuity

(B)   Tendency to alcoholism

(C)   Tendency to speak without thinking

(D)   Overeating and excessive smoking

(170) During which ages does the period of latency occur according to Freud's psychosexual theory of development?

(A)   Puberty onward

(B)   0 to 2 years

(C)   3 to 5 years

(D)   5 to 13 or 14 years

Answers to Exam 2

(1)   (B) Attention deficit hyperactivity disorder.

Ritalin and Adderall are stimulants and are used to treat most ADHD symptoms.

(2)   (D) Vicodin.

The client suffered a back injury a few months ago. She is most likely exhibiting the physiological symptoms of Vicodin withdrawal, since Vicodin is a popular painkiller prescribed to such patients.

(3)   (B) 1 to 2 years.

Where children are between one and two years of age, they go through the anal stage of psychosexual development, as proposed by Freud.

(4)   (C) Thoughts and feelings that the client is unaware of.

The unconscious is that element of awareness that consists of thoughts and feelings that the client is unaware of. Though they are unconscious, these elements affect behavior and personality.

(5)   (D) Dystonicity.

Idealization, twinship and mirroring are the three main self-object needs of children in the realm of self-psychology. Dystonicity is not a self-object need.

(6)   (A) Identity vs. role confusion.

This is a stage of psychosocial development during which adolescents make the transition from childhood to adulthood. Restrictions during this period can result in serious role confusion in later life.

(7)   (C) Object constancy.

During the object constancy stage from ages 24 to 38 months, children start viewing themselves as separate individuals.

(8)   (D) They have to accept personal losses and live as independently as possible.

Elders are individuals who are 80 years and older. At this stage of life, they have to come to terms with interpersonal changes, such as the deaths of spouses, friends, etc. They also have to learn how to live as independently as possible.

(9)   (B) Object constancy.

According to Piaget's theory of cognitive development, the four stages of development are sensorimotor, preoperational, concrete operations and formal operations. Object constancy is not a stage of cognitive theory.

(10)   (A) Imaginary friends are very common between two and seven years of age.

During the preoperational stage of cognitive development, imaginary friends are a very common phenomenon. The mother should be reassured and be educated properly.

(11)   (B) Enjoy listening to stories.

Young children enjoy listening to stories a lot, but that is not an indicator of physical growth. It is an indicator of mental growth.

(12)   (C) Self-actualization needs.

Self-actualization needs are at the top of Maslow's hierarchy of needs, and it is the only need that is not characterized as a deficiency need. Instead, it is referred to as a growth or being need.

(13)   (B) Bargaining.

The five stages of grief, as proposed by Elizabeth Kubler-Ross, are denial, anger, bargaining, depression and acceptance.

(14)   (D) Coping with one's own physical decline.

Coping with one's own physical decline is an element of the family life cycle stage also known as "Later family life," *not* "Launching the children."

(15)   (C) Uninvolved parenting.

The child's parents are largely absent from his life and do not show any interest. This is clearly a case of uninvolved parenting, which is the worst parenting style.

(16) (C) Hypersexuality.

Hypersexuality is not a physical manifestation of trauma. However, insomnia, sleeping disorders, anxiety, pain, fatigue, etc. are.

(17) (B) Genetic factors – chronic diseases, genetic conditions, etc.

When risk factors are assessed in the realm of social work, genetics, such as chronic diseases, genetic conditions, etc., are not counted.

(18) (B) Depression and a marked increase in behavioral issues.

If a person has been discriminated against on the basis of ethnicity and race, the person can suffer from depression. In several cases, these morph into increased long-term behavioral issues.

(19) (A) The client is married to a recovering alcoholic.

Being married to a recovering alcoholic is not an example of a risk factor for addictive behavior, such as substance abuse, alcohol abuse, gambling, etc.

(20) (C) The genetic matrix model.

Here are the theories of addiction that have been proposed throughout the history of social work: the medical model, biopsychosocial model, social model, family and environmental model and self-medication model. There is no genetic matrix model.

(21)   (C) A very low IQ and traits of very low empathy.

In the context of social work, a very low IQ score and low level of empathy may *not* be used as predictors of future violence or instances of abuse.

(22)   (A) Clients develop an aversion to sex in general. In some cases, they may also develop hypersexual behavior in an effort to compensate.

People who were sexually abused as children routinely display tendencies of sex aversion. In some cases, they are also reported to develop hypersexual behavior in an effort to compensate and regain control over this aspect of their lives.

(23)   (B) Development of online personas different from real-life ones

Many people are active on social media platforms and have an online persona. This does not imply that a largely differing online persona is somehow a psychological defense mechanism.

(24)   (C) People channel their maladaptive impulses into an activity that is constructive and good.

Sublimation is a process in which people channel their maladaptive and unacceptable impulses into something constructive and good. For example, a person who is prone to anger issues takes on an aggressive sport, such as football.

(25)   (D) Rational choice theory.

Rational choice theory says that humans are rational and cogent beings and that all of their behaviors and actions are measured and oriented toward objectives.

(26)   (A) The client is the center of attention in PIE theory.

In person-in-environment theory states that the client is the center of attention. This theory examines an individual's behavior in the context of the environment the person resides in. It is most beneficial for the client.

(27)   (C) The couple learns to live together practically and emotionally.

The couple learns to live together practically and emotionally in the immediately previous stage of the family life cycle, which is also known as the childless couple stage.

(28)   (B) Margaret Mahler.

Object relations theory was developed by Hungarian physician and psychologist Margaret Mahler in the 1920s and 1930s. She was a central psychoanalytic expert.

(29)   (C) The knowledge that impulses and desires have to be delayed to meet the needs of the real world.

The reality principle can be best defined as the knowledge that base desires and impulses have to be delayed or held in check to meet the needs of the real world.

(30)   (A) Autonomy vs. shame.

According to Erikson's psychosocial stages of development, the toddler is in the autonomy vs. shame stage. This stage usually occurs between one and three years of age.

(31)   (D) The instigator.

In a dysfunctional family, the roles include the addict, the enabler, the hero, the lost child, the scapegoat and the mascot. Instigator is not one of the roles.

(32)   (B) John Bowlby.

John Bowlby was a British psychologist and psychiatrist and one of the greatest minds in the field in the 20th century. He is responsible for developing the theory of bonding and attachment.

(33)   (D) A willingness to conduct experiments.

This is not a sign of mental growth in older children between ages seven and 12. Good signs of mental growth in older children include a sense of industry, a willingness to learn, an understanding of cause and effect, reading skills and mathematical skills.

(34)   (C) Encourage him to stay secretive and avoid open communication.

This advice is not appropriate for this client. During the vulnerable teenage years, clients should be encouraged to communicate in an open and transparent manner. This sets the stage for proper development and communication skills with peers, parents, romantic partners, etc.

(35)   (C) Females have lower levels of self-esteem during adolescence.

It is true that girls have a lower level of self-esteem than males do, especially during adolescence.

(36)   (B) Inform the client that the social worker will be getting in touch with law enforcement with a report of domestic violence.

Social workers are mandated reporters, according to the *Code of Ethics,* and it is their job to report all instances of violence. It is clear that this client is suffering intimate partner abuse at the hands of his wife. He needs immediate help.

(37)   (A) Conversion.

Conversion is a defense mechanism in which people repress their urges, and this repression is converted and expressed as some kind of bodily function, such as nervous tics, flatulence, hiccups, blinking, etc.

(38)   (D) The abuser's occupation at the time of abuse.

The abuser's occupation has no bearing on the way sexual abuse would affect the family life of someone who has been abused.

(39)   (A) Development of an eating disorder.

In many instances, those who have been abused—either physically, emotionally or sexually—develop some kind of eating disorder, such as anorexia or bulimia.

(40)   (A) Understand that the grandparents are an integral part of the child's support system and incorporate them into the treatment plan.

The child is Indian-American, and in Indian culture, the whole family usually plays a role in decision-making with regards to crises. The social worker should incorporate the grandparents into the nine-year-old's treatment plan.

(41)   (D) Expletives are often used to demonstrate affection.

This is not a communication trait in African American culture. In this culture, communication is often animated and passionate. A history of racism and prejudice has an impact on all interactions, which is why people tend to speak up and let their opinions be known. Physical touch and direct communication are highly valued, and respect always needs to be shown.

(42)   (B) LGBTQ+ youth have a lot of advantages growing up.

This is false. LGBTQ+ youth are extremely vulnerable and can be subjected to a lot of prejudice, harassment and social stigma.

(43)   (B) Try to speak with people of different cultures by developing a set of stereotypical responses.

This is not something a social worker should do. Social workers should use a language that is culturally and professionally appropriate.

(44) (D) Humorous quips.

This is not a technique a social worker should use. Some helpful interview techniques that social workers can use include reframing, confrontation, interpretation, clarification and universalization.

(45) (B) Universalization.

The social worker makes use of universalization, which is the generalization of behavior or experiences being faced by clients in an effort to reassure them that their experiences are valid.

(46) (C) Academic record.

Even though academic and professional history is a part of the social section, a complete academic record of the client is not kept.

(47) (A) 16.

Under the Myers-Briggs Personality Type Indicator test, there are 16 personality types that can be assigned.

(48) (D) An immense mistrust of other people.

This is not something that can be classified as a temperamental factor while conducting a client assessment.

(49)   (C) Being completely transparent and forthcoming with feelings.

This is not an indicator of resistance. Usually, someone resistant to treatment is always censoring and editing his or her thoughts and feelings before divulging them to the social worker. Such a person is not transparent and forthcoming at all.

(50)   (B) Injuries and pain.

Physical injuries and reports of pain are usually not part of the primary components of a mental status examination. They can be considered secondary components.

(51)   (C) Psychosis.

Moban and Clozaril are examples of antipsychotic drugs, which are used to treat the symptoms of psychosis.

(52)   (D) Klonopin.

Klonopin is an antianxiety drug that can become addictive. Therefore, it is commonly abused. It is prescribed under very specific conditions and can be dangerous when taken with alcohol.

(53)   (B) Lithium.

Lithium can be used as a mood stabilizer. It needs to be dispensed in a very controlled way, since even a slight overdose can have serious consequences on kidney and liver functions.

(54)   (C) Typical drugs work on the dopaminergic system, and atypical drugs work on the serotonergic system.

Typical antipsychotic drugs affect the dopaminergic system. On the other hand, atypical psychotropic drugs are designed to have a higher affinity for the serotonergic system.

(55)   (C) A tendency to experience manic and depressive episodes.

This is a symptom of bipolar disorder, not an expected trait in a person who has suffered psychological abuse.

(56)   (A) Subjective – Objective – Assessment – Plan.

The SOAP treatment framework consists of the following elements: Subjective (S) data, Objective (O) data, Assessment (A) and Plan (P).

(57)   (C) Traumatic stress.

The markers listed are clear indicators of traumatic stress. The client has undergone serious trauma.

(58)   (D) The client is part of a criminal gang in the city.

The client's affiliation with a criminal gang in the city is not a risk factor for suicide.

(59)   (B) Parnate.

Parnate or tranylcypromine is a popular monoamine oxidase inhibitor antidepressant. It inhibits the functions of the monoamine oxidase enzyme, which is responsible for removing serotonin and norepinephrine.

(60)   (C) Intellectual function.

Intellectual function is a separate category of the mental status examination and is not a component of the appearance category of the exam.

(61)   (B) Wechsler Intelligence Scale for Children (WISC).

Developed by David Wechsler, the WISC is an intelligence scale and one of the simplest measures of a child's intelligence and cognitive abilities. It is in its fifth edition.

(62)   (C) Sexual identity issues or concerns.

Sexual identity issues or concerns are a part of the social section of a client's biopsychosocial history. They are not part of the biopsychosocial history's psychological section.

(63)   (B) Reframing or relabeling.

The social worker is using the reframing technique by presenting the client's narrative in a different context. This allows the client to view the issue from a very different point of view.

(64)   (C) Punitive.

There are three purposes of social work interviews: diagnostic, therapeutic and informational. More often than not, all three are used at the same time. The purpose is never punitive.

(65)   (A) 21.

Developed by Aaron T. Beck, the Beck Depression Inventory test consists of 21 items. It is the most widely used psychometric test for evaluating depression severity.

(66)   (C) Minnesota Multiphasic Personality Inventory (MMPI).

The Minnesota Multiphasic Personality Inventory is a standard psychoanalytic test used all over the world. It consists of a verbal objective inventory with 550 statements.

(67)   (D) Participant with the role of evaluator.

Social workers can take on multiple roles if they are working in a participatory or observer capacity. However, they are typically not granted the roles of participant and evaluator.

(68)   (A) They are completely removed from the activity and are only allowed to observe the participants' actions and interviews remotely.

A complete observer is a social worker who observes the proceedings remotely without including him or herself in it.

(69)   (B) The ability to make good investments.

The client's ability to make good financial investments does not tell the social worker anything at all about the person's defense and coping mechanisms. It is not an element of the strength and weakness test.

(70)   (D) Precontemplation.

The precontemplation stage is when clients are unaware or unwilling to admit their need to make changes to their lives. There is a marked lack of motivation and a great deal of resistance.

(71)   (B) Awareness and orientation.

The social worker is clearly checking her client's awareness and orientation. This is why she asks for the date and details regarding a recent basketball game.

(72)   (B) Abilify.

Abilify is an example of an atypical (not typical) antipsychotic drug, which works by responding to the serotonergic system instead of the dopaminergic system.

(73)   (A) It's unclear, but it affects the central nervous system.

It is unknown how exactly lithium salts help in regulating mood disorders. However, extensive research has shown that they have an effect on the CNS.

(74)   (D) None of the above.

Remeron is an example of an atypical antidepressant, which does not help with the problem by affecting dopamine or serotonin levels in brain chemistry. It is powerful and is mainly used to treat MDD.

(75)   (D) Intense gastrointestinal pain.

Gastrointestinal pain may occur due to a variety of reasons and cannot be said to be a clear indicator of sexual abuse in a child.

(76)   (C) A 20-year-old male who was bullied as a child and therefore has a lot of anxiety that he channels into aggression.

Clients who engage with drugs, guns, etc., are more prone to violence than the client described in Option C. This is true if they are involved with gangs, criminals or delinquent peers. Someone who has already committed violence will show a tendency to commit serious crimes as he grows.

(77)   (A) Clients' opinions regarding their well-being.

Clients' opinions regarding their well-being are included in the Subjective (S) portion of the SOAP format test. In the Objective (O) portion, test results, medical stats, legal issues, etc., are added.

(78)   (B) Whether the same results or answers can be reproduced by another social worker or researcher in a similar setting.

Reliability is a criterion that applies to experimental research findings that tries to corroborate the findings of one researcher by attempting to reproduce the results, answers and findings of another.

(79)   (D) Assessment.

This is the assessment stage of the SOAP framework, where the social worker consolidates the S and O findings into one report.

(80)   (B) The unhealthy behavior that the client needs to eliminate.

The healthy behavior is listed, so all the unhealthy behaviors that need to be eliminated are not separately outlined while making the measurable objectives.

(81)   (D) Playing football very aggressively and injuring others.

This is a sign of aggression, not of self-destructive behaviors.

(82)   (C) Ativan or Lorazepam.

Ativan or lorazepam is a benzodiazepine that is used widely for the treatment of panic and anxiety disorders. It is a very powerful medication that can also be used to treat status epilepticus or epilepsy.

(83) (A) Emails or texting.

Social workers need to invest in the appropriate channels of communication. Younger clients are more receptive to informal methods of communication, such as text, email, calls, etc.

(84) (C) Client-to-superior feedback.

This is not a valid method of feedback within the realm of social work.

(85) (C) Adiabatic system.

There are many terms in physics that find their place in systems theory, but adiabatic is not one of them. *Adiabatic system* is a term that is mostly seen in the field of thermodynamics. It is used to describe processes in which no heat energy is transferred.

(86) (B) Buspar.

Buspirone, known popularly by its brand name Buspar, is a short-term anxiety medication that can be very helpful. It acts as an agonist of the serotonergic system.

(87) (D) Insight.

Insight is the client's ability to predict the consequences of his or her current behavior. This allows a person to make decisions that are sensible and understand how the decisions can contribute to a person's own problems.

(88)   (A) The client is demonstrating resistance. She is using flattery in an effort to manipulate the social worker.

This is one of the most telltale signs of resistance. The client is refusing to engage in a proper conversation with the social worker. Instead, she is wasting time by engaging in banal small talk. She is trying to soften up and manipulate the social worker by flattering her.

(89)   (B) Whether the client prefers to use a car or public transportation.

Whether or not a client prefers to use a car or a means of public transportation does not have any bearing on the person's strengths and weaknesses. This is not used by social workers while conducting an examination.

(90)   (A) Patience.

While conducting strength and weakness analyses of clients, patience is one of the factors that fall under the aegis of a cognitive skill. It is one of the most important cognitive skills.

(91)   (B) Temperamental factors.

An extreme distrust of others and a failure to take responsibility for one's own actions and self is a temperamental weakness. This is one of the things that the social worker will need to address during the client's course of treatment.

(92) (A) Confrontation.

When the social worker deliberately calls attention to a problem in an effort to highlight it in front of the client, the social worker is using the confrontation technique. It can be one of the most effective interview techniques.

(93) (C) Behaviorist.

The behaviorist approach to cognitive crisis intervention was jointly developed by Ivan Pavlov and B. F. Skinner. Here, learning is viewed through a change in behavior or stimulus.

(94) (D) The family hero.

The family hero tends to excel at academics or work to cover up the dysfunction that exists in the person's family.

(95) (A) Self-destruction and violence.

When working with traumatized clients, social workers need to guide them through three very well-defined stages—safety and stability, mourning and remembrance and reconnection and reintegration. Self-destruction and violence are not a phase that social workers need to work through with clients.

(96) (A) Yes, because it is important to identify feedback from someone who is critical.

It is tempting to ask for feedback only when things are going well with a client. However, feedback also has to be taken while working with difficult clients. This feedback can provide a lot of valuable insight.

(97)   (C) Superficial behavioral changes that do not affect family structure.

In the context of strategic family therapy, first-order changes are superficial behavioral changes that do not affect the internal structure of the family.

(98)   (B) Cognitive-behavioral therapy.

Cognitive-behavioral therapy is a psychosocial intervention that can improve the client's overall mental health condition. The goal of CBT is to change the underlying thought patterns contributing to the problem. CBT is not used for couples therapy.

(99)   (D) The social worker encourages verbal communication and intimacy and removes barriers.

The Gottman method focuses on the promotion of intimacy, affection, trust and verbal communication.

(100) (A) Differentiation.

In the differentiation stage, individual members realize and consider their individuality. They start to exist as individuals and as group members. This is also called performing.

(101) (D) They widen the members' social circles.

Groups are not meant to widen members' social circles because this can be done through friends and family. Groups are focused on helping members gain hope and universality.

(102) (A) The members' stability.

The stability of the group members is one of the main factors that can affect the cohesion of the group. If members change frequently, cohesion is negatively affected.

(103) (C) Religion.

Religion is not one of the main causes of groupthink, which is a phenomenon in which the group makes bad decisions due to faulty collective thinking or planning.

(104) (D) Reproductive health.

Reproductive health is not one of the eight constructs that are needed to understand the way Bowenian family therapy works.

(105) (B) Using humor in a tense situation.

Using jokes and humor in a tense situation to dispel anger is a technique under the communication approach (not environmental approach) of anger management.

(106) (D) None of the above.

Summarization can be done during the course of the conversation. It can be done right at the beginning by reviewing the discussion of the last meeting. It can also be done at the end or periodically during the session.

(107) (C) Display empathy and form a bond with the client.

Empathy is very important, and it helps the social worker reach out and form a bond with clients.

(108) (D) Hostility.

Social workers are expected to never resort to hostility as a form of nonverbal communication. They are encouraged to make use of nonverbal communication methods (such as silence), questioning, active listening and paraphrasing and clarifying.

(109) (B) Recipients seek feedback from everybody around them.

In 360° feedback, recipients seek feedback from their entire surroundings, including peers, superiors, community members, etc. This feedback can paint a very complete picture.

(110) (B) The social worker needs to financially support the client through treatment.

This statement is false. The social worker is under no obligation to provide the client with financial assistance during the treatment. However, she can do pro bono sessions if she wishes.

(111) (D) Do a comprehensive medical examination of the client.

A comprehensive medical examination of the client would fall under the biological sphere and not the spiritual sphere.

(112) (A) A system that uses up all of its energy and then dies.

In the context of systems theory, a closed system is one that uses up all of its energy and then dies.

(113) (C) Energy that makes its way into a system permanently.

In the context of systems theory, throughput is the energy that is integrated into the system so that the system can attain its goals. That energy may not remain in that specific system permanently.

(114) (D) Preservation.

Problem-solving does not involve preservation. The components or steps of problem-solving in the context of social work are engagement, assessment, plan generation, intervention, evaluation and termination.

(115) (B) Albert Bandura.

Albert Bandura was a psychologist who was responsible for the social approach to client crisis intervention. His theory posits that clients can learn by being placed in a stimulating environment.

(116) (A) Sexual arousal.

Sexual arousal is an example of respondent behavior, which includes behaviors that are involuntary. The other answer options are operant, which means that they are totally voluntary.

(117) (A) Fight or flight.

This case is a classic example of fight-or-flight respondent behavior, in which the client responds to a stimulus without thinking about it.

(118) (A) In situ.

This is not a level of social work intervention. Social work interventions are usually one of three kinds: macro, micro or meso.

(119) (D) Deflection of trauma through humor.

Deflection of trauma or issues through humor is a dysfunctional family role typically known as the mascot. It is not a role seen in a typical functional family.

(120) (C) Providing financial benefits to those involved.

Providing financial benefits to those involved is not an interaction-structuring technique that can help in conflict management and resolution.

(121) (B) Regular medical tests and screenings.

Providing clients with access to regular medical tests and screenings is an example of a secondary prevention strategy. This prevention strategy comes into play when the disease, injury or unwanted behavior has already occurred.

(122) (B) Secondary.

Heart patients being advised to take small doses of aspirin on a daily basis is an example of a secondary prevention strategy. It mitigates the risk of heart attacks or similar events occurring in the future.

(123) (A) They are abstract and need proper specification.

This is false. Behavioral objectives need to be observable and noted down by the social worker. When setting aims, social workers try to avoid using abstract and loose definitions.

(124) (B) Strength and weakness assessment.

The next step for the social worker is to conduct a thorough strength and weakness assessment. During this phase, the social worker collects data on the client and figures out the person's problem areas.

(125) (A) Providing clients with a hefty financial reward as a goal.

Inducing clients to change by providing them with a hefty financial reward is an unsustainable way of motivation. This does not persuade the clients to change their toxic practices and other unhealthy behaviors.

(126) (C) Relying on medication to achieve ideal results.

Relying on medication to achieve ideal results is not an example of a self-motivation strategy that clients can use during treatment.

(127) (D) Elaborate on the purpose and aspects of the intervention plan.

Being transparent and clarifying the purpose of the intervention plan with the client is the best way to deal with someone who is being noncooperative and hostile. Moreover, the social worker can listen to the client's experiences.

(128) (B) Engaging in risky behavior with friends.

Engaging in risky behavior with friends is not a healthy or sustainable way to deal with the stress of academics, work, dysfunctional family life, etc. It is important to find an outlet that is healthy, constructive and realistic.

(129) (A) Teaching the client to force himself to use logic.

Using logic to dissuade oneself from anger and rage is a part of the cognitive approach to anger management. As a part of the relaxation approach, clients are introduced to constructive outlets they can use to relax and calm down.

(130) (A) Families are resistant to change and tend to preserve their communication and structural patterns.

In the context of strategic family therapy, family homeostasis refers to the fact that families are resistant to change and preserve their communication and organization patterns very easily.

(131) (B) The social worker helps clients come to terms with emotions, feelings and life experiences and gain insight into their problems.

The aim of psychodynamic approaches to crisis intervention is to help clients come to terms with their thoughts, emotions and feelings. Life experiences are examined so that the clients can gain insight into their problematic behaviors and tendencies.

(132) (A) Binge eating.

Behavioral modification techniques can be best applied to the treatment of phobic disorders and compulsive behaviors. For example, smoking, binge eating, compulsive cleaning, etc., can be addressed by using behavioral modification.

(133) (C) Meso.

The meso level of intervention applies to large groups and communities in the context of social work. It is located between macro (the largest level of intervention) and micro (the narrowest level).

(134) (B) Resource provision and supply.

The boy thinks that his father is failing to provide him with resources that his peers take for granted. This is the basic reason why he has developed resentment toward his father.

(135) (A) Mourning and remembrance.

The social worker is helping the client with the mourning and remembrance stage, during which the client acknowledges trauma and addresses the events that she went through. In this stage, proper psychoeducation is paramount.

(136) (D) They need to recognize and acknowledge that there is a conflict.

The first step of conflict resolution and management lies in the parties acknowledging the fact that they have a conflict. Only after this can they begin to reach a consensus.

(137) (D) Indian Child Welfare Act.

Enacted by the 95th United States Congress in 1978, the Indian Child Welfare Act or ICWA was put in place to ensure the proper treatment of American Indian children who have been abused or displaced.

(138) (A) HIPAA.

The Health Insurance Portability and Accountability Act (HIPAA) of 1996 is federal legislation designed to provide individuals with unfettered access to their health information and medical records. It provides medical privacy protection to all US citizens.

(139) (A) It should be written only in English.

Nowhere is it specified that official written communications between the social worker and their client have to be conducted only in English. If both have a common language between them other than English, then they can use it for effective communication.

(140) (D) The social worker's sexual orientation.

The social worker's sexual orientation may not be used by social work agencies or superiors to evaluate the social worker's professional performance. Doing so is considered a form of discrimination under federal law.

(141) (D) Unethical, because this constitutes an impermissible dual relationship.

This case is a dual relationship, which is impermissible under the *Code of Ethics* that all social workers are obligated to follow.

(142) (C) The social worker keeps all dilemmas hidden from superiors.

This is not a step in the ethical problem-solving process in the context of clinical social work practices.

(143) (B) Unethical, because the clients' consent is not obtained.

According to the *Code of Ethics*, it is very important to ask for clients' express written consent before they can be recorded.

(144) (A) Ethical, because the client has been terminated and sufficient time has passed.

The social worker is no longer responsible for the client's treatment. Also, a lot of time has passed since the treatment. While definitely not ideal, there are no ethical issues here for the pair to address.

(145) (D) Religion.

Religion is not a value that can inhibit the therapeutic relationship between a client and a social worker. In fact, the opposite is usually true.

(146) (B) Universalism.

Universalism is a flawed way of thinking wherein a single and universal norm of behavior is assumed for all people. In reality, there are different behavioral standards.

(147) (A) Ethnocentric point of view.

An ethnocentric point of view is not an acceptable trait in social workers. They need to understand, value and celebrate different cultural differences.

(148) (A) Contact law enforcement because social workers are mandated reporters.

Social workers are mandated reporters, and they have a duty to report any and all instances of sexual abuse—especially those committed against minors. Law enforcement agencies must be informed about this situation immediately.

(149) (D) Janitorial staff.

Janitorial staff are not mandated to report instances of physical or sexual abuse, but they can choose to do so voluntarily if they come across it.

(150) (B) Lawyer-served mandate.

Social workers are not bound under papers served by lawyers under threat to sue, such as a cease and desist letter. They need to follow only mandates specified by judicial institutions like the court.

(151) (C) Verify the child's ethnic or tribal identity.

According to the Indian Child Welfare Act of 1978, the first step the social worker needs to take is to verify the ethnic and tribal identity of the abused child.

(152) (B) Child Abuse Prevention and Treatment Act.

The Child Abuse Prevention and Treatment Act of 1974 is a large-scale federal act designed to prevent and address the physical, emotional and sexual abuse of children.

(153) (D) Education for Handicapped Children Act.

Enacted in 1975, the Education for Handicapped Children Act provides supportive services, education, therapy and IEPs for physically, intellectually and behaviorally disabled children between the ages of three and 21.

(154) (B) They can collect money for clients to encourage charity drives.

It is inappropriate for social workers to collect money from clients to encourage charity drives as a form of advocacy. It is better to lobby for or modify existing policies.

(155) (D) The social worker's use of professional supervision.

While evaluating a social worker, an agency or superior should note how the social worker makes use of professional supervision. Gender, sexual orientation, race, educational levels, etc., do not matter.

(156) (D) Power is harmony gained with people in the environment.

In the context of social work, power is defined as obtained through harmony and sharing with other people in the environment. Sharing leads to expansion.

(157) (A) It can lead to an increase in remuneration and funding.

While multidisciplinary collaboration among social work professionals can lead to better funding and remuneration, this is not a direct advantage of the process. The main goal is to contribute to the advancement of the field of client care.

(158) (C) Client financial statement.

Usually, an overview of the client's financial condition is enough when it pertains to the problem at hand. Otherwise, it is not appropriate to have the client's financial statement in the case presentation.

(159) (A) Reports should be punctual.

In the context of social work case recording, all reports have to be clear, concise and unbiased. They should be objective, and all decisions have to be recorded in a written format. Lastly, the reports should be punctual.

(160) (C) Discussing payment methods and financial considerations with the client.

While payment methods and financial considerations are a valid consideration, they do not to be addressed during the referral process. All administrative aspects can be taken care of later.

(161) (D) The social worker and the client prepare for their first meeting with the consultant.

During the initial contact phase, the social worker needs to work with the client and prepare the person for initial contact with the consultant. The social worker also needs to take all of the steps to facilitate this contact and make sure that responsibility is transferred in a proper way.

(162) (A) Establish a clear chain of command.

The chain of command should only be established if the social worker is in charge of the interdisciplinary project. If the social worker is a team member, then it is not the person's burden to shoulder.

(163) (B) Patient Self-Determination Act.

Enacted in 1991, the Patient Self-Determination Act is a federal law that grants individuals the right to have the final say in all treatment matters.

(164) (D) Treatment of minors.

During the treatment of minors, there can be various conflicts of interest between the social worker and the minor's legal guardian. A social worker in this field can face various ethical dilemmas.

(165) (A) Dignity and worth of the person.

Dignity and worth of the person is one of the most basic values that every social worker is expected to appreciate. It is outlined very clearly in the *Code of Ethics*.

(166) (C) Legislative groundwork.

While lobbying is important for many social work agencies, it is not a necessary part of their responsibilities. Case supervision, workload management, etc., are more pressing matters.

(167) (B) Equitable redistribution of resources.

The ultimate goal of advocacy in social work is to come up with policies that can ensure a more equitable distribution of resources among those who are in need of it.

(168) (C) PPACA.

The Patient Protection and Affordable Care Act (PPACA) is a federal medical insurance act passed in 2010 by the Obama administration. It is commonly known as Obamacare.

(169) (D) Overeating and excessive smoking.

According to Freud, anyone who develops an oral fixation (in which the child is gratified or frustrated to a large extent) likely has a tendency to overeat or indulge in smoking at an excessive level.

(170) (D) 5 to 13 or 14 years.

During the period between five years old and adolescence, usually at 13 to 14 years of age, the child's psychosexual stage is called dormant. It is also referred to as the latent stage in various literature.

ASWB Clinical Exam 3

(1) Which contemporary of Freud is responsible for the individual psychology field?

(A)   Alfred Adler

(B)   Jean Piaget

(C)   B. F. Skinner

(D)   Margaret Mahler

(2) What is the first stage of Erik Erikson's psychosocial stages of development?

(A)   Autonomy vs. shame

(B)   Initiative vs. guilt

(C)   Trust vs. mistrust

(D)   Identity vs. role confusion

(3) During which stage of psychosocial development do children initiate pet projects and collaborate with their peers?

(A)   Industry vs. inferiority

(B)   Trust vs. mistrust

(C)   Initiative vs. guilt

(D)   Intimacy vs. isolation

(4) Which is the stage that occurs between one and five months of age in object relations theory?

(A) Practicing

(B) Normal symbiotic

(C) Rapprochement

(D) Object constancy

(5) What happens during the rapprochement stage of object relations theory?

(A) Increase in self-awareness

(B) Increased interest in the outside world

(C) Free exploration

(D) Becoming close to the mother

(6) What is the age group for middle adults?

(A) 35 to 65 years

(B) 40 to 64 years

(C) 30 to 70 years

(D) None of the above

(7) What is the Piaget cognitive stage of development that occurs during the ages of two to seven years?

(A)   Preoperational

(B)   Formal operations

(C)   Concrete operations

(D)   Formal operations

(8) During which ages do children start to play games that have proper rule structure?

(A)   Formal operations

(B)   Preoperational

(C)   Concrete operations

(D)   Sensorimotor

(9) Who is the main proponent of object relations theory?

(A)   Sigmund Freud

(B)   Margaret Mahler

(C)   B. F. Skinner

(D)   Aryabhatta

(10) When does the ego identity vs. despair stage come in the individual's life cycle?

(A)   Toward the end of life

(B)   Toward the middle of life

(C)   During the start of senescence

(D)   Adolescence

(11) During which stage do infants begin to see themselves as complete individuals?

(A)   Rapprochement

(B)   Object constancy

(C)   Practicing

(D)   Normal autism

(12) Which of the following is not a style of parenting?

(A)   Uninvolved parenting

(B)   Authoritative parenting

(C)   Authoritarian parenting

(D)   None of the above

(13) During which stage of the family life cycle do adults have to establish adult-adult relationships with their children?

(A)   Later family life

(B)   Launching the children

(C)   Family with teens

(D)   Leaving the home

(14) Which of the following is not a stage of grief?

(A)   Hysterical rage

(B)   Acceptance

(C)   Denial

(D)   Bargaining

(15) Which of the following is not a biopsychological response to disease and disability?

(A)   Stress due to financial burden

(B)   Emotional strain to caregiver

(C)   Physical strain to the caregiver

(D)   Jealousy and envy

(16) Who is responsible for coming up with the five stages of grief model?

(A)   Sigmund Freud

(B)   George Bonnano and Erich Lindemann

(C)   Elisabeth Kübler-Ross

(D)   Colin Murray Parkes

(17) At which stage of the life cycle do most individuals have a remarkably high level of self-esteem and self-importance?

(A)   Later adulthood

(B)   Adolescence

(C)   Childhood

(D)   Young adulthood

(18) Which of the following is not an effective method of care for adolescent clients?

(A)   Treating them with proper respect

(B)   Using threats to force them to follow rules

(C)   Providing them with proper information

(D)   Encouraging them to be more self-dependent

(19) Which of the following is not a form of growth expected in adolescent clients?

(A)   Sexual and gendered growth

(B)   Physical and physiological growth

(C)   Mental and cognitive growth

(D)   Socioemotional and communicative growth

(20) What percentage of the population can be expected to operate at the self-actualization stage of Maslow's hierarchy (pyramid) of needs?

(A)   0.01%

(B)   Less than 10%

(C)   Approximately 1%

(D)   More than 70%

(21) Which of the following is classified as a deficiency need according to Maslow?

(A)   Need for sexual intercourse / reproduction

(B)   Need for self actualization

(C)   Need for constructive social bonds

(D)   Need for stable level of self-respect

(22) Who is responsible for developing the theory of attachment, which posits that personality is shaped by caregivers' responses to an infant's needs?

(A)   Anthony Alfred Bowlby

(B)   John Mostyn Bowlby

(C)   John Edward Olmos Bowlby

(D)   Mary Dinsmore Ainsworth

(23) What is the study of the physical and mental aspects of aging also called?

(A)   Geriatry

(B)   Gerontology

(C)   Ilikialogy

(D)   Epistemology

(24) Which involuntary defense mechanism usually involves the development of intermittent periods of a fugue state?

(A)   Dissociation

(B)   Conversion and compensation

(C)   Denial

(D)   Acting out

(25) Which of the following options is a very common defense mechanism in which repressed mental urges are expressed as some kind of involuntary bodily function, such as burps, flatulence, etc.?

(A) Compensation

(B) Conversion

(C) Acting out

(D) Projection

(26) Which theory of human behavior attributes most aspects of human behavior to the sustained competition for resources and self-interest?

(A) Social constructionist theory

(B) Social behavioral theory

(C) Conflict theory

(D) Rational choice theory

(27) Which of the following is not a risk factor for an abuser?

(A) High anger score with low empathy

(B) Bad financial or professional record

(C) Documented psychiatric disorder

(D) Antisocial behavior and criminal history

(28) Which of the following is not a type of neglect?

(A)   Physical

(B)   Emotional

(C)   Medical

(D)   Sports or extracurricular activities

(29) Which of the following is not a risk that individuals might face if they disclose some kind of abuse they have suffered from?

(A)   Homicide or assault

(B)   Disbelief by loved ones

(C)   Subjected to blame for the abuse

(D)   Rejection by other people

(30) Which of the following is not a healthy family dynamic?

(A)   Members help one another in times of need.

(B)   Members have realistic expectations of one another.

(C)   One member is blamed for any problems the family may have.

(D)   The family has a structure and a regular routine.

(31) Which is the best way to diagnose normality and abnormality in a person's behavior?

(A)   *Diagnostic & Statistical Manual for Mental Disorders (DSM-5)*

(B)   *International Classification of Diseases (ICD)*

(C)   *Manual for Mental and Physical Disorders (MMPD)*

(D)   *Physician's Desk Reference for Psychiatric Disorders (PDRPD)*

(32) Which of the following is a tendency displayed by those who have been sexually abused?

(A)   Anger management issues

(B)   Affinity to self-destructive behaviors

(C)   Depressive disorders

(D)   Homosexuality

(33) Which of the following is a way in which sexual abuse can affect the life of the family?

(A)   Extent and duration of the abuse

(B)   Kind of sexual abuse

(C)   Profession of the abuser

(D)   Educational background

(34) Which of the following is not a risk factor for substance abuse?

(A)   Psychiatric disorders

(B)   Family dysfunction and issues

(C)   Sexual orientation and gender identity

(D)   Behavioral history

(35) Which theory of addiction posits that substance abuse relieves the addict's physical and mental discomfort?

(A)   Self-medication model

(B)   Social model

(C)   Family and environmental model

(D)   Medical model

(36) The use of which drug results in dilated pupils, irritability, excessive hyperactivity and going without meals for long periods of time?

(A)   Heroin

(B)   Methamphetamine or speed

(C)   Marijuana

(D)   Cocaine

(37) Which of the following is not a sign of substance abuse?

(A)   Neglect of family, academic and professional responsibilities

(B)   Dangerous and destructive behavior

(C)   Coming out as homosexual

(D)   Abandonment of hobbies

(38) What is the standard method or language of communication for Caucasian or White American individuals and families?

(A)   Standard American English

(B)   Regional dialects of English

(C)   Conversational Spanish

(D)   None of the above

(39) Which of the following is not a step that an LGBTQ+ youth will usually follow in the process of developing a positive self-image?

(A)   The person feels different from others.

(B)   The person tries out substance use to discover him or herself.

(C)   The person embraces and accepts who he or she is.

(D)   The person feels confused and can feel ashamed.

(40) Which of the following is not a long-term effect of discrimination due to race, ethnicity, culture, sex, gender and/or sexual orientation?

(A)   An increased mistrust of similar people

(B)   A loss of motivation or drive

(C)   A difficulty in communication

(D)   A lack of education and professional achievement

(41) Which of the following is not a normal occurrence?

(A)   A toddler talking about loving his friend at daycare

(B)   A teenager who develops a crush on her classmate

(C)   An adult male who drives recklessly

(D)   An older adult who has an active social or sexual life

(42) Which of the following is not a technique used during social work interviews?

(A)   Universalization

(B)   Cohesion

(C)   Confrontation

(D)   Interpretation

(43) Which of the following components is not included in the biological section of the client's biopsychosocial history?

(A)   History of education and work

(B)   Medical history

(C)   Current and past list of medications

(D)   Family history of medical conditions

(44) In which section of the biopsychosocial history will the client's legal history be included?

(A)   Psychological section

(B)   Medical and biological section

(C)   Social section

(D)   None of the above

(45) Which of the following is not included in the Myers-Briggs Personality Type Indicator test?

(A)   Extraversion or introversion

(B)   Sensation or intuition

(C)   Thinking or feeling

(D)   None of the above

(46) How many items are a part of the Beck Depression Inventory test?

(A)   18

(B)   19

(C)   20

(D)   21

(47) Which of the following is not a temperamental factor used in the strength and weakness assessment?

(A)   A belief in justice

(B)   A sense of humor

(C)   An ability to regulate impulses

(D)   A sense of trust in others

(48) Which of the following subsets of the strength and weakness analysis does a sense of security and empathy fall into?

(A)   Cognitive skills

(B)   Interpersonal skills

(C)   Temperamental factors

(D)   None of the above

(49) Which of the following situations is best tackled by using collateral sources of information?

(A)   A child custody battle

(B)   A sexual abuse case

(C)   Providing resources to refugees and immigrants

(D)   An LGBTQ+ youth suffering from depressive disorder

(50) Which is an interview technique in which social workers assure clients that their experiences are valid and are faced by many people in the same situation as them?

(A)   Clarification

(B)   Universalization

(C)   Reframing and relabeling

(D)   Symbiotic questioning

(51) What is the most important objective of any interview conducted in the realm of social work?

(A)   To minimize harm to society

(B)   To enact change through policy and law

(C)   To serve the best interests of the client

(D)   To ensure the implementation of law and order

(52) Which of the following is not a valid reason for a social work interview?

(A)   Financial or tax benefits for the client

(B)   Therapeutic purpose for the client

(C)   Diagnostic purpose for the client

(D)   Informational purpose for the client

(53) Which of the following items is not an element of the mental status exam used in the realm of social work?

(A)   Speech

(B)   Orientation

(C)   Hypertension

(D)   Impulsivity

(54) Which of the following is a sign of resistance on the part of clients?

(A)   Censoring their thoughts before speaking

(B)   Talking with family members instead of professionals

(C)   Speaking with a physician

(D)   None of the above

(55) During which stage does the client have a lack of motivation and impetus to change behaviors and habits?

(A)   Planning

(B)   Medication and treatment

(C)   Precontemplation

(D)   Contemplation

(56) Which of the following is an important aspect of the mental status exam in the context of social work?

(A)   The client's awareness regarding things like time, place, etc.

(B)   The amount of money in the client's bank account

(C)   The social worker's mood and behavior

(D)   The client's grooming, face and clothing

(57) What is the client's ability to predict the consequences of his or her current behavior?

(A)   Insight

(B)   Intellectual function

(C)   Speech

(D)   Impulsivity

(58) A client is claiming that she forgets to make payments to the social worker. She makes many delays before she pays the social worker. She also makes a lot of small talk and refuses to answer the social worker's questions. What is the most likely reason for this behavior?

(A)   She is struggling financially and is distracted by that.

(B)   She is struggling emotionally and cannot bring herself to ask for help.

(C)   She is too proud to ask for help from the social worker.

(D)   She is displaying the classic signs of resistance.

(59) Which of the following is not a factor present during strength and weakness analysis?

(A)   Problem-solving skills

(B)   Being a member of institutions

(C)   Common sense and presence of mind

(D)   A fulfilling and complete sexual life

(60) Which kind of observing capacity would have the social worker completely removed from all activity?

(A)   Complete participant

(B)   Complete observer

(C)   Participant, as an observer

(D)   Observer, as a participant

(61) Which of the following options is not an example of a typical antipsychotic drug?

(A)   Haldol

(B)   Moban

(C)   Zyprexa

(D)   Navane

(62) Which of the following drugs is used to treat the symptoms of bipolar disorder and can be extremely dangerous if over-consumed?

(A)   Depakene

(B)   Lithium

(C)   Xanax

(D)   Ritalin

(63) How is a selective serotonin reuptake inhibitor (SSRI) antidepressant different from a tricyclic antidepressant?

(A)   SSRIs are more selective toward the neurotransmitters they interact with.

(B)   Tricyclics are more selective toward the neurotransmitters they interact with.

(C)   SSRIs work with the brain, while tricyclics work with the nervous system.

(D)   SSRIs have lasting impacts on the person's brain chemistry, while tricyclic antidepressants have none.

(64) Which of the following is not a monoamine oxidase inhibitor antidepressant?

(A)   Phenelzine

(B)   Parnate

(C)   Nardil

(D)   Zoloft

(65) Which of the following drugs is very commonly abused and should never be consumed along with alcohol?

(A)   Ritalin/Concerta

(B)   Amphetamine/Adderall

(C)   Nardil

(D)   Xanax/Ativan

(66) Which of the following drugs is used to treat the symptoms of alcoholism and alcohol abuse disorder?

(A)   Ativan

(B)   Anafranil

(C)   Acamprosate

(D)   Pamelor

(67) Which of the following options is not an antianxiety drug?

(A)   Xanax

(B)   Valium

(C)   Phenelzine hydrazine

(D)   Buspar

(68) Which of the following is not a category of antidepressant medication?

(A)   Monoamine oxidase inhibitors

(B)   Antimanic serotonin level-stabilizing agents

(C)   Selective serotonin reuptake inhibitors

(D)   Tricyclic antidepressants

(69) Which of the following options is not an SSRI antidepressant drug?

(A)   Tofranil

(B)   Paxil

(C)   Prozac

(D)   Zoloft

(70) Which of the following drugs is the best choice for someone who is having trouble focusing in class and is acting out?

(A)   Zoloft/Celexa

(B)   Xanax

(C)   Dextrostat/Dexedrine

(D)   Valium/Buspar

(71) Which of the following is not an indicator of sexual abuse?

(A)   An interest in or curiosity about sex in someone who is young

(B)   Injuries in the genital or rectal area

(C)   Nightmares and enhanced sense of anxiety and fear

(D)   Children who have knowledge of inappropriate sexual matters

(72) Which of the following options is not an indicator of physical abuse?

(A)   A very low sense of empathy toward other people

(B)   An acute sense of wariness about other people

(C)   A tendency to resort to extreme aggressiveness or withdrawal

(D)   A number of unexplained injuries and bruises

(73) Which of the following behaviors is a likely indicator of psychological abuse?

(A)   Using humor as a coping mechanism

(B)   Tending to do extremely well in school

(C)   Engaging in risky, dangerous and self-destructive behavior

(D)   Incredible academic pressure

(74) Which of the following can be said to be the most common indicator of violence?

(A)   A history of doing drugs

(B)   A family history of violence

(C)   A history of mental disorders

(D)   A past history of violence

(75) Which of the following is not a risk factor relating to suicide?

(A)   An experience of loss—relationship, financial, professional, etc.

(B)   A violent youth involved in gangs

(C)   Easy access to firearms, dangerous substances, etc.

(D)   A history of psychiatric disorder and substance abuse

(76) Which of the following can be said to be the most likely predictor of suicide or self-harm?

(A)   Little access to social support

(B)   A life of isolation and depression

(C)   A history of substance abuse

(D)   An attempted suicide

(77) Which of the following is not an indicator of traumatic stress?

(A)   Dissociation

(B)   A tendency to lash out

(C)   Eating disorders or poor eating habits

(D)   Impulsive spending

(78) Which of the following is not part of the Subjective (S) section of a SOAP framework?

(A)   Client's recent activity

(B)   Client's current well-being

(C)   Client's blood sugar level

(D)   Client's recent social life

(79) Which of the following is not a part of the Objective (O) section of a SOAP framework?

(A)   Descriptive assessment of the client

(B)   Client's heart rate

(C)   Client's blood pressure reading

(D)   Client's test scores

(80) What does the SMART acronym, used for objectives that social workers must use to break down the intervention process into measurable steps, stand for?

(A)   Sustainable, Measurable, Analyzable, Relevant and Timebound

(B)   Specific, Measurable, Achievable, Relevant and Time-Specific

(C)   Specific, Measurable, Analyzable, Related and Timebound

(D)   Situational, Medical, Attributable, Relatable and Time-Specific

(81) Which of the following is the best advantage of generic questions in the context of a social work interview?

(A)   They help establish a friendly relationship with the client.

(B)   They help familiarize the client with interviews.

(C)   They help social workers glean helpful insights from the interview.

(D)   None of the above.

(82) Which of the following is not a helpful technique that social workers can use during an interview?

(A) Screaming at clients so that they can snap out of their reverie

(B) Deliberately bringing up problems to give them attention

(C) Generalizing clients' behaviors and experiences to reassure them

(D) Asking clients to reformulate the problem in their own words

(83) In which section of the biopsychosocial history do relationship status and marital status fall?

(A) Psychological

(B) Biological

(C) Social

(D) Legal and marital

(84) Which projective test makes use of a series of pictures, each of which depicts an ambiguous scene?

(A) Wechsler Intelligence Scale

(B) Emotional Intelligence Test

(C) Minnesota Multiphasic Personality Inventory

(D) Thematic Apperception Test

(85) Which of the following options is the latest edition of the Wechsler Intelligence Scale for Children?

(A)   Sixth edition

(B)   Fifth edition

(C)   Fourth edition

(D)   Second edition

(86) How many statements are repeated in the 550 statements of the Minnesota Multiphasic Personality Inventory test?

(A)   16

(B)   17

(C)   18

(D)   19

(87) Select the statement that is the most appropriate about the following claim: "Silence can be one of the most helpful and insightful types of communication."

(A)   Generally true, but sometimes false

(B)   Generally false, but sometimes true

(C)   Never true

(D)   Always true

(88) Which of the following is not a good temperamental indicator that would be included in a client's strength assessment?

(A)   Trust in other people

(B)   Tendency to be hostile and angry

(C)   Healthy sense of humor

(D)   Ability to cope with negative events

(89) Which of the following is a good interpersonal indicator of strength?

(A)   An ability to receive and use feedback in a constructive way

(B)   An ability to deal with problems

(C)   An ability to construct, develop and maintain healthy relationships with others

(D)   A sense of direction and purpose

(90) Which of the following is an antipsychotic drug that is sold under the brand name Mellaril?

(A)   Haloperidol

(B)   Thioridazine

(C)   Alprazolam

(D)   Thiothixene

(91) Which of the following medications used to treat bipolar disorder can also be used to treat epilepsy and neuropathic pain?

(A)   Carbatrol

(B)   Topamax

(C)   Lithium salts

(D)   Lamictal

(92) Which of the following antidepressants is not dangerous to brain or cognitive function if used correctly?

(A)   Elavil

(B)   Pamelor

(C)   Surmontil

(D)   Zoloft

(93) During which situation do social workers use texting or messaging platforms as a way to reach out to their clients?

(A)   If clients are physically disabled and cannot make regular visits

(B)   If clients are young people who have social anxiety

(C)   If clients are elderly people confined to their homes

(D)   If clients are children

(94) Which of the following is not a property of appropriate communication methods?

(A)   Empathetic

(B)   Genuine

(C)   Displays positive regard

(D)   Culturally inappropriate and humorous

(95) Which of the following is the best description of active listening?

(A)   Asking relevant questions to glean insights

(B)   Maintaining eye contact, making relevant comments, etc., to show clients that they are being listened to

(C)   Repeating back what the client said to clarify

(D)   None of the above

(96) Which of the following feedback methods best describes a situation in which the client directly gives service delivery feedback to the social worker?

(A)   360° feedback

(B)   One-to-one feedback

(C)   Group-to-group feedback

(D)   Intragroup feedback

(97) Which of the following options is a form of feedback in which the social worker seeks feedback from clients, superiors and the entire community at large?

(A)   Consultative feedback

(B)   Superior feedback

(C)   360° feedback

(D)   Group-to-group feedback

(98) Select the most appropriate option about the following statement: "It is very important for workers to critically assess the clients' feelings and provide them with judgment."

(A)   Generally true, but sometimes false

(B)   Generally false, but sometimes true

(C)   Always true

(D)   Always false

(99) What is a communication technique in which social workers assure clients that they are worthy of care and assistance?

(A)   Positive regard

(B)   Self-esteem regard

(C)   Upliftment

(D)   Empathy

(100) When is not the best time for a social worker's total summarization of the conversation?

(A)   At the beginning of the conversation

(B)   In the middle of the conversation

(C)   At the end of the conversation

(D)   At the beginning of the next meeting

(101) Which of the following is not a property of empathetic communication?

(A)   Constructive

(B)   Rational

(C)   Problem-solving

(D)   Helps to calm the client

(102) Which is the best communication method when a client is prone to using anger and violence as a coping mechanism against frustration?

(A)   Consultative communication

(B)   Empathetic communication

(C)   Rational communication

(D)   Active listening and problem-solving

(103) Which is the most important property of any relationship between social workers and clients?

(A)   The preservation of trust

(B)   Emotional openness

(C)   The promotion of self-determination

(D)   Consent

(104) Which of the following is not appropriate in a social worker and client relationship?

(A)   The establishment of trust

(B)   Mutual listening on both ends

(C)   An establishment of empathy

(D)   The broadcast of private information for academic purposes

(105) Which of the following forms of feedback is not obligatory?

(A)   Intragroup feedback

(B)   360° feedback

(C)   Group-to-group feedback

(D)   Consultative feedback

(106) Which of the following is a term included in the systems theory terminology?

(A)   Closed system

(B)   Throughput

(C)   Homeostasis

(D)   Spontaneous processes

(107) Which is the correct definition of *throughput* in the context of systems theory?

(A)   Amount of a product or service that a company can produce and deliver in a given period

(B)   A measure of energy integrated into the system to attain the goals of the system

(C)   A measure of how many units of information a system can process in a given period

(D)   None of the above

(108) What does *differentiation* mean in the context of systems theory?

(A)   When a system becomes specialized in functioning and structure

(B)   When a system breaks into many cohesive parts

(C)   When a system disintegrates

(D)   None of the above

(109) Who is responsible for the development of the social approach to crisis intervention?

(A)   B. F. Skinner

(B)   Margaret Mahler

(C)   Albert Bandura

(D)   Abraham Maslow and Ivan Pavlov

(110) Who is responsible for the development of the cognitive approach to crisis intervention in social work?

(A)   B. F. Skinner

(B)   Sigmund Freud

(C)   Margaret Mahler

(D)   Jean Piaget

(111) Which of the following is not a dimension in the context of social work intervention processes?

(A)   Psychological

(B)   Financial

(C)   Social

(D)   Spiritual

(112) Which of the following terms refers to the state of chaos or disorder endemic to a system that uses up all of its energy?

(A)   Entropy

(B)   Homeostasis

(C)   Negentropy

(D)   None of the above

(113) Which of the following is not a stage of the problem-solving process?

(A)   Engagement

(B)   Assessment

(C)   Plan generation

(D)   Objective data collection

(114) Which of the following options is the best definition of a maladaptive client?

(A)   A client who does not have the skills required to solve problems

(B)   A client who does not have the motivation to solve problems

(C)   A client whose mental, cognitive and emotional capacities have been impaired

(D)   A client who is resorting to unhealthy tendencies

(115) Which psychologists were responsible for the development of the behaviorist approach to crisis intervention?

(A)   Abraham Maslow and Sigmund Freud

(B)   Burrhus Frederic Skinner and Ivan Pavlov

(C)   Carl Rogers and Douglas McGregor

(D)   Margaret Mahler and Jean Piaget

(116) Which of the following is not an example of operant behavior?

(A)   Walking

(B)   Running for exercise

(C)   Drinking water

(D)   Running from danger

(117) Which of the following conditions can be best corrected with the help of behavioral modification?

(A)   Major depressive disorder

(B)   Postpartum anxiety

(C)   Binge eating tendencies

(D)   Anxiety disorder

(118) Who is responsible for the development of cognitive-behavioral therapy?

(A)   Alfred Adler

(B)   Aaron T. Beck

(C)   John B. Watson

(D)   Arnold Lazarus

(119) Which of the following is not a property of cognitive-behavioral therapy?

(A)   Depends on the physician

(B)   Active

(C)   Collaborative

(D)   Structured

(120) Which level of social work intervention can be said to be the broadest in its scope?

(A)   Micro

(B)   Meso

(C)   Macro

(D)   Mega

(121) At which level of social work interventions do social workers interact with large groups and communities?

(A)   Micro

(B)   Meso

(C)   Macro

(D)   Mega

(122) Which of the following is a functional role in a healthy family dynamic?

(A)   Being in charge of family management and decisions

(B)   Blaming one member for everything

(C)   Restricting members' access to resources

(D)   None of the above

(123) Which of the following is not a dysfunctional family role?

(A)   The scapegoat

(B)   The lost child

(C)   The resource provider

(D)   The enabler

(124) What does the person with the lost child role do in a dysfunctional family?

(A)   Run away from home and try to get lost

(B)   Stir up trouble and get blamed for everything

(C)   Try to make everybody laugh all the time

(D)   Blend into the background to escape dysfunction

(125) What does the person with the mascot role do in a dysfunctional family?

(A)   Enable the addict and try to cover up for them

(B)   Try to make everybody laugh all the time

(C)   Try to compensate for the dysfunction by doing well at school or work

(D)   None of the above

(126) Which of the following is not a technique that can be used for anger management?

(A)   Using deep breathing to calm oneself down

(B)   Using humor and jokes to avoid rage-inducing situations

(C)   Taking out anger on loved ones by yelling at them

(D)   Avoiding people and situations that may lead to anger

(127) Which of the following is not an element used in the communication approach to anger management?

(A)   Using humor and jokes to avoid getting angry

(B)   Using physical exercise to get over anger

(C)   Trying to stop getting defensive during a tense situation

(D)   Deliberately slowing down speech and calming down properly

(128) Which of the following is not an element used in the cognitive approach to anger management?

(A)   Using meditation to sharpen one's senses and calm down

(B)   Using empathy to see differing perspectives

(C)   Using problem-solving methods

(D)   Using logic and rationality to make a balanced perspective

(129) Which of the following is not a way to engage with a mandated client?

(A)   Listening to the client's experiences and opinions

(B)   Telling the client why he or she is there

(C)   Viewing clients as more than their problems

(D)   Giving clients some punitive ultimatums

(130) Which of the following is not a self-motivation technique?

(A)   Reminding

(B)   Criticizing

(C)   Visualizing

(D)   Forgiving

(131) Which of the following is not a healthy motivational approach?

(A)   Using the allure of financial rewards to motivate the client

(B)   Setting clear and measurable goals

(C)   Elaborating on how the change is going to help clients

(D)   Preventing a relapse of past dysfunctional behavior

(132) Which of the following is an example of the visualization technique?

(A)   Looking at images of things that make you happy

(B)   Looking at images of friends on social media

(C)   Looking at an inspirational image and internalizing it

(D)   None of the above

(133) Which of the following is not a stage of intervention?

(A)   Engagement with client

(B)   Strength and weakness assessment

(C)   Applying the intervention

(D)   Accepting payment from the client

(134) Which of the following is not an important property of behavioral objectives?

(A)   Clear and easy to understand

(B)   Observable and measurable

(C)   Oriented toward the social worker

(D)   Contains the desired client behavior

(135) A 50-year-old man discovers he has a high cholesterol level. The doctor advises him to change his diet and lifestyle. He also asks him to take one baby aspirin every day to prevent the risks of heart attacks. What prevention strategy is this?

(A)   Primary prevention strategy

(B)   Secondary prevention strategy

(C)   Tertiary prevention strategy

(D)   Preemptive prevention

(136) A two-year-old is taken by his parents for his set of immunizations against diseases like diphtheria, polio, etc. What prevention strategy is this?

(A)   Primary prevention strategy

(B)   Secondary prevention strategy

(C)   Tertiary prevention strategy

(D)   Preemptive prevention

(137) Which of the following is not a phase in trauma treatment plans?

(A)   Safety and stabilization

(B)   Confrontation

(C)   Mourning and remembrance

(D)   Reconnection

(138) Which of the following is not an interaction structuring technique used for conflict management?

(A)   Implementing long gaps between the conflict-management sessions

(B)   Making use of third-party mediators

(C)   Decreasing contact between parties in conflict

(D)   Limiting the scope of issues being discussed

(139) Which of the following is not a tertiary prevention strategy?

(A)   Membership in support groups

(B)   Membership in pain-management groups

(C)   Hospice care

(D)   Screenings and MRI examinations

(140) Which of the following is not a form of family therapy?

(A)   Structural family therapy

(B)   Bowenian family therapy

(C)   Piaget's family therapy

(D)   Strategic family therapy

(141) Which of the following is not a first-order family strategic change?

(A)   There is a change in the family's overall structure.

(B)   The father does not yell at the mother in front of children.

(C)   The mother is emotionally withholding but does not neglect children.

(D)   None of the above.

(142) Which of the following is not a construct needed in Bowenian family therapy?

(A)   Differentiation

(B)   Family homeostasis

(C)   Emotional fusion

(D)   Emotional triangle

(143) Which 1965 federal act aims to protect the rights of senior citizens in the United States?

(A)   Parents and Senior Citizens Protection Act (PSCPA)

(B)   Older Americans Act (OAA)

(C)   Age Discrimination in Employment Act (ADEA)

(D)   Elderly Act (EA)

(144) Which federal law transfers the rights of educational records to children once they turn 18?

(A)   Family Educational Rights and Privacy Act (FERPA)

(B)   Educational Rights Transfer Act (ERTA)

(C)   Federal Educational Rights and Privacy Act (FERPA)

(D)   None of the above

(145) When was the Americans with Disabilities Act (ADA) passed?

(A)   1989

(B)   1990

(C)   1991

(D)   1992

(146) Which 1978 federal law guarantees the protection of the rights of Native American children who have been abused or displaced?

(A)   Federal Native American Child Welfare Act (FNACWA)

(B)   Indian Child Displacement Prevention Act (ICDPA)

(C)   Indian Child Welfare Act (ICWA)

(D)   None of the above

(147) What is the last course of action that the ICWA allows with regard to the welfare and placement of a Native American child?

(A)   Placed in a home that is not indigenous

(B)   Placed in a family member's home

(C)   Placed in a home that is indigenous

(D)   Placed in the tribe's jurisdictional care

(148) Which 1994 federal law prevents US agencies from refusing foster care and social services to people of color?

(A)   Title VI of the Civil Rights Act (CRA)

(B)   Multiethnic Placement Act (MEPA)

(C)   Protection Against Multiethnic Non-Placement Act (PAMENA)

(D)   None of the above

(149) What is the Patient Protection and Affordable Care Act (PPACA) also known as?

(A)   Medicare

(B)   Fedicare

(C)   Obamacare

(D)   None of the above

(150) Which of the following is false about written communications between a social worker and a client?

(A)   There should be a huge block of text without indents.

(B)   The language should be clear and simple.

(C)   The recommendations should be purely data driven.

(D)   Client confidentiality should be maintained.

(151) Which of the following is not a model of peer supervision and collaboration?

(A)   Epistemological model

(B)   Psychodynamic model

(C)   Developmental model

(D)   Role-centered model

(152) Which of the following is not an appropriate approach to consultation?

(A)   The role of the consultant has to be clearly defined.

(B)   The consultation process should be transparent.

(C)   The purpose of consultation has to be clearly defined.

(D)   Deliberate obfuscations should be made to the client.

(153) Which of the following is not an element of a standard case presentation?

(A)   Identifying information

(B)   Presenting problem and assessment

(C)   Medical and psychiatric history

(D)   Opinions and value judgments

(154) Which of the following is not an advantage of multidisciplinary collaboration?

(A) Cross-fertilization of skills

(B) Fulfillment of aspects of client care

(C) Provision of peer support and service delivery

(D) Better remuneration

(155) Which of the following is not a helpful idea in the context of interdisciplinary collaboration?

(A) Articulating responsibility

(B) Looking for common ground

(C) Establishing dominance over team members

(D) Addressing underlying conflicts

(156) Which of the following is not an element of client reports?

(A) The representation of facts should be long and excessively detailed.

(B) The decisions should be written down.

(C) The report should be free of value judgments.

(D) The report should be punctual.

(157) Which of the following is not a step of client referral?

(A)   Looking up available resources

(B)   Keeping the referral's need clear

(C)   Setting up an initial contact phase

(D)   None of the above

(158) Should a social worker limit clients' access to reports?

(A)   No, because the reports ultimately belong to clients.

(B)   Yes, but with certain exceptions.

(C)   No, because social workers cannot withhold information from clients.

(D)   Yes, to protect confidentiality.

(159) Which of the following is prohibited according to the *Code of Ethics*?

(A)   Maintaining a sexual relationship with the client

(B)   Belonging to the same church congregation as the client

(C)   Avoiding any social interaction or contact with the client

(D)   None of the above

(160) Which of the following is not a type of legal mandate that social workers need to obey or pay heed to?

(A)   Statutory

(B)   Regulatory

(C)   Privately served

(D)   Court-ordered

(161) Which of the following can inhibit a social worker's relationship with a client?

(A)   Open-mindedness

(B)   Cultural sensitivity

(C)   Dichotomous thinking

(D)   Professional appropriateness

(162) Which of the following is a flawed way of thinking that considers only a universal fixed norm of values and behaviors?

(A)   Generalism

(B)   Catechism

(C)   Universalism

(D)   None of the above

(163) Which is not a core social work value?

(A)   Integrity

(B)   Discrimination and systemic barriers

(C)   Dignity and worth of the person

(D)   Integrity

(164) What is a perspective called in which one takes only one's own culture and values into account?

(A)   Ethnocentricity

(B)   Ethnofascism

(C)   Ethnosuperiority

(D)   Ethnoplurality

(165) What is wrong with the view "Power is power over others"?

(A)   Power should be defined as power over subordinates.

(B)   Power should be defined as power over superiors.

(C)   Power should be defined as power through sharing.

(D)   None of the above.

(166) Which of the following do social workers not need to be aware of?

(A)   Personal biases about race

(B)   At least one additional language

(C)   Traditions and beliefs of other cultures

(D)   Beliefs of their own culture and traditions

(167) Which of the following professions is not a mandated reporter?

(A)   A doctor or a nurse

(B)   A janitorial staff member

(C)   A social worker and therapist

(D)   A lawyer

(168) What should social workers do first if they are served with a subpoena by a court?

(A)   Ignore the subpoena, citing confidentiality

(B)   Cooperate fully with the court and divulge everything

(C)   Respond to the subpoena and claim privilege

(D)   Contact a lawyer

(169) What standard should social workers follow with regard to confidentiality and client privacy?

(A) NASW *Code of Ethics*

(B) NASW Code of Client Confidentiality and Information

(C) NASW Codicil of Privacy

(D) None of the above

(170) Which of the following options is not a step in the ethical dilemma or problem-solving process?

(A) Monitor the situation for new dilemmas or issues.

(B) Identify the dilemma or issue and look for its root cause or causes.

(C) Immediately contact a superior for specialized advice.

(D) Make use of the *Code of Ethics* to understand what needs to be done.

Answers to Exam 3

(1)   (A) Alfred Adler.

Alfred Adler was an Austrian physician and psychologist who was ultimately responsible for the foundation of the school of individual psychology.

(2)   (C) Trust vs. mistrust.

The first stage in Erik Erikson's psychosocial stages of development is trust vs. mistrust, which usually occurs between birth and 12 months.

(3)   (A) Industry vs. inferiority.

During the industry vs. inferiority stage of psychosocial development, children collaborate with their peers, initiate projects and take pride in their work.

(4)   (B) Normal symbiotic.

According to object relations theory, from ages one to five months, an infant is in the normal symbiotic self. This is when infants start to be aware of parents and caregivers.

(5)   (D) Becoming close to the mother.

According to object relations theory, from ages 15 to 24 months, infants undergo rapprochement. They start to become close to their mothers.

(6)   (B) 40 to 64 years.

Individuals between the ages of 40 and 64 are known as middle adults. During this period, they begin to age, enter menopause and more.

(7)   (A) Preoperational.

During the ages of two to seven years, a child undergoes the preoperational stage of cognitive development.

(8)   (C) Concrete operations.

During the ages of seven to 11 years, children go through the concrete operations stage of normal cognitive development. They play games and have proper rule structure.

(9)   (B) Margaret Mahler.

Margaret Mahler was a Hungarian physician and psychologist responsible for the development of object relations theory.

(10)   (A) Toward the end of life.

Toward the end of life, individuals have to explore life and learn new things and develop their ego identity. Otherwise, they can develop a sense of despair.

(11)   (B) Object constancy.

During the stage of object constancy, infants begin to see themselves as unique individuals.

(12)   (D) None of the above.

Uninvolved, authoritarian and authoritative are all different parenting styles.

(13)   (B) Launching the children.

During the launching the children stage of the family life cycle, parents have to establish adult-adult relationships with their kids.

(14)   (A) Hysterical rage.

Anger is a commonly observed stage during grief, but hysterical rage is extremely rare. It is not viewed as a stage of grief.

(15)   (D) Jealousy and envy.

Jealousy and envy are not commonly seen biopsychological responses to a loved one or family member having some kind of disease, infirmity or disability.

(16)   (C) Elisabeth Kübler-Ross.

The five stages of grief is a model developed by the Swiss-American psychologist and physician Elisabeth Kübler-Ross in her 1969 seminal work *On Death and Dying*.

(17)   (C) Childhood.

Usually, small children have a remarkably high level of self-esteem. This falls as they grow and begin to develop a more balanced portrayal of their own selves.

(18)   (B) Using threats to force them to follow rules.

While working with adolescents, using threats to force them to follow rules is not a very effective method. It is a much better idea to form a healthy rapport by treating them with respect.

(19)   (A) Sexual and gendered growth.

Despite adolescence being the time that individuals start to discover their sexuality and explore their gender identity, it is not a form of growth.

(20)   (C) Approximately 1%.

It has been theorized that approximately 1% of people operate at the self-actualization layer consistently.

(21)   (A) Need for sexual intercourse/reproduction.

The need for sexual intercourse is classified as a part of deficiency needs according to Maslow.

(22)   (B) John Mostyn Bowlby.

John Mostyn Bowlby was a British psychologist responsible for the development of attachment theory. He was one of the most prolific psychologists of the 1900s.

(23)   (B) Gerontology.

Gerontology is a term used to describe the study of the physical, social, cultural and mental aspects of the entire aging process.

(24)   (A) Dissociation.

This is a defense mechanism in which a person's mental state splits, and the person gives in to unconscious desires. During this stage, a fugue state usually occurs.

(25)   (B) Conversion.

This is a defense mechanism in which people repress innate urges that are then involuntarily expressed in the form of bodily functions.

(26)   (C) Conflict theory.

The conflict theory of human behavior states that people always see themselves in competition with others for scarce resources. All social change is driven by conflict.

(27)   (B) Bad financial or professional record.

A bad financial or professional record is not a risk factor that can point to an affinity for physical, sexual, psychological or emotional abuse.

(28)   (D) Sports or extracurricular activities.

There are three kinds of neglect: physical (a child is denied food, clothing, etc.), emotional (a child is denied affection, comfort, etc.) and medical (a child is denied access to medical attention). Sports or extracurricular activities are not a form of neglect.

(29)   (A) Homicide or assault.

When someone says that they have been abused, homicide or assault is not a typical risk. It can happen in fringe cases, but it is usually rare.

(30)   (C) One member is blamed for any problems that the family may have.

In a dysfunctional family, one member may be assigned the role of the scapegoat and always be blamed for anything that goes wrong. This is not a healthy family dynamic.

(31)   (A) *Diagnostic & Statistical Manual for Mental Disorders (DSM-5)*.

The *Diagnostic & Statistical Manual for Mental Disorders, Edition 5* is a taxonomic and diagnostic tool published by the American Psychiatric Association. It is the ideal tool for differentiating normal from abnormal behavior.

(32) (B) Affinity to self-destructive behaviors.

Those who have been subjected to sexual abuse feel shame and guilt. They also tend to display self-destructive behavior patterns, such as substance abuse.

(33) (A) Extent and duration of the abuse.

The extent and duration of the abuse is one of the major factors that can affect the life of the abused, as well as family dynamics.

(34) (C) Sexual orientation and gender identity.

A person's sexual orientation and gender identity are not risk factors that can result in substance abuse.

(35) (A) Self-medication model.

The self-medication model of addiction behavior theorizes that substance abuse relieves the addict's physical or emotional discomfort. Thus, self-medication is reinforced by symptom relief.

(36) (D) Cocaine.

Dilated pupils, irritability, excessive hyperactivity, abstention from meals, etc., are all the classic symptoms of cocaine use.

(37)   (C) Coming out as homosexual.

Coming out as homosexual is not a sign of substance abuse.

(38)   (A) Standard American English.

Usually, White (Caucasian) American families and individuals use Standard American English.

(39)   (B) The person tries out substance use to discover him or herself.

While LGBTQ+ youth are at risk for developing substance abuse issues, it is not a concrete step they need to follow on the path to self-discovery and acceptance.

(40)   (A) An increased mistrust of similar people.

Discrimination can cause negative experiences that can result in trauma, but that does not result in a mistrust of those in similar situations.

(41)   (C) An adult male who drives recklessly.

Driving recklessly is a dangerous risk-taking behavior and is not normal. It can be a by-product of a self-destructive tendency.

(42)   (B) Cohesion.

Cohesion is not an example of a helpful technique that a social worker can use with a client in the context of a social work interview process.

(43)   (A) History of education and work.

A history of the client's education and work experience is not included in the biopsychosocial history, but it is in the social section.

(44)   (C) Social section.

The client's legal history is a pertinent addition to the social section of the biopsychosocial history. It can provide valuable context and information.

(45)   (D) None of the above.

All of the other answer options are actual criteria and parameters used in the MBTI test. They measure general attitude, perception and process style, respectively.

(46)   (D) 21.

The Beck Depression Inventory is a psychometric test used to assess the severity of depression. It consists of a total of 21 statements and questions.

(47)   (C) An ability to regulate impulses.

An ability to regulate impulses is part of the section on defenses and coping mechanisms, not on the strength and weakness assessment. It is a reliable way to assess clients.

(48)   (B) Interpersonal skills.

Empathy and a sense of security are all aspects of interpersonal skills. These points feature under this subsection of the strength and weakness assessment.

(49)   (A) A child custody battle.

Child custody is an inherently adversarial process, and the separating couple cannot be counted on to have objective opinions. In this situation, the social worker needs collateral sources of information.

(50)   (B) Universalization.

Universalization is a useful technique in which the social worker generalizes the client's behavior or experiences. This reassures the person that his or her experiences and feelings are valid.

(51)   (C) To serve the best interests of the client.

The goal of any process conducted in the realm of social work is to serve the best interests of the client. This is especially true in the context of interviews.

(52) (A) Financial or tax benefits for the client.

Social work interviews are not conducted with the goal of providing financial or tax benefits to the client. The main goal of interviews is to aid in diagnosis, intervention, information and therapy.

(53) (C) Hypertension.

Hypertension is a medical condition, and it is usually included in the physical section of the biopsychosocial history, not in the mental status examination.

(54) (A) Censoring their thoughts before speaking.

Censoring or editing one's thoughts and feelings while talking to a social worker is one of the classic signs of resistance to treatment.

(55) (C) Precontemplation.

In the stage of precontemplation, clients are unaware that they need to make changes to their lives. There is a lot of resistance and less motivation.

(56) (B) The amount of money in the client's bank account.

The amount of money in the person's bank account is not a component of the client's mental status exam.

(57)   (A) Insight.

Insight is the person's ability to predict the consequences of one's own behavior. This allows individuals to make decisions properly.

(58)   (D) She is displaying the classic signs of resistance.

Just forgetting to make payments or delaying payments is not a sign of resistance. But in this case, the client is also wasting time on small talk. She is displaying the classic resistance signs.

(59)   (D) A fulfilling and complete sexual life.

While a good sign in itself, a fulfilling and complete sexual life is not a usual element of the standard social work strength and weakness analysis.

(60)   (B) Complete observer.

As a complete observer, the social worker would be removed from any and all activity. He or she would purely observe the proceedings.

(61)   (C) Zyprexa.

Zyprexa is an example of an *atypical* antipsychotic drug, one that is designed to affect the serotonergic system instead of the dopaminergic.

(62) (B) Lithium.

Lithium is a mood stabilizer that can treat the symptoms of bipolar disorder. However, it can be extremely toxic and dangerous if it is over-consumed.

(63) (A) SSRIs are more selective toward the neurotransmitters they interact with.

Most physicians prefer SSRI antidepressants because they can be used to interact specifically with certain neurotransmitters.

(64) (D) Zoloft.

Zoloft is the brand name for the drug sertraline, which is a powerful and popular SSRI antidepressant. It is not a monoamine oxidase inhibitor.

(65) (D) Xanax and Ativan.

Xanax and Ativan are antianxiety drugs, and they are very commonly abused. They are also very dangerous if they are consumed with alcohol.

(66) (C) Acamprosate.

Acamprosate, also known as Camprosal, is a medication that can be used to treat alcohol use disorder.

(67)   (C) Phenelzine hydrazine.

Phenelzine hydrazine is a tricyclic antidepressant, which works by affecting the dopamine neurotransmitter. It is not an antianxiety drug.

(68)   (B) Antimanic serotonin level-stabilizing agents.

Antimanic serotonin level-stabilizing agents are not a category of antidepressants. There are three main categories of antidepressants—SSRIs, MAOIs and tricyclics. There is also an additional class of antidepressants, atypicals.

(69)   (A) Tofranil.

Tofranil is a tricyclic antidepressant, not a selective serotonin reuptake inhibitor.

(70)   (C) Dextrostat and Dexedrine.

Dextrostat is an enantiomer of amphetamine that can act as a stimulant, making it the drug of choice for treating hyperactivity disorder. Dexedrine is another name for the same enantiomer of amphetamine, also known as dextroamphetamine.

(71)   (A) An interest in or curiosity about sex in someone who is young.

Most young people have an interest in or curiosity about sex and sexual matters. This in itself cannot be said to be a sign that they have been sexually abused.

(72)   (A) A very low sense of empathy toward other people.

A low sense of empathy about other people is one of the indicators of psychological abuse. It is not a very strong indicator of physical abuse.

(73)   (C) Engaging in risky, dangerous and self-destructive behavior.

People who have been psychologically abused tend to engage in dangerous and risky behavior, which can be detrimental to their safety. For example, they may start binge drinking, driving recklessly, etc.

(74)   (D) A past history of violence.

A person who has engaged in an act of violence toward others in the past is likely to do so again. This is especially true for offenders who were minors at the time of the assault.

(75)   (B) A violent youth involved in gangs.

A history of violence or a criminal youth can be said to be a predictor of violence or crime. However, it is not necessarily a risk factor for suicide.

(76)   (D) An attempted suicide.

If a person attempted suicide in the past, then this is the most likely indicator of suicidal or self-harm behavior later.

(77)   (B) A tendency to lash out.

A tendency to lash out at others can be a sign of many underlying problems. But it is not necessarily an indicator of traumatic stress.

(78)   (C) Client's blood sugar level.

The client's blood sugar level is an example of medical information. It is usually part of the Objective (O) section of the SOAP plan, not the Subjective section.

(79)   (A) Descriptive assessment of the client.

A descriptive assessment of the client is part of the Assessment section of the SOAP plan. The social worker combines all of the subjective and objective data into a short, precise and descriptive assessment of the client.

(80)   (B) Specific, Measurable, Achievable, Relevant and Time-Specific.

SMART stands for Specific, Measurable, Achievable, Relevant and Time-Specific—all of which are properties that intervention plan objectives need to have.

(81)   (D) None of the above.

In the context of social work interviews, generic questions without a specific purpose are not recommended. Specific inquiries are required for the different situations.

(82)   (A) Screaming at clients so that they can snap out of their reverie.

Screaming at clients is never a good technique to use, especially in social work interviews.

(83)   (C) Social.

The marital and relationship history is usually included in the social section of the client's biopsychosocial history.

(84)   (D) Thematic Apperception Test.

The Thematic Apperception Test (TAT) is a projective test consisting of ambiguous pictures. Clients are required to make up stories using the images.

(85)   (B) Fifth edition.

The Wechsler Intelligence Scale for Children is a simple intelligence measuring scale test, which is currently in its fifth edition.

(86)   (A) 16.

In the Minnesota Multiphasic Personality Inventory test, there are 550 statements in total, of which 16 are repeated over the test.

(87)   (D) Always true.

Silence is one of the most powerful tools in the social worker's inventory. Cutting across all cultural backgrounds and experiences, it is a very powerful type of nonverbal communication.

(88)   (B) Tendency to be hostile and angry.

A tendency to be hostile and angry is actually a temperamental weakness, not an example of a temperamental strength factor.

(89)   (C) An ability to construct, develop and maintain healthy relationships with others.

An ability to construct, develop and maintain healthy relationships with others is one of the strengths included in the interpersonal skills section.

(90)   (B) Thioridazine.

Thioridazine is a typical antipsychotic, which directly affects the dopamine receptors in the brain.

(91)   (A) Carbatrol.

Carbamazepine, sold under the brand name Carbatrol, is a popular drug that can be used to treat bipolar disorder. It can also treat epilepsy and neuropathic pain.

(92)   (D) Zoloft.

Sertraline, sold under the brand name Zoloft, is one of the most popular SSRI antidepressant medications available worldwide. It has no long-term side effects on brain function.

(93)   (B) If clients are young people who have social anxiety.

Communication methods like texting, emails, etc., are best used with young clients. In this context, a young person with social anxiety is best communicated with by using texting.

(94)   (D) Culturally inappropriate and humorous.

While being humorous is a great idea, being culturally inappropriate and insensitive is absolutely not allowed. All social work communication needs to be appropriate.

(95)   (B) Maintaining eye contact, making relevant comments, etc., to show clients that they are being listened to.

Active listening is a very simple technique in which clients are shown that they are being listened to by maintaining eye contact, making relevant comments, etc.

(96)   (B) One-to-one feedback.

One-to-one is a feedback method in which clients give their feedback about service delivery directly to the social worker in question.

(97)   (C) 360° feedback.

360° feedback is one of the most effective forms of feedback, in which social workers seek feedback from the entire community they are involved in.

(98)   (D) Always false.

Social workers are required to suspend all judgments while talking to their clients.

(99)   (A) Positive regard.

Positive regard is a method in which clients are shown that they are worthy of care and assistance. This can be done via respect and nonverbal communication.

(100) (A) At the beginning of the conversation.

There is no point in summarizing a conversation that has not happened yet. Summarization should be done in the middle, the end or before the next conversation.

(101) (D) Helps to calm the client.

Empathetic communication can help to establish a relationship of trust between the social worker and the client. However, it does not always help to calm the client.

(102) (B) Empathetic communication.

Empathetic communication is one of the best ways to work with someone who resorts to anger and violence as a coping mechanism for his or her own frustrations.

(103) (C) The promotion of self-determination.

In the context of social work and therapy, it is very important to emphasize to clients the importance of their own self-determination and independence.

(104) (D) The broadcast of private information for academic purposes.

Unless written and informed consent is granted by the client, social workers may not use private information for academic purposes.

(105) (D) Consultative feedback.

Consultative feedback is a type of feedback in which a group of professionals provides feedback to each other. However, the advice and suggestions are not obligatory.

(106) (D) Spontaneous processes.

Spontaneous processes is a term found in thermodynamics, a field from which systems theory derives a lot of its main terminology.

(107) (B) A measure of energy integrated into the system to attain the goals of the system.

In the context of systems theory, throughput is a measure of the resources and energy integrated into the system so that its goals and objectives can be achieved.

(108) (A) When a system becomes specialized in functioning and structure.

In the context of systems theory, differentiation is a process in which the system becomes specialized in terms of function and overall structure. It becomes a highly capable unit.

(109) (C) Albert Bandura.

Canadian-American psychologist Albert Bandura is responsible for developing the social approach to crisis intervention models.

(110) (D) Jean Piaget.

Jean Piaget was a Swiss psychologist best known for developing the cognitive approach to crisis intervention in the context of social work and therapy.

(111) (B) Financial.

In the context of social work intervention processes, social workers do not need to take financial factors solely into account. These are usually subsumed under another sector.

(112) (A) Entropy.

Derived from thermodynamics, entropy is a state of chaos or disorder that is endemic to each and every system. It uses up all of the available energy.

(113) (D) Objective data collection.

Objective data collection is not a separate step outlined in the standard problem-solving model. The collection of objective data will usually fall into assessment.

(114) (C) A client whose mental, cognitive and emotional capacities have been impaired.

A client whose problem-solving capacity has been impaired is referred to as a maladaptive client. Usually, the person's mental, cognitive and emotional capacities have been stifled.

(115) (B) Burrhus Frederic Skinner and Ivan Pavlov.

The behaviorist approach to crisis intervention was developed by two of the greatest minds in the history of the psychological field—B. F. Skinner and Ivan Pavlov.

(116) (D) Running from danger.

Running from danger is an example of the fight-or-flight response in action. It is an example of respondent or involuntary behavior. Operant behavior is voluntary and always controlled.

(117)   (C) Binge eating tendencies.

A tendency to binge eat is an example of a compulsive behavior, and behavioral modification can be extremely helpful with tackling this kind of crisis.

(118)   (B) Aaron T. Beck.

Although many academicians and physicians are responsible for the early development of CBT, Aaron T. Beck is credited with formalizing the treatment process.

(119)   (A) Depends on physician.

Cognitive-behavioral therapy is a form of therapy that is active, collaborative, problem-focused, structured, time limited and goal oriented.

(120)   (C) Macro.

The broadest level of social work intervention that a social worker or a social work agency can indulge in is the macro level. This involves making changes at the very systemic level.

(121)   (B) Meso.

This is the second level of intervention, where the social worker has to interact with large communities and groups. This falls right between the micro and macro levels.

(122) (A) Being in charge of family management and decisions.

This is one of the main roles in a functional and healthy family, and it is usually fulfilled by the adults in the family. In a small nuclear family with two adults and two children, the adults would be responsible.

(123) (C) The resource provider.

In any healthy family dynamic, one or more members may be responsible for providing the family with essential resources, such as shelter, financial security, food, education, etc.

(124) (D) Blend into the background to escape dysfunction.

The lost child in a dysfunctional family attempts to blend into the background or escape in an attempt to stay far away from the dysfunction.

(125) (B) Try to make everybody laugh all the time.

In a dysfunctional family, mascots try to distract themselves and their family members from the dysfunction surrounding them by making everyone laugh. They crack jokes, act out, etc.

(126) (C) Taking out anger on loved ones by yelling at them.

It is not a healthy or constructive form of anger management to take out one's rage and frustration by yelling at loved ones.

(127) (B) Using physical exercise to get over anger.

Using physical exercise as a way to manage one's anger is a very effective technique used by a lot of people. However, it is a part of the relaxation management approach.

(128) (A) Using meditation to sharpen one's senses and calm down.

Meditation is a really effective method of anger management. However, it is part of the relaxation approach, not the cognitive management approach.

(129) (D) Giving clients some punitive ultimatums.

A social worker is more likely to make headway with a mandated client by avoiding any punitive ultimatums.

(130) (B) Criticizing.

Criticizing is not a self-motivation technique. Instead, people should remind themselves why they need a change, forgive themselves and be less self-critical.

(131) (A) Using the allure of financial rewards to motivate the client.

It is not a sustainable idea to use the allure of financial rewards to motivate the client. Instead, clients should be motivated to strive for change from within.

(132) (C) Looking at an inspirational image and internalizing it.

A good way to engage in visualization is to pin up an inspirational picture on the fridge or in the bedroom. This picture will help a client internalize goals.

(133) (D) Accepting payment from the client.

Accepting payment from the client is not an element of the intervention plan.

(134) (C) Oriented toward the social worker.

Behavioral objectives are client-oriented, not oriented toward the social worker's needs.

(135) (B) Secondary prevention strategy.

People who are at risk of developing heart conditions are advised to take baby aspirin regularly. This is an example of secondary prevention strategies.

(136) (A) Primary prevention strategy.

Primary prevention is the first line of defense designed to protect the client from a condition that is ultimately preventable. Immunizations are a good example.

(137) (B) Confrontation.

Confrontation may be an element of mourning or remembrance or reconnection. It is not a separate phase of the trauma treatment plan.

(138) (A) Implementing long gaps between the conflict-management sessions.

This is false. Social workers are advised to leave short gaps between conflict-resolution sessions. This increases overall efficiency.

(139) (D) Screenings and MRI examinations.

Screenings and regular MRI examinations are part of secondary prevention strategies, not tertiary ones.

(140) (C) Piaget's family therapy.

Psychologist Jean Piaget was responsible for the cognitive approach to behavioral modification, but he did not contribute to family therapy.

(141) (A) There is a change in the family's overall structure.

A change in the family's overall structure is a second-order change, which is not superficial.

(142) (B) Family homeostasis.

Family homeostasis describes the tendency of family systems to be resistant to change. It is a construct in strategic family therapy, not in Bowenian family therapy.

(143) (B) Older Americans Act (OAA).

The Older Americans Act (OAA) was a 1965 federal law that protects the rights of senior citizens in the United States. It also established the Administration and Agencies of Aging.

(144) (A) Family Educational Rights and Privacy Act (FERPA).

The Family Educational Rights and Privacy Act (FERPA) of 1974 is a federal law that guarantees the privacy of educational records.

(145) (B) 1990.

The Americans with Disabilities Act (ADA) was passed by Congress and the Senate in 1990. It was recommended by the National Council on Disability (NCD) and signed into law by President Bush.

(146) (C) Indian Child Welfare Act (ICWA).

The Indian Child Welfare Act of 1978 is a federal law designed to protect the rights of Native American children who have been abused, displaced or threatened.

(147) (A) Placed in a home that is not indigenous.

The last course of action is to place the displaced child in a foster family or a home that is not indigenous or Native American.

(148) (B) Multiethnic Placement Act (MEPA).

MEPA is a federal law that prohibits child welfare agencies in the United States from discriminating against adoptive and foster parents on the basis of their ethnicity or race.

(149) (C) Obamacare.

The Patient Protection and Affordable Care Act (PPACA) is also known widely as Obamacare because it was passed in 2010 under the presidency of President Barack Obama.

(150) (A) There should be a huge block of text without indents.

This is false. Any written communication between the social worker and the client should be formatted properly, along with appropriate headings.

(151) (A) Epistemological model.

The epistemological model is not a verified model of peer supervision.

(152) (D) Deliberate obfuscations should be made to the client.

This is false. While collaborating with other professionals, the client should be informed about the consultation process with the utmost clarity and transparency.

(153) (D) Opinions and value judgments.

Any case presentation should be completely free of all opinions or value judgments. It is important to maintain fact-based elements.

(154) (D) Better remuneration.

While better funding does accompany multidisciplinary collaboration, better remuneration is not a necessary advantage of it.

(155) (C) Establishing dominance over team members.

It is not the social worker's job to establish dominance over the members of the team. Any team effort is collaborative.

(156) (A) The representation of facts should be long and excessively detailed.

In client reports, it is important to represent the facts in a clear and concise manner. Excessive detailing and bias should be avoided.

(157) (D) None of the above.

Looking up resources, clarifying the referral's need and establishing initial contact are all steps in the client referral process.

(158) (B) Yes, but with certain exceptions.

Social workers should limit client access to their own reports unless not doing so can cause serious harm to the client. All situations should be taken very seriously.

(159) (A) Maintaining a sexual relationship with the client.

A social worker is completely forbidden from engaging in a romantic or sexual relationship with a client.

(160) (C) Privately served.

Social workers do not need to abide by any privately served mandates or orders, such as a cease and desist letter.

(161) (C) Dichotomous thinking.

Dichotomous thinking or looking at events as "black or white" can sorely impede the therapeutic relationship.

(162) (C) Universalism.

Universalism is a flawed way of thinking that considers a universal or fixed norm of behavior and values that people all must adhere to.

(163) (B) Discrimination and systemic barriers.

It is the social worker's job to remove all discrimination and system barriers that someone may face.

(164) (A) Ethnocentricity.

Ethnocentricity is a flawed way of thinking that uses one's culture as the yardstick for other cultures.

(165) (C) Power should be defined as power through sharing.

Social workers need to recognize that power is actually accrued through sharing.

(166) (B) At least one additional language.

While knowing a language is a definite advantage, social workers are not required to speak another language.

(167) (B) A janitorial staff member.

While members of janitorial staff are encouraged to come forward when there are any suspected cases of abuse, they are not mandated to do so.

(168) (C) Respond to the subpoena and claim privilege.

If a social worker is served with a subpoena, the person needs to respond to it and claim privilege. This helps to protect clients' confidentiality.

(169) (A) NASW *Code of Ethics*.

Social workers are mandated to refer to the NASW *Code of Ethics* for any ethical considerations they may have—especially ones regarding client confidentiality.

(170) (C) Immediately contact a superior for specialized advice.

Going to a superior is not a mandatory step in the ethical problem-solving process. The social worker may do so if he or she feels it is necessary.

ASWB Clinical Exam 4

(1) What is the collective name for theories that seek to explain the origins and mechanisms of an individual's personality?

(A)   Personality theories

(B)   Psychodynamic theories

(C)   Psychosexual theories

(D)   None of the above

(2) Which of the following is not a psychosexual stage of development?

(A)   Oral

(B)   Anal

(C)   Haptic

(D)   Phallic

(3) Which of the following is a consequence of fixation during the oral stage of psychosexual development?

(A)   Anal-retentive behavior

(B)   Guilt with respect to sex

(C)   Excessive smoking tendencies

(D)   None of the above

(4) What is the age period during which a child goes through the anal stage of psychosexual development?

(A)   2 to 5 years

(B)   0 to 2 years

(C)   5 to 13 years

(D)   Puberty onward

(5) What is the age period during which a child experiences the latency stage of psychosexual development?

(A)   Puberty onward

(B)   5 years to adolescence

(C)   0 to 2 years

(D)   None of the above

(6) During the age period of three to five years, what stage of psychosexual development do children go through?

(A)   Phallic

(B)   Genital

(C)   Anal

(D)   Oedipal or Electra

(7) Which of the following is not a level of awareness according to Freud?

(A)   Preconscious

(B)   Conscious

(C)   Unconscious

(D)   None of the above

(8) Which component of the human personality is composed entirely of unconscious psychological energy containing the base urges of the flesh?

(A)   Ego

(B)   Id

(C)   Superego

(D)   Syntonic ego

(9) Which of the following is the underlying drive for the personality's id component?

(A)   Pain principle

(B)   Pacifist principle

(C)   Poly perspective principle

(D)   Pleasure principle

(10) Which component of the human personality is responsible for the moral component?

(A) Ego

(B) Superego

(C) Syntonic ego

(D) Dystonic ego

(11) Which of the following options is the underlying drive behind the human ego?

(A) Reality principle

(B) Acceptance principle

(C) Pleasure principle

(D) None of the above

(12) What is the term used to describe the capability of a person's ego to keep up with the demands of the id and the superego?

(A) Ego power

(B) Ego tensile

(C) Ego strength

(D) None of the above

(13) What is behavior called when it is in line with the overall ego?

(A)   Ego syntonic

(B)   Ego dystonic

(C)   Ego agreeable

(D)   Ego conformant

(14) Which of the following is not a main self-object need in the realm of self-psychology?

(A)   Idealization

(B)   Twinship

(C)   Mirroring

(D)   Abject frustration

(15) Who was responsible for the establishment of individual psychology as a field?

(A)   Margaret Mahler

(B)   Alfred Adler

(C)   Jean Piaget

(D)   Sigmund Freud

(16) Which of the following is not a topic that ego psychology addresses?

(A)   The client's behavior in specific situations

(B)   The ego's strengths, called coping abilities

(C)   The client's perception of reality, called reality testing

(D)   The client's ability to dominate peers

(17) Who is responsible for the establishment of the psychosocial stages of development?

(A)   Erik Erikson

(B)   Gustaf Gustafson

(C)   David Davidson

(D)   Arthur Jeffries

(18) How many stages make up the basic theory of psychosocial development?

(A)   Five

(B)   Six

(C)   Seven

(D)   Eight

(19) During which stage of psychosocial development do children start to be more independent in their play and pet projects?

(A)   Autonomy vs. shame

(B)   Initiative vs. guilt

(C)   Industry vs. inferiority

(D)   Latency stage

(20) What is the first stage of psychosocial development?

(A)   Trust vs. mistrust

(B)   Initiative vs. guilt

(C)   Industry vs. inferiority

(D)   Autonomy vs. shame

(21) What is the very last stage of psychosocial development?

(A)   Intimacy vs. isolation

(B)   Generativity vs. stagnation

(C)   Ego identity vs. despair

(D)   Dystonicity

(22) Who is responsible for the development of object relations theory?

(A)   Helene Deutsch

(B)   Margaret S. Mahler

(C)   Jean Piaget

(D)   Benjamin M. Spock

(23) What is the stage of object relations during which a child is aware of his or her parents but has not yet developed a sense of self?

(A)   Normal autism

(B)   Individualizing

(C)   Normal symbiotic

(D)   Practicing

(24) At what age do children go through the rapprochement stage, during which they become close to their mothers?

(A)   2 to 6 months

(B)   24 to 38 months

(C)   15 to 24 months

(D)   5 to 9 months

(25) Margaret Mahler's stage of object constancy in object relations theory was based on _____'s work regarding object permanence.

(A)   Jean Piaget

(B)   Alfred Adler

(C)   Erik Erikson

(D)   Ivan Pavlov and B. F. Skinner

(26) Which of the following is not a physical change that young adults experience?

(A)   Physical maturity

(B)   Sexual maturity

(C)   Nutritional needs for maintenance, not growth

(D)   Menopause

(27) Which of the following is not an interpersonal change usually exhibited by young adults?

(A)   Seeking intimacy and relationships

(B)   Starting a family

(C)   Taking on a role as a grandparent

(D)   Setting career goals

(28) Which of the following is a mental change that elderly adults have to come to terms with?

(A)   Active learning

(B)   Confusion due to dementia

(C)   Acquiring new skills

(D)   Desiring intimacy

(29) During which stage of cognitive development do children start to develop a sense of time?

(A)   Sensorimotor

(B)   Preoperational

(C)   Concrete operations

(D)   Cognitive

(30) During which age does a child engage in the concrete operations stage of cognitive development?

(A)   11 and older

(B)   13 and older

(C)   18 and older

(D)   Between 7 and 11

(31) During which stage of cognitive development do children engage in copycat playing and object retention?

(A)   Sensorimotor

(B)   Preoperational

(C)   Concrete operations

(D)   Formal

(32) Who was responsible for the theory of the stages of cognitive development?

(A)   Jean Picard

(B)   Jean Pinochet

(C)   Jean Poseur

(D)   Jean Piaget

(33) Which of the following is the best explanation for why life expectancy has increased dramatically over the last 100 years?

(A)   Better political leadership

(B)   More scientific awareness

(C)   Better standards of living, hygiene and preventive medicine

(D)   Better income and availability of food

(34) Which of the following factors does not play a role in the physical changes a person undergoes over a lifetime?

(A)   Financial history

(B)   Genetics

(C)   Lifestyle

(D)   Medical history

(35) Who developed the theory of attachment and bonding?

(A)   Edward John M. Bowlby

(B)   James T. Bowlby

(C)   Jack F. Bowlby

(D)   Jerome Bowlby

(36) Which of the following is not a sign of mental growth in young children?

(A)   Vivid imagination

(B)   Sensitivity to the feelings of other people

(C)   Fear of things

(D)   Memory decline

(37) Which of the following is a sign of socioemotional growth in infants and toddlers?

(A)   Mathematics and quantitative abilities

(B)   Trust in others

(C)   Independence and assertiveness

(D)   Advanced and developed sense of self

(38) Which of the following is not a deficiency need, as described by Abraham Maslow in his hierarchy of needs?

(A)   Self-actualization needs

(B)   Social needs

(C)   Survival and basic needs

(D)   Social and esteem needs

(39) Who was responsible for developing the five stages of grief model?

(A)   Elisabeth Ross

(B)   Elizabeth Rossetti

(C)   Elisabeth Kübler-Ross

(D)   Elisabeth Heinrich Ross

(40) Which of the following is not a stage of grief?

(A)   Denial

(B)   Anger

(C)   Depression

(D)   Self-harm and violence

(41) Which of the following is not a stage of the life cycle of the family?

(A)   Pre-marriage

(B)   Celibacy

(C)   Family with young children

(D)   Experiences with family of origin

(42) Which of the following is not an aspect of the family with young children stage of the family life cycle?

(A)   Selecting a partner to marry or settle down with

(B)   Perfecting and adopting the role of the parent

(C)   Helping young children develop successful relationships

(D)   Family of origin realigning to new roles

(43) Which parenting style can be said to be the best one?

(A)   Authoritarian

(B)   Authoritative

(C)   Uninvolved

(D)   Permissive

(44) Which of the following is not likely to cause emotional trauma?

(A)   The abuser was intentionally cruel.

(B)   The event happened without warning.

(C)   The event happened during childhood.

(D)   None of the above.

(45) Which of the following is not a physical symptom of some kind of trauma?

(A)   Insomnia, nightmares and sleep disorders

(B)   Numbness

(C)   Agitation and irritability

(D)   Increase in muscle tension

(46) Which of the following is not a sign of domestic violence?

(A)   Irrational anger and a tendency to lash out

(B)   A suspicious injury and history of injuries

(C)   A controlling, coercive and overly concerned partner

(D)   A tendency to buy things on impulse

(47) Which of the following is not an example of a psychological defense mechanism?

(A)   A 13-year-old child with divorcing parents who keeps getting into trouble at school for misbehaving during class

(B)   A closeted homosexual repeatedly making jokes at the expense of other gay people

(C)   A person whose repressed urges are expressed as hiccups and nervous tics

(D)   A person prone to anger starts to meditate to calm down

(48) Which of the following psychological defense mechanisms is associated with a fugue state?

(A)   Dissociation

(B)   Conversion

(C)   Denial

(D)   None of the above

(49) Which of the following is not a functional family dynamic?

(A)   Connecting with the extended family and community

(B)   Each and every member is a separate individual

(C)   One person is blamed for all the family's problems

(D)   Members spending time with each other

(50) Which of the following is the best predictor of violence or abuse?

(A)   A history of owning and collecting illegal firearms

(B)   A documented psychiatric disorder, such as narcissistic personality disorder

(C)   A case of alleged assault and battery in the past

(D)   A very high score of anger with low empathy

(51) Which of the following options is not a healthy interview technique that social workers can use?

(A)   Universalization

(B)   Clarification

(C)   Interpretation

(D)   Extrapolation

(52) Which of the following is a social work interview technique in which the problem is deliberately and explicitly referred to?

(A)   Confrontation

(B)   Reframing

(C)   Antagonization

(D)   Realizing

(53) Which of the following is not an overall aim of a social work interview?

(A)   Therapeutic

(B)   Antagonistic

(C)   Diagnostic

(D)   Informational

(54) What is the overarching objective for any intervention or interview in the realm of social work?

(A)   To help improve the client's health

(B)   To satisfy the client's needs

(C)   To provide support to the client

(D)   To serve the client's primary interests

(55) When a client tells the social worker that she feels incapable and incompetent while taking care of her new baby, the social worker tells her that almost every new mother experiences baby blues. Then she provides the client with words of reassurance. What technique did the social worker use?

(A)   Universalization

(B)   Globalization

(C)   Affirmation and reassurance

(D)   Reframing and relabeling

(56) Which of the following is not included in the biological section of a client's biopsychosocial history?

(A)   Developmental history

(B)   Sexual orientation

(C)   Current list of medications

(D)   Complete medical history

(57) A social worker sees a client who has all the symptoms of emphysema. What should the social worker do?

(A)   Provide the client with the right medication.

(B)   Get the client an appointment with a doctor as soon as possible.

(C)   Provide the client with alternative medicine options.

(D)   None of the above.

(58) Which of the following is included in the social section of the client's biopsychosocial history?

(A) History of psychiatric illnesses

(B) Family history of medical conditions

(C) History of the family of origin

(D) Mental status

(59) Which of the following is an appropriate situation for using collateral to glean information?

(A) A child who has been sexually abused

(B) A child custody case with a divorcing couple

(C) A teenager with a case of depressive disorder

(D) None of the above

(60) What is a social work information-gathering technique in which multiple sources are used at the same time?

(A) Source collation

(B) Quadrilation

(C) Triangulation

(D) None of the above

(61) Which psychometric test is used to gauge the severity of an individual's depression?

(A)   Beck Depression Checklist

(B)   Beck Depression Inventory

(C)   Beck Depression Test

(D)   Beck Depressive Outline

(62) Which of the following is not an aspect used by the Myers-Briggs Personality Type Indicator?

(A)   General attitude – extraversion or introversion

(B)   Perception style – sensing or intuiting

(C)   Processing style – thinking or feeling

(D)   Empathy – high or low

(63) How many question statements are in the Minnesota Multiphasic Personality Inventory?

(A)   >500

(B)   <500

(C)   600

(D)   No more than 400

(64) What is not a factor that social workers should use while assessing a client's communication skills?

(A)   Trauma and experiences

(B)   Medication

(C)   Cultural background

(D)   Silence and nonverbal communication

(65) Which of the following is not a professional position as an observer?

(A)   Participant, but as a judge

(B)   Pure observer

(C)   Pure participant

(D)   Observer, as a participant

(66) Which social observation role is completely removed from activity?

(A)   Observer, as a participant

(B)   Participant, as an observer

(C)   Pure or complete observer

(D)   Pure or complete participant

(67) Which of the following is not a strength that falls under the defense mechanism category?

(A)   A belief in justice

(B)   An ability to cope with stressors

(C)   An ability to soothe oneself

(D)   An ability to control impulses

(68) Which of the following is not a temperamental factor in the strength and weakness test?

(A)   A good sense of humor

(B)   An ability to grieve in a healthy way

(C)   An ability to receive and use feedback

(D)   A sense of confidence and optimism

(69) Which of the following is not an interpersonal skill?

(A)   A sense of security

(B)   A large capacity for empathy

(C)   Standard intellectual and problem-solving abilities

(D)   An ability to confide in other people

(70) Which of the following is not an element included in the strength and weakness assessment?

(A)   Food habits

(B)   Supportive circle of loved ones

(C)   Proper source of income

(D)   Membership of societal institutions

(71) A client is exhibiting a lack of motivation and is resistant to treatment. Which stage of motivation is this person in?

(A)   Contemplation

(B)   Resistance

(C)   Precontemplation

(D)   Informal thoughts

(72) What should a social worker not do in order to establish a rapport with a client?

(A)   Keep conversations formal

(B)   Keep the client engaged in discussions

(C)   Recognize the client's thoughts and feelings

(D)   Acknowledge the client's fears and concerns

(73) Which of the following behaviors is not an example of resistance?

(A)   A client who fixates on past issues instead of present problems

(B)   A client who shows up to appointments regularly

(C)   A client who is reticent about providing information

(D)   A client who constantly flatters the social worker

(74) Which of the following is not a primary component of the mental status exam?

(A)   The client's pattern and tone of speech

(B)   The client's basic thinking style

(C)   The client's relationship status

(D)   The client's grooming and dress

(75) What is the term used to describe clients' ability to understand the consequences of their behavior?

(A)   Intellectual function

(B)   Insight

(C)   Orientation

(D)   Thought processes

(76)   Which of the following is not a typical antipsychotic drug?

(A)   Haloperidol or Haldol

(B)   Moban or Molindone

(C)   Navane or Thiothixene

(D)   Depakene

(77) What adverse effects can an overdose of lithium have on a person?

(A)   Psychosis and mental issues

(B)   Impacts on the renal and thyroid functions

(C)   Digestive issues and body odor

(D)   Cancer of the lymphatic system

(78) Which of the following is not a mood stabilizer drug?

(A)   Amphetamine salts

(B)   Lamictal

(C)   Tegretol

(D)   Topamax

(79) Why have doctors stopped prescribing tricyclic antidepressants lately?

(A)   They can cause chemical dependence.

(B)   They can adversely alter brain chemistry.

(C)   They cause cardiovascular and CNS instability.

(D)   They are not reliable.

(80) Which of the following antidepressant drugs is not an MAOI antidepressant?

(A)   Nardil

(B)   Parnate

(C)   Marplan

(D)   Elavil

(81) Which of the following drugs is very commonly abused and can result in dangerous side effects if overused?

(A)   Remeron

(B)   Dextrostat

(C)   Vicodin or hydrocodone

(D)   Haldol

(82) What is the brand name under which the drug alprazolam is sold in the United States?

(A)   Abilify

(B)   Thorazine

(C)   Xanax

(D)   Lamictal

(83) What is the difference between a typical antipsychotic and an atypical antipsychotic?

(A)   One affects the brain, and the other affects the CNS.

(B)   One has side effects, and the other has no side effects.

(C)   One affects the dopamine receptors, and the other affects the serotonin receptors.

(D)   One is easier to produce, and the other is difficult.

(84) Which of the following is a side effect of haloperidol, also known as Haldol?

(A)   Xerostomia

(B)   Cardiac arrhythmia

(C)   Diaphoresis

(D)   Excessive coughing

(85) A decrease in sexual desire and impotence are side effects of which popular SSRI antidepressant?

(A)   Lexapro

(B)   Celexa

(C)   Zoloft

(D)   Amphetamine salts

(86) Which of the following is ~~not~~ *not* an indicator of psychological abuse?

(A)   Very little sense of empathy toward others

(B)   Excessive eye contact and a balanced outlook

(C)   Relating to others in a flat or superficial way

(D)   Engaging in risky and destructive behaviors

(87) Which of the following is not a risk factor for suicide?

(A)   A tendency to be aggressive

(B)   A previous attempt at suicide

(C)   A family history of suicide

(D)   Struggles with substance abuse

(88) Which of the following is not an indicator of traumatic stress and violence?

(A)   A sustained job and finances

(B)   Repeated thoughts of suicide and self-harm

(C)   Eating disorders and poor eating habits

(D)   Paranoia of people, places, etc.

X (89) Which of the following is a trait that social workers ~~need to~~ exhibit in their communication?

should not
_is 50_

(A)   Empathy

o (B)   Condescension

(C)   Positive regard

(D)   Suspension of judgments

(90) Which of the following is neither a verbal nor nonverbal communication method?

(A)   Interrupting while speaking

(B)   Silence

(C)   Active listening

(D)   Paraphrasing and clarifying

(91) Which of the following is a form of feedback in which the social worker consults superiors, clients, peers, subordinates and the entire community?

(A)   Consultative feedback

(B)   Commensurate feedback

(C)   Holistic feedback

(D)   360° feedback

(92) Which of the following options is not a dimension in most biopsychosocial models of intervention?

(A)   Spiritual

(B)   Social

(C)   Psychiatric

(D)   Biological and medical

(93) Which of the following is a term used to describe the steady state of a system? In this state, all the values of the system grow at constant rates.

(A)   Homeopathis

(B)   Homeostatis

(C)   Homogeneous

(D)   Homeostasis

(94) Which term, borrowed from thermodynamics, describes a system that can exchange resources and information with others?

(A)   Adiabatic system

(B)   Open system

(C)   Free border system

(D)   None of the above

(95) Which of the following is the first step in the problem-solving process?

(A)   Engagement

(B)   Contact

(C)   Intervention

(D)   None of the above

(96) Which term describes when a client's problem-solving capacity has been impaired?

(A)   Malappropriation

(B)   Maladaptive

(C)   Malcontent

(D)   Maldirection

(97) Who, along with Burrhus Frederic Skinner, was responsible for the development of the behaviorist school of thought in crisis psychology?

(A)   Ivan Chekhov

(B)   Abraham Maslow

(C)   Ivan Pavlov

(D)   None of the above

(98) Who was responsible for developing the humanistic approach to crisis intervention?

(A)   Abraham Marlowe

(B)   Margaret Mahler

(C)   B. F. Skinner

(D)   Abraham Maslow

(99) Which of the following is not an example of operant behavior?

(A)   Talking to someone on the phone

(B)   Being sexually aroused while being intimate with a partner

(C)   Playing rugby with classmates

(D)   Drinking a glass of water

(100) Which of the following traits is not expected from cognitive-behavioral therapy?

(A)   Active

(B)   Collaborative

(C)   Time-limited

(D)   Unstructured and random

(101) Which of the following is not a phase in the three-phase model that is used while working with clients who have been traumatized?

(A)   Safety and stabilization

(B)   Mourning and remembrance

(C)   Therapy and assistance

(D)   Reconnection and reintegration

(102) Which of the following is not a step in conflict management?

(A)   Acknowledgment of conflict

(B)   Assessment of conflict

(C)   Selection of strategy

(D)   A complete stop in communication

(103) Which interaction-structuring technique can help in resolving conflicts?

(A)   Increasing the time between sessions

(B)   Limiting the scope of discussion

(C)   Increasing the amount of contact outside discussions

(D)   Not using third-party mediators

(104) What kind of prevention strategy is an immunization booster shot against COVID-19?

(A)   Primary

(B)   Secondary

(C)   Tertiary

(D)   Quaternary

(105) Wearing a seat belt while driving and using a helmet while riding a motorcycle are examples of what kind of prevention?

(A)   Primary

(B)   Secondary

(C)   Tertiary

(D)   Quaternary

(106) What is the goal of secondary prevention strategies?

(A)   Avoid unwanted diseases, injuries, etc.

(B)   Limit the long-term impact of disease, injury, etc.

(C)   Mitigate the costs of disease, injury, etc.

(D)   Provide long-term care

(107) Which of the following is not an important element of behavioral objectives?

(A)   Client-oriented

(B)   Clear and easy to understand

(C)   Abstract

(D)   Contains the desired behavior

(108) Why do doctors recommend elderly patients take baby aspirin pills on a daily basis?

(A)   Aspirin increases blood flow.

(B)   Aspirin improves heart health.

(C)   Aspirin decreases the heart's muscle fiber density.

(D)   Aspirin slows down blood clotting.

(109) Can secondary strategies be put into place even if clients are asymptomatic?

(A)   Yes, because prevention is better than a cure.

(B)   No, because symptoms alone betray a risk of disease.

(C)   Yes, because it is put in place once the disease, injury, etc., has already occurred.

(D)   None of the above

(110) What is the first step of the intervention process?

(A)   Developing a plan

(B)   Engaging with the client

(C)   Performing a strength and weakness assessment

(D)   Applying and evaluating the plan

(111) What is the very last step of the intervention process?

(A)   Anticipating any future needs

(B)   Providing evaluation and feedback

(C)   Applying the intervention

(D)   None of the above

(112) Which of the following is not a motivation technique?

(A)   Slapping the client

(B)   Identifying and addressing barriers

(C)   Explaining why change is important

(D)   Preventing a relapse

(113) Which of the following is a constructive self-motivation technique?

(A)   Checking progress

(B)   Visualizing goals

(C)   Punishing

(D)   None of the above

(114) Which of the following is not a tried and tested approach to mandated or involuntary clients?

(A)   Simply listening to the clients' experiences

(B)   Elaborating on a client's personality

(C)   Engaging in clear communication

(D)   None of the above

(115) Which of the following approaches does not fall into the cognitive approach to anger management?

(A) Slowing down speech when angry

(B) Using logic to balance the approach

(C) Not jumping to "all-or-nothing" conclusions

(D) Focusing on goals and problems to solve

(116) Which of the following approaches does not fall into the relaxation approach to anger management?

(A) Doing cardio exercises at the gym

(B) Participating in guided meditation sessions

(C) Walking away from tense situations

(D) Deep breathing and Lamaze

(117) Which of the following is a healthy way to deal with anger?

(A) Punching the wall

(B) Getting defensive and berating others

(C) Making crass jokes at the expense of others

(D) Avoiding people who aggravate you

(118) Which of the following is not a type of family therapy?

(A)   Strategic family therapy

(B)   Structural family therapy

(C)   Freudian family therapy

(D)   Bowenian family therapy

(119) Which of the following terms is a concept used in Bowenian family therapy?

(A)   Multigenerational transgression

(B)   Multigenerational transportation

(C)   Societal retardation

(D)   Family projection process

(120) Which of the following is not an intervention technique that can be used in couples therapy?

(A)   Piaget method

(B)   Insight-oriented psychotherapy

(C)   Gottman method

(D)   Behavior modification

(121) What federal institution was established by the Older Americans Act of 1965 to provide supportive services and funds to people over 60?

(A)   Agencies on Aging

(B)   Support for the Elderly

(C)   Administration on Aging

(D)   Department of Aging

(122) When was the Child Abuse Prevention and Treatment Act (CAPTA) passed?

(A)   1902

(B)   1974

(C)   2001

(D)   1969

(123) How does CAPTA prevent the neglect and abuse of children?

(A)   It provides federal funding to states to prevent, assess, investigate, treat and prosecute all cases of child abuse.

(B)   It provides states with information about suspected abuse cases.

(C)   It established CPS, which is responsible for assessing cases of child abuse.

(D)   None of the above.

(124) When was the Family Educational Rights and Privacy Act (FERPA) passed?

(A)   1969

(B)   1972

(C)   1980

(D)   1974

(125) What age group of affected children does the Education for Handicapped Children Act (EHCA) provide Individual Educational Plans for?

(A)   5 to 18 years

(B)   3 to 18 years

(C)   3 to 21 years

(D)   7 to 18 years

(126) Which federal law enacted in 1978 gives tribal leadership exclusive jurisdiction over children who are residents of a reservation?

(A)   Indian Child Welcoming Act

(B)   Indian Child Wellness Act

(C)   Indian Child Welfare Act

(D)   None of the above

(127) Which of the following is not a step specified in the ICWA?

(A)   Verify the child's ethnic or tribal identity.

(B)   Allow for presumptive tribal jurisdiction.

(C)   Place the child with a family member.

(D)   Contact CPS and place the child with foster parents.

(128) Which of the following federal health-care laws is also known as Obamacare?

(A)   Family & Medical Leave Act

(B)   Affordable Care Act

(C)   Medicaid Act

(D)   None of the above

(129) Which federal law provides individuals with full and complete access to all of their medical records and related information?

(A)   HIPPA

(B)   HIPPO

(C)   HIIPA

(D)   HIPAA

(130) Which law requires employers to provide their employees with at least 12 weeks of job-protected and insured leave for family or medical reasons?

(A)   Family and Medical Leave Act

(B)   Medical Leave Act

(C)   Employment Protection Leave Act

(D)   Employment Guarantee

(131) When was the No Child Left Behind Act passed?

(A)   1999

(B)   2000

(C)   2001

(D)   2002

(132) Which of the following is not a trait that needs to be exhibited in any written communication between a social worker and a client?

(A)   Culturally appropriate

(B)   Short and concise

(C)   Confidential

(D)   Guesswork and assumptions

(133) True or false: Social work reports should contain only objective opinions.

(A)   True

(B)   False

(C)   True, but with exceptions

(D)   False, but with exceptions

(134) True or false: The Violence Against Women Act (VAWA) was enacted in 1980.

(A)   True

(B)   False

(C)   This law does not exist

(D)   None of the above

(135) True or false: Social workers' use of supervision is not included in their evaluations.

(A)   True, because this is a subjective area.

(B)   False, because this is a necessary criterion.

(C)   True, but it is included in the appendices.

(D)   False, because it is confidential.

(136) Which of the following is not a standard case management activity in social work?

(A)   Assessment

(B)   Termination of services

(C)   Monitoring

(D)   Advocacy

(137) True or false: An illusion of unanimity is one of the main causes of groupthink.

(A)   True

(B)   False

(C)   It depends on the group

(D)   Only in some cases

(138) True or false: Teamwork can always lead to group polarization.

(A)   True

(B)   False

(C)   It depends on the type of team

(D)   Only in some cases

(139) What term describes self-appointed members of the group who protect leaders and other members from information contradictory to their point of view?

(A)   Guards

(B)   View guards

(C)   Mindguards

(D)   None of the above

(140) When group members do not heed warnings and fail to reconsider assumptions, what is it called?

(A)   Groupthink

(B)   Lemming behavior

(C)   Risky behavior

(D)   Collective rationalization

(141) True or false: The size of a group can affect group cohesion.

(A)   True

(B)   False

(C)   Insufficient information

(D)   Only sometimes

(142) Which of the following is not a factor that can affect the cohesion of the group?

(A)   Homogeneity

(B)   Level of participation

(C)   Stability of members

(D)   Background of the members

(143) True or false: Groups can provide members with a sense of hope in some cases.

(A)   True

(B)   False

(C)   It depends on the type of group

(D)   Only in some cases

(144) True or false: Groups provide a sense of corporeality to members.

(A)   True

(B)   False

(C)   Cannot say for sure

(D)   Only in some cases

(145) Which stage of group processes is also called storming?

(A)　Preaffiliation

(B)　Power and control

(C)　Separation

(D)　None of the above

(146) Which of the following is not a stage of group processes?

(A)　Forming

(B)　Norming

(C)　Terraforming

(D)　Performing

(147) True or false: Adjourning is the first stage of group development.

(A)　True

(B)　False

(C)　It depends on the type of group

(D)　In some cases

(148) What is the basis of the Gottman method in couples therapy?

(A)   Members of the couple know each other's worries and stresses.

(B)   Members of the couple need time away from one another.

(C)   Couples need to be studied.

(D)   Couples need to modify behaviors.

(149) True or false: The main goal of advocacy is to obtain public support for policies.

(A)   True

(B)   False

(C)   It depends on the policy

(D)   It depends on the kind of advocacy

(150) Which of the following is not a stage that indicates readiness to change?

(A)   Precontemplation

(B)   Contemplation

(C)   Preparation

(D)   Protective maintenance

(151) Which of the following is a value that can inhibit the therapeutic relationship between a social worker and client?

(A)   Dichotomous thinking

(B)   Expressiveness

(C)   Understanding of cultural norms

(D)   Good sense of humor

(152) True or false: There is only one acceptable norm of behavior and morals.

(A)   True

(B)   False

(C)   In specific cases

(D)   It depends on culture

(153) True or false: The importance of human relationships is an important ethos for a social worker.

(A)   True

(B)   False

(C)   In specific cases

(D)   It depends on the type of relationships

(154) Which of these is not a core value of social work practice?

(A)   Integrity

(B)   Competence

(C)   Institutional power

(D)   Service

(155) In which situation would disclosure of information about clients be permissible?

(A)   Imminent threat of service termination

(B)   Legal issue faced by social worker

(C)   Imminent harm to the client or an identifiable person

(D)   No situation

(156) What should a social worker do if served with a subpoena?

(A)   Ignore it.

(B)   Challenge it.

(C)   Divulge information.

(D)   Respond and claim privilege.

(157) Which of the following professionals are mandated reporters?

(A)   Journalists

(B)   Law enforcement officers

(C)   Museum curators

(D)   Bankers

(158) True or false: Statutory is an example of a legal mandate.

(A)   True

(B)   False

(C)   In specific cases

(D)   This used to be true but isn't any longer

(159) What is the last step of ethical problem-solving?

(A)   Suggest systemic modifications.

(B)   Review the *Code of Ethics*.

(C)   Report the dilemma to superiors.

(D)   Monitor for new ethical issues.

(160) Which of the following is not an example of a dual relationship?

(A)   A client is the social worker's cousin.

(B)   A client is the social worker's home contractor.

(C)   A client is a member of the social worker's congregation.

(D)   A client is the social worker's friend.

(161) True or false: Videotaping client sessions always requires written consent.

(A)   True

(B)   False

(C)   In specific cases

(D)   It depends on the client's age

(162) Which of the following is not a step in the client referral process?

(A)   Looking up resources

(B)   Transferring payment

(C)   Initial contact phase

(D)   Follow-ups

(163) True or false: All social work intervention decisions have to be written.

(A)   True

(B)   False

(C)   In specific cases

(D)   It depends on the kind of intervention

(164) True or false: The client's educational history is seldom included in the case presentation.

(A)   True

(B)   False

(C)   In specific cases

(D)   It depends on the level of education

(165) Which of the following is not a model of peer supervision?

(A)   Role-centered model

(B)   Psychodynamic model

(C)   Developmental model

(D)   Cognitive model

(166) Which of the following is not a social risk factor for substance abuse?

(A)   Drugs and alcohol are easy to access.

(B)   There is a low tolerance for stress.

(C)   Peers use drugs and alcohol regularly.

(D)   Existing social norms allow substance abuse.

(167) Which of the following is not a behavioral risk factor for substance abuse?

(A)   A history of aggressive behavior

(B)   Academic problems due to behavior

(C)   Substandard interpersonal relationships

(D)   Presence of family trauma

(168) True or false: The medical model is the most widely accepted theory of addiction.

(A)   True

(B)   False

(C)   In specific cases

(D)   It used to be true but isn't any longer

(169) Which of the following is not a sign of substance abuse?

(A)   Substance abuse that results in financial trouble

(B)   Psychological issues like paranoia, hysteria, etc.

(C)   Sudden change in attitudes toward family

(D)   Neglect of other responsibilities

(170) True or false: Inappropriate laughter and extreme sleepiness are signs of heroin abuse.

(A)   True

(B)   False

(C)   In specific cases

(D)   This used to be believed to be true but isn't any longer.

Answers to Exam 4

(1) (B) Psychodynamic theories.

Theories that aim to uncover the origin of human personalities are referred to as psychodynamic theories.

(2) (C) Haptic.

According to Sigmund Freud, the five stages of psychosexual development are oral, anal, phallic, latency and genital. Haptic is not one of these stages.

(3) (C) Excessive smoking tendencies.

Those who have a fixation during the oral stage of psychosexual development tend to indulge in excessive smoking. Some also tend to overeat or binge eat.

(4) (A) 2 to 5 years.

The anal stage occurs during the age period of two to five years.

(5) (B) 5 years to adolescence.

During the period between five years of age and adolescence, a child's sexuality lies latent or dormant.

(6)   (A) Phallic.

During the age period of three to five years, a child goes through the phallic development stage.

(7)   (D) None of the above.

According to Freud, the three levels of awareness can be classified into the preconscious, conscious and unconscious.

(8)   (B) Id.

The id is the component of personality that contains all of the unconscious base desires of the human: sex, survival, aggression, etc.

(9)   (D) Pleasure principle.

The pleasure principle is the underlying drive behind the human personality. It states that all humans want more pleasure and act in order to avoid pain.

(10)   (B) Superego.

The superego is responsible for all moral decisions. It contains all of the moral standards imparted by guiding figures.

(11)   (A) Reality principle.

The reality principle is the underlying drive behind a person's ego. It is the knowledge that all impulses have to be delayed to meet the demands and needs of the real world.

(12)   (C) Ego strength.

Ego strength is the ability of a person's ego to deal with all of the demands of the id and superego.

(13)   (A) Ego syntonic.

Ego syntonicity describes an individual's behavior that is in line with the overall ego.

(14)   (D) Abject frustration.

According to self-psychology, the three main self-object needs of a child are idealization, twinship and mirroring. Abject frustration is not one of these self-object needs.

(15)   (B) Alfred Adler.

Alfred Adler was one of Freud's contemporaries who broke away from him to establish the theory of individual psychology.

(16)　(D) The client's ability to dominate peers.

Ego psychology addresses whether clients can relate to their peers, not dominate them.

(17)　(A) Erik Erikson.

Erik Erikson was a German-American psychologist who established the psychosocial stages of development. Here, personality is the result of social interactions.

(18)　(D) Eight.

Erikson's theory of psychosocial development is made up of eight specific stages.

(19)　(B) Initiative vs. guilt.

During the initiative vs. guilt stage of the psychosocial stages of development, children start to become more independent during play.

(20)　(A) Trust vs. mistrust.

From the period of birth until 12 months of age, a child goes through a stage of trust vs. mistrust. This is the first stage of psychosocial development.

(21)   (C) Ego identity vs. despair.

The very last stage of the psychosocial stages of development is between ego identity and despair, which happens toward the end of one's life.

(22)   (B) Margaret S. Mahler.

Margaret Mahler was a Hungarian physician and psychoanalyst responsible for developing the theory of object relations.

(23)   (C) Normal symbiotic.

When children are between one and five months of age, they are aware of their parents. However, they do not have a clearly defined sense of self. This is also called normal symbiotic.

(24)   (C) 15 to 24 months.

When children are between the ages of 15 and 24 months, they go through rapprochement. During this time, they become close to their mothers once again.

(25)   (A) Jean Piaget.

Jean Piaget was a famous Swiss psychoanalyst who came up with the concept of object permanence. Mahler incorporated this concept in her seminal object relations theory.

(26)   (D) Menopause.

Menopause is not a stage that young adults go through. Women go through the stage of menopause in their later life, usually starting around the age of 45 and continuing until 55.

(27)   (C) Taking on a role as a grandparent.

Young adults usually do not have to take on a role as grandparents. Their job is to seek intimacy, start a family, work on their career and ensure financial security.

(28)   (B) Confusion due to dementia.

Confusion due to elderly-onset diseases like dementia and Alzheimer's is something that elderly adults have to cope with.

(29)   (B) Preoperational.

During the preoperational stage of cognitive development (between the ages of two and seven years), children start to develop a solid sense of time.

(30)   (D) Between 7 and 11.

Between the ages of seven and 11 years, a child starts to think in abstract terms, play games with rules, understand cause and effect, etc. This is called the concrete operations stage of development.

(31) (A) Sensorimotor.

During the sensorimotor stage of cognitive development, children begin to display object retention. They also engage in a copycat playing phase.

(32) (D) Jean Piaget.

Swiss psychoanalyst Jean Piaget is responsible for laying the groundwork for the cognitive development stages.

(33) (C) Better standards of living, hygiene and preventive medicine.

Life expectancy has increased considerably over the last 100 years owing to the development of preventive medicine (such as vaccines), better standards of living and better hygiene practices.

(34) (A) Financial history.

Financial history is not responsible for any physical changes that a person has to go through during his or her life.

(35) (A) Edward John M. Bowlby.

Edward John M. Bowlby was a British psychologist responsible for developing the theory of attachment and bonding.

(36) (D) Memory decline.

Young children, aged between four and six years, actually show signs of improving memory as they grow older.

(37) (B) Trust in others.

Trust in other people is a basic sign of socioemotional growth in infants and toddlers, aged between birth and three years in general.

(38) (A) Self-actualization needs.

Self-actualization needs are at the top of the Maslow pyramid and are categorized as growth needs. All other answer options are deficiency needs.

(39) (C) Elisabeth Kübler-Ross.

Elisabeth Kübler-Ross was a Swiss-American physician and psychologist responsible for theorizing the five stages of loss and grief, as published in *On Death and Dying*, which is her most renowned work.

(40) (D) Self-harm and violence.

Many people resort to self-harm and violence when they are grieving, but they do not do so as a separate stage of grief. It is usually a part of anger or depression.

(41)   (B) Celibacy.

Celibacy is a choice that many people make, especially due to religious or personal reasons. However, it is not a stage in the life cycle of the family.

(42)   (A) Selecting a partner to marry or settle down with.

Selecting a partner to marry or settle down with is a task in the pre-marriage stage of the family life cycle. It follows directly from the leaving the home stage.

(43)   (B) Authoritative.

Authoritative parenting is generally regarded as the best parenting style. This is because discipline is enforced while children are still given a voice.

(44)   (D) None of the above.

All of the answer options are likely to cause some sort of emotional or psychological trauma in a person.

(45)   (B) Numbness.

Numbness is classified as an emotional and psychological symptom of trauma, not a physical symptom.

(46) (D) A tendency to buy things on impulse.

Impulsive shopping is an unhealthy coping mechanism, but it cannot be classified as a sign or symptom of domestic abuse.

(47) (D) A person prone to anger starts to meditate to calm down.

A person who has anger management issues makes use of these anger management techniques to calm down. This is not a psychological defense mechanism, which is always involuntary. This is a conscious choice.

(48) (A) Dissociation.

The dissociation defense mechanism is associated with a fugue state, which is also referred to as daydreaming.

(49) (C) One person is blamed for all the family's problems.

In a dysfunctional family, one person is routinely blamed for any problems and is made into the scapegoat. This is absent in healthy family dynamics.

(50) (C) A case of alleged assault and battery in the past.

When it comes to violence or abuse, a past history of violence is the best predictor for future instances of abuse. In this case, a case of assault and battery in the past is the best indicator for future violence.

(51)   (D) Extrapolation.

Extrapolation is not a helpful technique in the context of social work interviews. It is better to interpret situations using different behaviors.

(52)   (A) Confrontation.

Confrontation is an effective technique in the context of interviews. The problem is highlighted by deliberately and explicitly calling attention to it.

(53)   (B) Antagonistic.

Social work interviews may never be antagonistic in nature. They are usually a mix of therapeutic, diagnostic and informational.

(54)   (D) To serve the client's primary interests.

The overarching aim in social work is to serve the client's primary interests. As a result, all interviews have to be planned, methodical and well thought out.

(55)   (A) Universalization.

The social worker makes use of the universalization technique. By generalizing the client's behavior and experiences, the social worker validates her feelings.

(56)   (B) Sexual orientation.

While pertinent, this piece of information is not included in the biological section. It is included in the biopsychosocial history's social section.

(57) (B) Get the client an appointment with a doctor as soon as possible.

If the client has symptoms of emphysema, the social worker should talk to the client and schedule a medical appointment as soon as possible.

(58) (C) History of the family of origin.

A complete history of the family of origin would be included in the social section of the biopsychosocial history.

(59) (B) A child custody case with a divorcing couple.

Most child custody cases are inherently adversarial, which is why social workers would need to resort to collateral information sources.

(60) (C) Triangulation.

When social workers gather data from multiple sources to ensure its basic validity and overall authenticity, it is referred to as triangulation.

(61) (B) Beck Depression Inventory.

The Beck Depression Inventory is a psychometric test consisting of 21 questions that can be used to gauge the presence and severity of depression. It was developed by Aaron T. Beck.

(62) (D) Empathy – high or low.

Empathy is not one of the aspects that is judged on the MBTI personality test.

(63) (A) >500.

The Minnesota Multiphasic Personality Inventory consists of 550 statements, of which 16 statements are repeated.

(64) (B) Medication.

A list of medications is sensitive information that social workers use. However, they do not use it to assess clients' overall communication skills.

(65) (A) Participant, but as a judge.

Usually, a social worker who participates in the activity takes on a partial role as an observer or no role at all. However, someone who is a judge will not participate at all.

(66) (C) Pure or complete observer.

A pure or complete observer is one who is usually removed from the entire activity. The person is isolated and is asked to observe without interfering.

(67) (A) A belief in justice.

A belief in justice and goodness is a temperamental factor and cannot be counted as a strength in the defense and coping mechanisms category.

(68)   (C) An ability to receive and use feedback.

An ability to receive and use feedback to improve oneself is a cognitive skill, not a temperamental factor in the strength and weakness test.

(69)   (C) Standard intellectual and problem-solving abilities.

Standard intellectual and problem-solving abilities do not fall under interpersonal skills. In a strength and weakness assessment, this is a cognitive skill.

(70)   (A) Food habits.

Food and dietary habits do not feature in the strength and weakness assessment.

(71)   (C) Precontemplation.

The client is currently in the precontemplation stage, which is why the person is displaying a lack of motivation and resistance to treatment.

(72)   (A) Keep conversations formal.

The best way to establish a rapport with clients is to talk to them in an informal manner. Formal conversations do not help in achieving this goal.

(73)   (B) A client who shows up to appointments regularly.

Showing up to appointments regularly and on time is a good sign and is not an indicator of resistance.

(74)   (C) The client's relationship status.

The client's relationship or marital status is not a factor that is taken into account while conducting a mental status exam.

(75)   (B) Insight.

Insight is the client's ability to predict the consequences of behavior. This allows clients to make sensible decisions and take ownership of their actions.

(76)   (D) Depakene.

Depakene is an antimanic agent and a mood stabilizer, not a typical antipsychotic drug.

(77)   (B) Impacts on the renal and thyroid functions.

An overdose of lithium can have an adverse effect on renal and thyroid functions. Someone who takes lithium needs to get tested on a regular basis.

(78)   (A) Amphetamine salts.

Amphetamine salts are used to help people focus. They are used for people who have ADHD and are not mood stabilizer drugs.

(79) (C) They cause cardiovascular and CNS instability.

Tricyclic antidepressants have a narrow function window, and they can result in cardiovascular and CNS instability. Even small doses can be fatal.

(80) (D) Elavil.

Elavil is a tricyclic antidepressant and is not a good example of an MAOI antidepressant.

(81) (C) Vicodin or hydrocodone.

Hydrocodone paracetamol, known popularly by the brand name Vicodin, is an opioid painkiller that is widely used. However, it can be very addictive.

(82) (C) Xanax.

Xanax is a short-acting tranquilizer for anxiety or sleeping disorders. It is the brand name of the drug alprazolam.

(83) (C) One affects the dopamine receptors, and the other affects the serotonin receptors.

Typical antipsychotic drugs affect the dopaminergic system receptors, while atypical ones affect the serotonergic system receptors.

(84)   (A) Xerostomia.

Xerostomia or dry mouth is one of the most common side effects of Haldol (or haloperidol).

(85)   (B) Celexa.

Celexa, the brand name for citalopram, is an SSRI class antidepressant that can result in decreased sexual drive and impotence.

(86)   (B) Excessive eye contact and a balanced outlook.

People who have been psychologically abused usually have an imbalanced outlook on life. They generally avoid eye contact.

(87)   (A) A tendency to be aggressive.

A tendency toward aggressiveness is not a definite risk factor related to suicide. However, it can be an indicator of many other problems.

(88)   (A) A sustained job and finances.

Someone who has undergone traumatic stress and violence in the past generally does not have a sustained job.

(89)   (B) Condescension.

Social workers are supposed to suspend all value judgments and speak to their clients in an empathetic and kind way. Condescension is very unhelpful.

(90)   (A) Interrupting while speaking.

Interrupting people while they are speaking is not an effective communication method. This can be disruptive and can adversely affect the clients' attitude toward therapy.

(91)   (D) 360° feedback.

In 360° feedback, social workers ask for opinions from each person associated with their work. This is an effective type of feedback, as it considers many differing perspectives.

(92)   (C) Psychiatric.

Biopsychosocial models of intervention do not have a psychiatric component, but they usually have a psychological component.

(93)   (D) Homeostasis.

Homeostasis is the state of a system in which all the values of a system grow at constant rates. It is the steady state of the system.

(94)   (B) Open system.

In systems theory, an open system can exchange resources and information across boundaries.

(95)   (A) Engagement.

Engagement is the first step to problem-solving.

(96)   (B) Maladaptive.

Impaired problem-solving capabilities are referred to as maladaptive tendencies.

(97)   (C) Ivan Pavlov.

The Russian psychologist and physician Ivan Pavlov was one of the first proponents of behaviorist crisis intervention, along with Dr. Skinner.

(98)   (D) Abraham Maslow.

Abraham Maslow was responsible for developing the humanistic model of crisis intervention. He is also known for the hierarchy of needs.

(99)   (B) Being sexually aroused while being intimate with a partner.

Sexual arousal is an example of respondent (not operant) behavior, which is involuntary. It comes about as a response to specific stimuli.

(100) (D) Unstructured and random.

Usually, cognitive-behavioral therapy is structured and preemptively planned out. There is very little room for random or impulsive practices.

(101) (C) Therapy and assistance.

Therapy and assistance is not a separate phase in supporting clients who have undergone serious trauma. It is part of the overall crisis intervention plan.

(102) (D) A complete stop in communication.

Bringing about a complete stop in communication is not an example of an effective strategy that should be adopted while resolving any conflicts.

(103) (B) Limiting the scope of discussion.

Limiting the scope of the discussion and focusing on issues is an effective conflict management interaction-structuring technique.

(104) (A) Primary.

Immunization is an example of primary prevention. It helps protect the client from preventable diseases and conditions.

(105) (A) Primary.

Taking road safety measures is a primary prevention strategy.

(106) (B) Limit the long-term impact of disease, injury, etc.

A secondary prevention strategy is put in place only after a disease, injury, accident, etc., has already taken place.

(107) (C) Abstract.

Behavioral objectives should never be abstract. They should be easy to note down and constructively designed.

(108) (D) Aspirin slows down blood clotting.

Aspirin is a medication that slows down the clotting of blood, which can decrease the severity and frequency of heart attacks. It decreases the size of the clot.

(109) (C) Yes, because it is put in place once the disease, injury, etc., has already occurred.

Yes, secondary prevention strategies can be put in place even if clients are asymptomatic.

(110) (B) Engaging with the client.

The first step of the intervention process requires the social worker to engage with the client, the group and the whole community at large.

(111) (A) Anticipating any future needs.

The very last stage of the intervention process is termination and the anticipation of future needs.

(112) (A) Slapping the client.

It is completely inappropriate for the social worker to assault a client in any way. This is not a motivation technique.

(113) (B) Visualizing goals.

Putting an image on the refrigerator or wall can be an effective motivational tool.

(114) (D) None of the above.

All of the options are tried and tested methods for working with mandated or involuntary clients.

(115) (A) Slowing down speech when angry.

Slowing down speech when angry to avoid saying things in the heat of the moment is an example of the communication approach to anger management.

(116) (C) Walking away from tense situations.

Walking away from tense situations is an approach under the environmental change approach to anger and stress management.

(117) (D) Avoiding people who aggravate you.

Avoiding people who aggravate you is a good way to manage anger.

(118) (C) Freudian family therapy.

There is no therapy method known as Freudian family therapy.

(119) (D) Family projection process.

The family projection process is one of the main theoretical constructs needed to understand how Bowenian family therapy works.

(120) (A) Piaget method.

There is no couples' intervention or treatment called the Piaget method.

(121) (C) Administration on Aging.

The OAA of 1965 established the Administration on Aging, a federal body in charge of providing support and funds to elderly individuals aged over 60.

(122) (B) 1974.

The Child Abuse Prevention and Treatment Act (CAPTA) was a piece of keystone federal legislation passed in 1974.

(123) (A) It provides federal funding to states to prevent, assess, investigate, treat and prosecute all cases of child abuse.

CAPTA is a federal law that provides large-scale funding to states, governmental organizations and NGOs so that they can prevent child abuse.

(124) (D) 1974.

The FERPA of 1974 is a federal law that governs access to educational information by public entities. It is also referred to as the Buckley Amendment, after Senator James L. Buckley.

(125) (C) 3 to 21 years.

The EHCA of 1975 provides children between the ages of three and 21 with Individual Educational Plans, along with support services and financial support.

(126) (C) Indian Child Welfare Act.

The ICWA of 1978 is a landmark law that provides presumptive jurisdiction of Native American children to tribal governments.

(127) (D) Contact CPS and place the child with foster parents.

This is not a step that is specified in the Indian Child Welfare Act.

(128) (B) Affordable Care Act.

The Patient Protection and Affordable Care Act, passed in 2010, is also known as Obamacare.

(129) (D) HIPAA.

The Health Insurance Portability and Accountability Act (HIPAA) of 1996 provides individuals with complete and unrestricted access to their complete medical history.

(130) (A) Family and Medical Leave Act.

The FMLA of 1993 is a US federal labor law that requires all employers to provide their employees with job-protected leave for all approved family or medical reasons.

(131) (C) 2001.

No Child Left Behind (NCLB) is a 2001 federal education act authorized by the Bush administration.

(132) (D) Guesswork and assumptions.

Assessments and recommendations made by social workers should be free of guesswork and assumptions.

(133) (A) True.

Social work reports should contain only objective assessments that are free of any value judgments or subjectivity.

(134) (B) False.

The VAWA legislation, supported by Joe Biden, was enacted in 1994.

(135) (B) False, because this is a necessary criterion.

A social worker's use of supervision during service delivery is a necessary criterion considered while conducting any agency performance appraisals.

(136) (B) Termination of services.

Termination of services is not included as a standard step in the case management process.

(137) (A) True.

An illusion of unanimity is one of the main causes of groupthink. Majority opinions are assumed to be unanimous, and fringe opinions are not considered at all.

(138) (B) False.

Group polarization happens only when the group adopts a dominant perspective. This results in the group collectively reaching an extreme position.

(139) (C) Mindguards.

Mindguards are self-appointed members of the group who decide to guard leaders and members from information that is contradictory to their group cohesion.

(140) (D) Collective rationalization.

When members of the group disregard warnings, it is called collective rationalization.

(141) (A) True.

The size of a group is one of the factors that can have an effect on cohesion.

(142) (D) Background of the members.

Background of group members is not a specific factor that can affect group cohesion. This can be subsumed under homogeneity.

(143) (D) Only in some cases.

In some cases and situations, a group can provide members with a sense of hope about their future.

(144) (C) Cannot say for sure.

Corporeality is an experience that groups can sometimes provide to members. However, it is impossible to say with certainty.

(145) (B) Power and control.

Storming or power and control is the stage of the group process in which individual members vie for control among themselves.

(146) (C) Terraforming.

Terraforming is a hypothetical process in science, not a group process.

(147) (B) False.

This is false. Adjourning or separation is the last stage of group development. Here, members act separately from one another.

(148) (A) Members of the couple know each other's worries and stresses.

The Gottman method of couples therapy posits that the members of each couple are familiar with each other's worries and stresses and share mutual admiration.

(149) (A) True.

The main goal of advocacy in social work is to obtain public support for policies that can lead to an equitable and efficient redistribution of available resources.

(150) (D) Protective maintenance.

The stages of indicators of readiness to change include precontemplation, contemplation, preparation and maintenance in general.

(151) (A) Dichotomous thinking.

Thinking in terms of either/or is known as dichotomous thinking. This is a fallacy that leads people to believe that differences in behavior are wrong or bad.

(152) (B) False.

There is no single universal norm of behavior or morals. This fallacy is also known as universalism.

(153) (A) True.

The *Code of Ethics* states that the importance of human relationships is a core value in social work.

(154) (C) Institutional power.

While institutional power can be a powerful tool in social work, it is not a core value of the discipline.

(155) (C) Imminent harm to the client or an identifiable person.

Social workers can disclose confidential information only if there is an imminent threat to the client or an identifiable person.

(156) (D) Respond and claim privilege.

If they receive a subpoena, social workers have a duty to respond to it and claim their privilege.

(157) (B) Law enforcement officers.

While all individuals have a moral duty to report instances of abuse or neglect, law enforcement officers are mandated to do so.

(158) (A) True.

A statutory mandate is one of the five kinds of binding, legal mandates that all social workers need to be aware of.

(159) (D) Monitor for new ethical issues.

Social workers need to monitor for new ethical dilemmas that may crop up. That is the last step of ethical problem solving.

(160) (C) A client is a member of the social worker's congregation.

Being a part of the same church congregation is not a dual relationship, provided that the contact is minimum.

(161) (A) True.

Any form of recording that involves the client always needs the client's express written and informed consent.

(162) (B) Transferring payment.

Transferring payment is not a step in the client referral process. This can be handled by the administrative department.

(163) (A) True.

Any and all decisions regarding social work interventions have to be recorded in writing.

(164) (C) In specific cases.

The client's educational and social history may not be included in the case presentation if it is not pertinent.

(165) (D) Cognitive model.

There are three kinds of peer supervision models: developmental, psychodynamic and role-centered. Cognitive is not one of these models.

(166) (B) There is a low tolerance for stress.

A low tolerance for stress is a psychiatric risk factor for substance abuse, not a social one.

(167) (D) Presence of family trauma.

The presence of family trauma is a familial risk factor for substance abuse, not a behavioral one.

(168) (A) True.

In recent times, the medical model of addiction has received the most credence, both from the scientific community and from empirical observations made by professionals such as police officers, social workers, etc.

(169) (C) Sudden change in attitudes toward family.

A sudden change in attitudes toward one's family is not necessarily a sign of substance abuse disorders.

(170) (B) False.

Inappropriate laughter and extreme drowsiness are signs of marijuana use, not necessarily of heroin abuse.

Milton Keynes UK
Ingram Content Group UK Ltd.
UKHW030809281123
433408UK00011B/1087